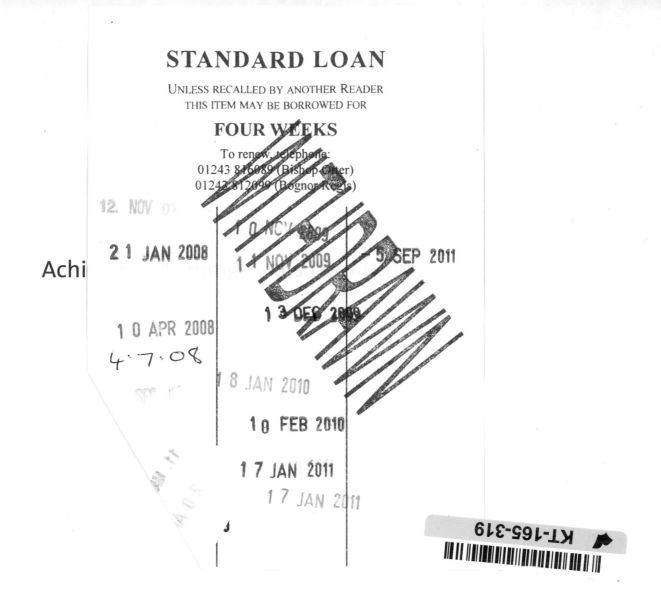

Achieving Learning Goals Through Play

Teaching Young Children
with Special Needs

Second Edition

by

Anne H. Widerstrom, Ph.D.

Baltimore • London • Sydney

Paul H. Brookes Publishing Co.
Post Office Box 10624
Baltimore, MD 21285-0624

www.brookespublishing.com

Typeset by A.W. Bennett, Inc., Hartland, Vermont.
Manufactured in the United States of America by
Sheridan Books, Inc., Fredericksburg, Virginia.

First edition published by Communication Skill Builders, 1995.

The case studies described in this book are composites based on the author's actual experiences. Individuals'
names have been changed, and identifying details have been altered to protect confidentiality.

Photographs on the front cover and pages 3, 15, 29, 41, 59, 75, 81, 93, 99, 149, 157, and 167 taken under
contract by Edward McCain.

Library of Congress Cataloging-in-Publication Data

Widerstrom, Anne H.
   Achieving learning goals through play : teaching young children with special needs / by Anne H.
Widerstrom.—2nd ed.
      p.   cm.
   Includes bibliographical references and index.
   ISBN 1-55766-698-9 (papercover)
   1. Children with disabilities—Education (Early childhood).   2. Children with disabilities—Development.
   3. Children and adults.   4. Curriculum planning.   I. Title.
   LC4019.3.W54 2005
   371.9'0472—dc22
                                                     2004016040

British Library Cataloguing in Publication data are available from the British Library.

Contents

About the Author

Anne H. Widerstrom, Ph.D., is Professor Emeritus of Early Childhood Special Education at San Francisco State University. She received her doctorate in educational psychology and early childhood special education at Temple University. The author of several books concerning young children with disabilities, Dr. Widerstrom has published numerous articles in early childhood and special education journals, both in the United States and in France. She has lectured in French at the University of Geneva and the University of Montpellier and in English at numerous professional conferences. For many years, Dr. Widerstrom worked as a consultant to Head Start and child care programs, helping teachers to include children with disabilities more effectively in preschool classrooms. Her special interest for many years has been play and developmentally appropriate practice for young children.

Preface

This book is intended for professionals who work in various settings with young children. It is written especially for those who work with children with developmental delays and disabilities of varying types or with children who are at risk for delay. The information is applicable in child care centers, early childhood education classrooms, and other settings in which young children with special needs are served. The suggestions presented will assist all adults who work with young children to more easily and more effectively include children with disabilities or delays in their programs.

Please note that the primary aim of this book is to support early childhood teachers in their efforts to fully include children with disabilities in their programs. Many early childhood and child care professionals are unaware of the legal requirement first mandated under the Individuals with Disabilities Education Act (IDEA) of 1990, PL 101-476, of inclusion for children with disabilities. Moreover, some are unaware that children with disabilities have access to professional support services, including individual and group therapy for speech-language problems, gross and fine motor delays, and psychological services.

Therefore, early childhood teachers should never feel that they bear the whole burden of individualizing a program for a child with a disability. Teachers should become familiar with each eligible child's individualized education program (IEP) in order to learn which specialists are available to help the child in the classroom and during home visits. Often these specialists include an early childhood special educator, an inclusion specialist, the therapists mentioned previously, or a teaching assistant with some training in special education.

Section I: The Role of Play in Early Childhood Education (Chapters 1–3) provides background on why play is important, the changing perceptions of play, and how play can be adapted for children with special needs. Planning matrices are introduced in Section II: Planning and Writing Goals and Objectives for Children with Disabilities (Chapters 4–5).

The suggested lessons and activities in Section III: Let's Play: Embedding Techniques and Learning Goals in Play Activities (Chapters 6–14) are labeled according to the target child's developmental age. These developmental ages are meant only as general ability indicators. The chapters are written for use primarily in preschool classrooms where the children's chronological ages are 3–6 years.

Section IV: Playing Together and Making Friends (Chapters 15–18) includes information on group play and social skills learned through play. The section also provides information on encouraging parents to participate in classroom and community activities. The last chapter is a case study that illustrates how one child achieved her learning goals through play.

The appendixes contain best practices guidelines, information on specific techniques, and resources for children with disabilities. Appendix A provides sources of adaptive equipment and learning materials. Appendix B includes guidelines for adapting developmentally appropriate practice for preschool children with disabilities. Appendix C contains information on adapting the learning environment for specific disabilities. Appendix D contains a sample of checklists for observing play skills, and Appendix E contains the planning matrices discussed in Chapter 4, as well as a true–false quiz on play.

Acknowledgments

I wish to thank Dr. Susan Sandall of the University of Washington for her valuable work on the first edition of this book, including the play matrix found in Chapter 4 and the information in Chapter 5 on individualizing play. Her contributions have been included in this second edition and are gratefully acknowledged.

A big thank you goes to Dr. M. Diane Klein, whose review of the first edition and whose suggestions for revision for the current edition I found invaluable. And without the extensive and expert editorial assistance of Heather Shrestha and Janet Betten, this edition would never have been completed. Thanks to all of you.

To my granddaughter Rachel Zoe

SHE WILL SOON TO BE ATTENDING AN EARLY CHILDHOOD PROGRAM HERSELF.
I HOPE, AS A TYPICALLY DEVELOPING 3-YEAR-OLD, SHE WILL HAVE MANY
OPPORTUNITIES TO INTERACT AND PLAY WITH CHILDREN WITH DISABILITIES,
AN EXPERIENCE THAT WILL BROADEN HER UNDERSTANDING AND APPRECIATION
OF CHILDREN WHO MAY BE DIFFERENT IN LANGUAGE, CULTURE, AND ABILITY.

I

The Role of Play
in Early Childhood Education

Why Is Play Important?

Children love to play. As an early childhood educator, you know how true this is! Play is considered to be important for all children because it is the most meaningful mode for them to learn. Children engage in play more readily than in other means of learning such as through memorization or direct teaching, and what they learn in play is generalizable to other situations, unlike rote learning.

This book will help you understand the role of play in early childhood education. It contains ideas for using play as a means for helping children with special needs achieve individualized learning goals. You will learn how to plan and write goals and objectives for children with disabilities, embed teaching and learning goals in play activities, and encourage children to play together and make friends. The suggested techniques and strategies also work with typically developing children.

Play is an excellent medium for achieving learning goals for several reasons related to acquisition, practice, mastery, and integration of learning. First, play creates a safe, noncompetitive arena for children to experiment with materials, objects, and people; to test hypotheses; and to try out new roles. Play also provides opportunities for learning through trial and error. As a result, through play children can acquire new skills and understandings in all of the developmental domains:

- *Physical knowledge*—Through playing alone or with a small group of peers, children can acquire knowledge about the surrounding environment. Kamii (Kamii & DeVries, 1978) referred to this as *physical knowledge,* based on Piaget's concept of logical-mathematical knowledge. Through manipulating objects and materials, children learn to categorize, seriate, and conserve. That is, children learn that objects are alike in some ways and different in other ways and that objects can be grouped according to these characteristics. As an example of categorization, a child might put all of the blue trucks in one pile and all of the red ones in another. In learning to seriate, a child comes to understand differences in size and can place a group of similar objects in order according to size (e.g., lining up five pencils with the longest first, the next longest second, and so forth until the shortest pencil is at the end of the row). Conservation refers to the idea that objects and materials don't change their weight, volume, or size when they are moved from one location to another. For example, when a cup of sand is dumped from a tall, thin container to a short, fat one, the weight and volume do not change, even though there appears to be less sand in the short container.

- *Fine motor skills*—Small muscle control is enhanced through play. For example, playing with a set of measuring cups and several large jars at the sand or water table (i.e., filling various-sized containers then dumping out the contents) helps children develop their ability to pick up and manipulate objects of various sizes and weights in addition to learning about quantity and volume.

- *Symbolic behavior*—Symbolic or pretend play is necessary for the later development of the ability to use symbols, including spoken and written language.

Playing dress-up and acting out roles that mirror real life (e.g., parents, cowboys, waiters, doctors) give children practice in making one idea, object, or activity stand for another, which is the basis of symbol use.

- *Language and communication*—As they become more skilled at using symbols in their play, children develop the ability to communicate in increasingly complex ways. From early gestures and eye contact, they progress to single word utterances such as "more!" or "bye-bye" and soon begin putting words together into phrases. Play enhances this developmental process by providing situations to practice using symbols (e.g., "Feed dolly") that result in language. Later, play activities such as drawing pictures and telling stories about those drawings extend the child's symbolic activity to writing.

- *Gross motor skills*—Through rough-and-tumble play, children develop their large muscles. Riding a tricycle, climbing on the jungle gym, running, crawling, and throwing a ball are all play activities that help develop children's gross motor abilities. Outdoor play activities provide opportunities to develop new movement skills and practice old ones.

- *Socialization*—Because it is the ideal medium for peer interactions, play is an effective way to enhance social development. Through play, children learn to resolve their differences and enjoy one another's company. They learn to cooperate in order to solve problems or accomplish goals. In short, they learn to be successful in their interactions with others. At the same time, they learn to communicate effectively with their peers, with adults, and with siblings.

- *Emotional development*—Another important reason for providing play opportunities is that significant emotional development can take place through play. Children can work through several developmental tasks, including separation from parents, independence, individuation (Mahler, Bergman, & Pine, 1975), and gender-role identification. In addition, play can provide an outlet for aggression and a means for satisfying sexual curiosity. When a little girl spanks her dolly after being scolded herself, an emotional need for retribution is satisfied. The game of doctor–nurse–patient—a favorite of preschool children—provides an opportunity for children to observe anatomical differences between boys and girls and to begin the important process of gender-role identification.

Play is also important because it offers opportunities to practice newly acquired skills and thus achieve mastery of the environment—a great self-esteem enhancer (Landy, 2002). According to Erikson, play assists children in organizing and integrating their life experiences (as cited in Cook, Tessier, & Klein, 2000). Practice is especially important for children with disabilities or developmental delays because they learn at a slower pace and need more practice than typically developing children to fully master new skills. Practicing a new skill during play is enjoyable. In fact, all children seem to enjoy repeating play activities. Just as they have favorite stories they enjoy hearing over and over again, children have favorite play activities of which they never seem to tire.

Play also promotes the development of creativity by allowing children to make their own choices and decisions and to experiment with materials and activities, using make-believe formats as they choose. There is no need to conform to adult standards or rules or to gain adult approval for most play activities. This aspect of play is crucial, for it places children in control of their own play environment, thus increasing their sense of mastery and independence. Gaining mastery over their environment is especially important for children with special needs, who may be more dependent on adults than other children.

Clearly, play is vital for many aspects of children's development. The next question is how play might be different for children with delays or disabilities. How can we adapt play to meet the needs of children who may not be able to plan and carry out independent play activities? How can we assure that individual learning goals are achieved in a program that is based primarily on play? To find answers to these questions, let's look more closely at children's play in Chapter 2.

Changing Perceptions of Play in Early Childhood Education

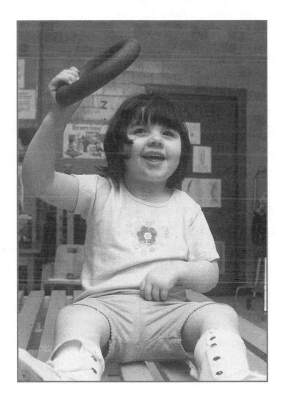

The importance of play in child development has been recognized for centuries, beginning with Plato and Aristotle in ancient Greece. The French 18th-century philosopher Rousseau also believed that children learn through play, and his writings influenced European and American educators. He felt that children had an intrinsic motivation to learn through their own self-initiated activities. Rousseau was perhaps the first person to claim that play is an important activity for children. He wrote,

> Work or play are all one to him. His games are his work; he knows no difference. . . . Is there anything better worth seeing, anything more touching or more delightful, than a pretty child, with merry, cheerful glance, easy contented manner, open smiling countenance, playing at the most important things or working at the lightest amusements? (as cited in Braun & Edwards, 1972, p. 134)

Apparently Rousseau held a rather idealistic view of children!

PAPA PESTALOZZI

Rousseau influenced a philosopher named Pestalozzi, who lived in Switzerland during a revolution that occurred there in the early 1800s. Pestalozzi (1890) began a school for children who were orphaned by the revolution and based the curriculum on play and learning through discovery. He believed that early education should parallel children's natural development. He did not view children's play as we do today, however; he allowed children little freedom of choice. Lessons were developed to teach children social values, such as the value of honest work, and various manual skills were practiced during highly structured outdoor play.

Pestalozzi developed a method of early education based on six principles. His method became widely accepted, giving impetus to the idea of training teachers, and he became known as "Papa" Pestalozzi. The six principles are as follows (as cited in Braun & Edwards, 1972):

1. Education must be religious.

2. Education must develop the child as a whole.

3. Education must guide and stimulate self-activity.

4. Education must be based on intuition and exercise.

5. Education must observe a natural progression in development.

6. Education must foster the development of ideas through use of number, form, and language.

KINDERGARTEN MOVEMENT

Pestalozzi, in turn, influenced Friedrich Wilhelm Froebel, who studied under Pestalozzi for 2 years and, in 1840, opened the first kindergarten in Germany. Borrowing ideas from Pestalozzi and Rousseau, Froebel based his curriculum on principles of play, children's natural development, and active participation. Froebel's curriculum was more open and child-directed than Pestalozzi's, but it still incorporated less freedom of choice for children than English and American kindergartens that were later developed based on his principles. Nevertheless, many activities commonly seen in today's kindergartens and preschools—such as block building, sand and water play, and clay modeling—were originally part of the Froebel kindergarten curriculum.

The kindergarten movement spread quickly from Germany to England and to the United States, retaining its emphasis on play as the natural setting for children's learning. It provided the foundation for what later became known as the child-centered curriculum, an approach proposed by John Dewey based on the premise that children have an intrinsic motivation to learn (Dewey, 1902, 1938). This idea had considerable influence on later American psychologists and educators.

For a more thorough discussion of Froebel, Pestalozzi, Rousseau, and other historical figures mentioned in this chapter, please refer to *History and Theory of Early Childhood Education* (Braun & Edwards, 1972) or *Contemporary Influences in Early Childhood Education, Second Edition* (Evans, 1975). For more recent information, please consult the following web sites: http://www.froebel foundation.org and http://www.froebelweb.com. To locate current books and articles related to any of the topics in this chapter, please visit http://www.questia.com, a large online library listing thousands of books and journals.

MARIA MONTESSORI

In the early 20th century in Italy, a physician named Maria Montessori started a program for children who were orphaned or abandoned by parents who could not afford to raise them. The Case dei Bambini (Children's Houses) were residential schools for young children with a practical, child-centered curriculum, and the first school opened in Rome in 1907. Much like Piaget, Montessori believed that children learn through their senses and through motor activity. She believed that learning experiences could be carefully constructed to take advantage of children's natural curiosity. Therefore, she developed a series of special, self-correcting activities and materials that remain the foundation of Montessori education today. The Montessori method also incorporates an emphasis on cleanliness, self-care, and independence through "practical life exercises" such as sweeping, pouring water, folding linens, and caring for plants and animals (Montessori, 1912).

The curriculum is highly structured and teacher directed, but as the children master each technique or activity according to the precise demonstration of the teacher, they are free to practice it whenever they wish. This method does not allow for creative use of materials, for there is a right and a wrong way to use each learning material. Montessori believed that children should first be observed in their own spontaneous learning environments and that learning experiences should then be carefully arranged to take advantage of their natural curiosity. Because these experiences are based on the child's natural curiosity, they are uniquely suited to children's learning and even today are very popular with early childhood educators (Evans, 1975).

For further reading about Montessori, refer to *The Imagination of Early Childhood Education* (Morgan, 1999). In addition, the Montessori web site, http://www .montessori.edu, lists numerous works about the model.

PLAY-BASED CURRICULUM MODELS

Modern early childhood education in the United States acknowledges children's intrinsic motivation to learn. Furthermore, it emphasizes that learning should be planned around their natural development because children do not learn in the same ways that adults do. It emphasizes, too, that children learn best through play. These ideas originate with Rousseau and are carried through the works of Pestalozzi, Froebel, Montessori, Dewey, and others.

Several early childhood curricula have been developed based on the principle of play. Two of the most popular are described briefly here. These models were developed for typically developing children, but some educators have adapted them for children with special learning needs.

Bank Street College of Education Model

Beginning in the 1940s, a group of psychologists and educators at Bank Street College in New York City became influential in early childhood educational theory. Most notable among them were Shapiro and Biber (1972), who developed a model of early childhood education known as the developmental-interaction model. *Developmental* refers to the child's natural pattern of developing increasingly more complex cognitive structures; *interaction* refers to the relationship between the child's cognitive and affective development, as well as to the child's interaction with the environment. The Bank Street model places primary emphasis on psychosocial development, with a major goal being development of self-esteem and a sense of autonomy. The emphasis is on process and

> Providing the experiences that make it possible for children to try out, shift backward as well as forward, to create . . . opportunities for the kind of interaction that is essential for the assimilation of experience, the achievement of new integrations, and the resolution of conflict—in both cognitive and emotional realms. (Shapiro & Biber, 1972)

Because children are thought to derive satisfaction from learning and to have a strong intrinsic motivation to learn, extrinsic rewards are not recommended. In the Bank Street model, the most important component of the ideal learning environment is the teacher, whose job it is to create a safe, healthy climate for learning and to respond positively to children. The teacher–child relationship is built on mutual trust. The model emphasizes dramatic and symbolic play, language-related activities, and "support-guided play" (Shapiro & Biber, 1972). This means that the teacher acts as a facilitator to guide children toward certain goals in their play. For more information on the Bank Street model, please visit http://www.bankstreet .edu.

The British Infant School and Open Education

At the same time as the developmental-interaction model was being created in the United States, early childhood educators in England were developing a model that gave children nearly absolute freedom of choice regarding the activities in which they could engage. This model, based on the idea that children's natural curiosity and desire to explore are the bases for learning, became known in the United States as *open education*. In Britain, open education became the foundation for the infant schools and nursery schools that served children 3–8 years of age.

Three main principles characterized these schools, namely the integrated day, vertical or family groupings, and the play-centered curriculum. The *integrated day* meant that there was no set schedule of activities, except perhaps for lunch. The classrooms were organized into learning centers, and children chose their activities freely throughout the day. Teachers took a reactive role, following children's lead and not getting involved unless children requested it. When children expressed an interest in a certain topic or event, then the teacher provided information and extended or elaborated on what the children were doing.

Vertical groupings were typical of this model. Children 3, 4, and 5 years of age or 6, 7, and 8 years of age shared a classroom, creating "family" groups. This arrangement made it possible for a group of children to remain with the same group of teachers for 2–3 years and provided opportunities for the younger and less able children to learn from older and more able peers.

The open education model was *play centered*. Materials were set out and organized into centers. Teachers did little advance preparation of either lessons or materials. Emphasis was on the present, with little concern for preparing the children for later schooling.

The Bank Street model offers some good ideas for adapting play to meet the special learning needs of children with delays or disabilities. The open education model, too, offers possibilities for adapting play as a means for achieving learning goals. You will recognize elements of these models in the activities and suggestions contained in the following chapters.

DEVELOPMENTALLY APPROPRIATE PRACTICE AND BEST PRACTICE

Experts in early childhood education and early childhood special education joined together to develop guidelines for educating children with and without disabilities

Table 2.1. Principles of child development and learning that inform developmentally appropriate practice

1. Domains of child development—physical, social, emotional and cognitive—are closely related. Development in one domain influences and is influenced by development in other domains.
2. Development occurs in a relatively orderly sequence, with later abilities, skills, and knowledge building on those already acquired.
3. Development proceeds at varying rates from child to child as well as unevenly within different areas of each child's functioning.
4. Early experiences have both cumulative and delayed effects on individual children's development; optimal periods exist for certain types of development and learning.
5. Development proceeds in predictable directions toward greater complexity, organization, and internalization.
6. Development and learning occur in and are influenced by multiple social and cultural contexts.
7. Children are active learners, drawing on direct physical and social experiences as well as culturally transmitted knowledge to construct their own understandings of the world around them.
8. Development and learning result from interaction of biological maturation and the environment, which includes both the physical and social worlds that children live in.
9. Play is an important vehicle for children's social, emotional, and cognitive development, as well as a reflection of their development.
10. Development advances when children have opportunities to practice newly acquired skills as well as when they experience a challenge just beyond the level of their present mastery.
11. Children demonstrate different modes of knowing and learning and different ways of representing what they know.
12. Children develop and learn best in the context of a community where they are safe and valued, their physical needs are met, and they feel psychologically secure.

in inclusive settings from birth to 8 years. The national organizations representing both groups have published guidelines for best practice. The National Association for the Education of Young Children (NAEYC) published the first guidelines for developmentally appropriate practice (DAP) in 1987 (Bredekamp, 1987).

These guidelines were written for early childhood educators and were not considered to be applicable to children with disabilities. The guidelines are sensible and child centered. They minimize adult control and direct instruction. Therefore, they were viewed by many special educators as not appropriate for children with special needs, who, it was thought, required a more structured environment involving more adult–child interaction than the NAEYC guidelines suggested (see Wolery & Odom, 1991).

A decade later, the views of early childhood special educators shifted, and DAP gradually became accepted as a means for fully including young children with disabilities in early childhood programs such as Head Start and child care. Revised guidelines published by NAEYC (Bredekamp & Copple, 1997; see Table 2.1) focused on general principles of child development and principles concerning how children learn best.

In addition, the Division for Early Childhood (DEC) of the Council for Exceptional Children in 1992 appointed a task force to review and recommend best practices for young children with disabilities. Their report, *DEC Recommended Practices: Indicators of Quality in Programs for Infants and Young Children and Their Families,*

Table 2.2. DEC recommended practices in early intervention/early childhood special education: Selected recommended practices in child-focused interventions

1. Physical space and materials, social dimensions, play routines, and transitions are structured and adapted to promote engagement, play, interaction, and learning.
2. Environments are designed and activities are conducted so that children learn or are exposed to multiple cultures and languages.
3. Services are provided in natural learning environments as appropriate. These include places in which typically developing children participate, such as home or community settings.
4. Interventionists facilitate children's engagement with their environment to encourage child-initiated learning that is not dependent on the adult's presence.
5. Practices target meaningful outcomes for the child that build on the child's current skills and behavior and promote membership with others.
6. Children's behavior is recognized, interpreted in context, and responded to contingently, and opportunities are provided for expansion or elaboration of child behavior by imitating the behavior, waiting for the child's responses, modeling, and prompting.
7. Interventionists are agents of change to promote and accelerate learning.
8. Planning occurs prior to implementation, and that planning considers the situation (e.g., home, center, community) to which the interventions will be applied.
9. Peer-mediated strategies are used to promote social and communicative behavior.
10. Specialized procedures (e.g., naturalistic strategies, prompt/prompt fading strategies) are embedded and distributed within and across activities.

From Sandall, S.R., McLean, M., & Smith, B. (Eds.). (2000). *DEC Recommended practices in early intervention/early childhood special education* (pp. 34–37). Reston, VA: Council for Exceptional Children; reprinted by permission.

was published a year later (DEC Task Force on Recommended Practices, 1993). See Table 2.2 for revised and updated DEC recommended practices (Sandall, McLean, & Smith, 2000). Together, the two sets of guidelines represent a child-centered, fully inclusive approach to early childhood education. Let's further explore the issue of adapting play for children with special needs in Chapter 3.

Adapting Play for Children with Special Needs

Many children with special needs are enrolled in early childhood care and education programs, and these children are often included in typical settings for most or all of their education. Federal legislation (Individuals with Disabilities Education Act Amendments of 1997 [IDEA '97], PL 105-17) mandates that services for children with disabilities be provided in the least restrictive environment. Federal law also states that a rationale must be provided if a child is *not* placed in a typical environment. This chapter provides guidelines for adapting play for children with special needs in inclusive environments including Division for Early Childhood (DEC) recommended practices and The National Association for the Education of Young Children (NAEYC) guidelines as well as information on developmentally appropriate environments, fully including children with special needs, the role of direct teaching, and practicing new skills through play.

RECOMMENDED PRACTICES

The DEC Task Force (1993) developed recommended practices for service delivery to children with special needs from birth to age 8. These practices are based on scientific evidence and experimental knowledge and include

1. Least restrictive and most natural environment

2. Family-centered services

3. Transdisciplinary intervention teams

4. Practices based on current empirical research and families' diverse values

5. Developmentally and individually appropriate practices

These principles are applicable in a variety of settings, from hospitals and clinics to special education classrooms and inclusive general education programs. Full inclusion of young children with disabilities in typical child care and early childhood centers provides an opportunity to extend these five principles beyond special education boundaries to programs that serve all children. Early childhood educators and child care specialists can benefit from the knowledge that early interventionists bring to their classrooms. Conversely, the principles of developmentally appropriate practice (DAP) developed by early childhood educators have enriched the education of young children with special needs.

Least Restrictive and Most Natural Environments

Natural environments are home and community settings that are typical for peers without disabilities. Full inclusion in natural environments (e.g., school; child care centers; community activities like playgroups, library story groups, Gymboree classes, and religious activities) recognizes the value of young children with special needs learning from typically developing peers. At the same time, typically developing children learn to accept and appreciate differences in ability and behavior as they interact with peers with special needs.

Family-Centered Services

In planning and carrying out interventions and services for young children, the field of early childhood special education has traditionally placed more emphasis on families and their priorities, concerns, and resources than the field of early childhood education has. Parents are a child's first and best teachers, and they must be involved in all decision-making concerning their child, especially in developing the individualized education program (IEP) and the individualized family service plan (IFSP) (see Chapter 4) and in planning transitions from one program to another.

Transdisciplinary Intervention Teams

The idea of several specialists working together in one classroom, sharing ideas and information, training others (e.g., parents, early childhood teachers and caregivers, other therapists and specialists), and working with small groups in the typical setting is an important contribution from special education to general education. Early childhood classrooms that have included children with special needs have inherited a wealth of resources from the special education network (see Appendix A), greatly enriching the teaching of all the children involved.

Practices Based on Current Empirical Research and Families' Diverse Values

Although it has been difficult to conduct research on early intervention outcomes due to small samples and a variety of uncontrollable variables, the body of literature consisting of this research has yielded several indicators of quality that are empirically sound, including adult–child ratios, barrier-free environments, and the importance of data collection to more accurately measure outcomes (see Guralnick, 1997, 2001, and McWilliam & Strain, 1993, for more information).

Areas for Future Research

In discussing goal domains for early childhood inclusion, Guralnick (2001) identified four areas for future research that may contribute to the development of more effective inclusion programs. The four goal domains are

- *Universal access*—Universal access refers to having inclusive programs in local communities as well as allowing children with disabilities to have as much participation as possible in typical activities with typically developing children. Data on inclusive child care options for infants and young children are very limited. In summarizing the existing research on school-based inclusion, Guralnick concluded that although progress has been made, we are far from achieving the goal of universal access. Many parents of young children with disabilities report having difficulty locating appropriate community-based child care.

- *Feasibility*—This concept refers to the ability of individual programs to maintain their integrity (fundamental assumptions and structure) while accommodating the individual needs of all children. Classrooms should provide a curriculum that is specifically adapted to the needs of each student, and training and resources should be available to help teachers as needed. Specialized services, such as occupational and physical therapy, must be available to children. Above all, quality education should be provided for all children, regardless of ability level. Despite its importance, feasibility is the least researched, least discussed, and least developed aspect of early childhood inclusion.

- *Developmental and social outcomes*—For inclusion to be a valid goal, it is necessary that children with and without disabilities do as well in the inclusive programs as they do in specialized or segregated ones. Guralnick (2001) concluded that well-designed inclusive programs produce no adverse effects on either group of children. In fact, these programs have been shown to increase peer interactions for the children with disabilities. Play is a strong component in most of these programs, as is the absence of a social stigma attached to children with disabilities.

- *Social integration*—Social integration refers to "typically developing children's ability and willingness to understand and then . . . move beyond differences in the developmental, behavioral, and even certain physical characteristics of their peers" (Guralnick, 2001, p. 23). In addition, children with disabilities develop better social skills and decrease behaviors that lead to social rejection (e.g., biting, withdrawal). Guralnick concluded that positive signs of social integration exist, but a more specific set of social interaction expectations needs to be developed in order to determine children's progress in this area.

Please see Guralnick (2001, pp. 8–27) for more details on these four areas for research.

Respecting Family Values

To ensure that practices accurately reflect the values of families, it may be necessary to individualize them for each family. McWilliam and Strain wrote, "The canon of individualization characterizes early intervention and distinguishes it from other early childhood services. . . . It reflects a strongly held value in our field" (1993, p. 44). According to the research of Hanson and Zercher (2001), little attention has been paid to the impact of the cultural and linguistic differences of children and families attending inclusive preschools. Their review of issues of diversity in early childhood programs yielded several recommendations for practice that would result in family-centered services becoming more culturally sensitive.

Among the recommendations for practice suggested by Hanson and Zercher (2001) are the following:

1. Promote cultural and linguistic diversity in preschool environments, including personnel who speak the children's languages and who understand the culture of the children and families being served, to ensure that practices match the families' expectations.

2. Coordinate and collaborate among fields and service systems to eliminate disciplinary barriers and provide a more comprehensive approach to meeting IEP goals.

3. Include strategies for developing *cross-cultural competence* (i.e., self-awareness that leads to being culturally sensitive) in personnel training and professional development.

4. Acknowledge families' preferences for service delivery and follow them as much as possible regardless of whether you agree with the families' wishes.

5. Encourage less socially competent children to participate in the classroom social environment by supporting all children's interactions and by recognizing the existence and importance of the social world created and occupied by the children in your classrooms.

See pages 424–426 of Hanson and Zercher (2001) for more information.

Developmentally and Individually Appropriate Practices

The principles underlying developmentally and individually appropriate practices recognize the need for personalized and one-to-one instruction for some children who learn best with more teacher support, including direct teaching. Nevertheless, the principles also recognize the benefit to all children of learning in natural environments within the context of play (Cook et al., 2000).

Updated Guidelines

Table 2.2 (see Chapter 2) provides information on how the original five DEC recommended practices have been updated (Sandall et al., 2000). Essentially, the recommended practices are now child focused, which is a major shift in concentration for many special educators. Historically, special education in the United States has followed a behavioral tradition in which professionals developed individual goals for children, then drilled the children—often through rote methods—to achieve the goals. For many years, parents were excluded from the intervention process. By contrast, early childhood education developed as child centered and family inclusive. Modern changes in both fields have drawn the two together, and special educators have adopted the child-focused methods of early childhood education.

The new DEC recommended practices for intervention consist of three general goals, listed next, and 27 specific objectives:

- Adults design environments to promote children's safety, active engagement, learning, participation, and membership.

- Adults individualize and adapt practices for each child based on ongoing data to meet children's changing needs.

- Adults use systematic procedures within and across environments, activities, and routines to promote children's learning and participation.

DEVELOPMENTALLY APPROPRIATE ENVIRONMENTS

There continues to be a great deal of interest in DAP for children in early childhood care and educational settings. Some controversy has emerged concerning whether practices can be developmentally appropriate and individually appropriate at the same time. Some special educators have raised concerns about placing children with disabilities in environments where teaching is "developmentally appropriate" and therefore presumably not appropriate for children who are not developing typically.

The concept of DAP was first proposed by the NAEYC and implied that an educational practice was both age appropriate and individually appropriate (Bredekamp & Copple, 1997). Leaders in the early childhood field agree that practices that are sound educationally and developmentally for young children are appropriate for all children. The guidelines simply represent practices that are considered to be the most successful ways for adults to interact with typically developing children in order to promote their optimal learning. A perusal of DAP guidelines adapted for children with special needs (see Appendix B) illustrates how little adaptation is really necessary to accommodate children of varying abilities and educational needs. At the same time, however, it is necessary to give careful attention to planning and implementing the learning goals of children with special learning needs. Appendix B contains some adaptations for young children to illustrate this point.

NAEYC has published guidelines for the early childhood curriculum, adult–child interaction, and relationships between home and school (Bredekamp 1987; Bredekamp & Copple, 1997). The guidelines are based on extensive research describing practices that foster optimal child development for typically developing children. There are separate guidelines for infants and toddlers, 3-year-olds, 4- and 5-year-olds, and 6- to 8-year-olds. The original curriculum guidelines included the following (adapted from Bredekamp, 1987):

1. The curriculum provides for all areas of a child's development—physical, emotional, social, and cognitive—through an integrated approach.

2. Curriculum planning is based on teachers' observations and recordings of each child's special interests and developmental progress.

3. Learning is viewed as an interactive process. Teachers prepare the environment so that children can learn through active exploration and interaction with adults, other children, and materials.

4. Learning activities are concrete, real, and relevant to the lives of young children.

5. Adults are prepared to meet the needs of children who exhibit unusual interests and skills outside the typical developmental range. Activities are planned for a wider range of interests and abilities than the chronological age range of the group would suggest.

6. Adults provide a variety of materials and activities at varying levels of difficulty, complexity, and challenge to meet the needs of children at different levels of understanding and skill development.

7. Many opportunities are provided for children to choose among a variety of activities, materials, and equipment. Time is provided for children to explore through active involvement while adults promote their engagement and extend their learning by asking questions or making suggestions that stimulate their thinking.

8. Multicultural and anti-bias experiences, materials, and equipment are provided for children of all ages. They ensure the individual appropriateness of the curriculum and, at the same time, strengthen ties between the home and the educational program by supporting the integrity of each child's family. In addition, they enrich the lives of all participants through respectful acceptance and appreciation of the differences and similarities among them.

9. Adults provide a balance of rest and active movement throughout the program day.

10. Outdoor experiences are provided daily for all children.

In the revised guidelines, the emphasis was broadened to include principles of child development, including the following (Bredekamp & Copple, 1997):

• Development occurs in a predictable and orderly sequence for all children.

• The domains of development are closely interrelated.

• Early experiences and the social context of those experiences influence the individual child's rate of development.

• Development and learning result from the interaction of biological maturation and the environment.

Other principles state how children learn best, such as through play, while being actively engaged, while in a safe and secure community context, and through different modalities (visual, auditory, tactile). See Table 2.1 in Chapter 2.

The revised DAP guidelines focus more on sound general principles of learning and development deemed appropriate for all children and less on the concrete activities and curriculum found in the 1987 version. This was done in order to make the case for applying DAP to children with disabilities; however, in both versions there is a strong emphasis on play as the preferred vehicle for child learning.

A brief review of these curriculum guidelines (found in Appendix B) reveals that some modifications may be necessary for children with delays, disabilities, or special health concerns. In these guidelines, the adult is seen exclusively as a facilitator, whereas some children with special needs may require more individual and direct teaching of certain skills. In addition, it may be necessary to individualize learning experiences for every child in the group and to offer activities at varying levels of difficulty, complexity, and challenge. For example, the sixth curriculum guideline (see page 194) involves making sure 3-year-olds take naps or do restful activities during the day. Children with special needs, however, may need a greater amount of rest during the day and may not be able to participate in active movement activities to the extent that many of their peers wish to.

In general, however, the guidelines address sound principles of development that are as appropriate for children with delays or disabilities as they are for typically developing children. The original emphasis is on *increasing* the level of complexity as children advance in their learning. Although this emphasis is appropriate for all children, it is also necessary to *decrease* complexity for children who function below their chronological age level.

Adult–Child Interaction

Guidelines for adult–child interaction generally require adults to be attentive to children's needs, to be available when children require companionship or assistance, and to be able to facilitate children's optimal development. Such guidelines seem appropriate, with some modifications, for adults who work with children with special needs. The guidelines are summarized next, followed by a discussion of recommended modifications for children who may not be developing typically.

1. Adults respond quickly and directly to children's needs, desires, and messages and adapt their responses to children's differing styles and abilities.

2. Adults provide many varied opportunities for children to communicate.

3. Adults facilitate each child's successful completion of tasks by providing support, focused attention, physical proximity, and verbal encouragement. Adults recognize that children learn through trial and error and that children's misconceptions reflect their developing thought processes.

4. Adults are alert to signs of undue stress in children's behavior and are aware of appropriate stress-reducing activities and techniques.

5. Adults facilitate the development of self-esteem by respecting, accepting, and comforting children, regardless of the children's behavior.

6. Adults facilitate the development of self-control in children.

7. Adults are responsible for all children under their supervision at all times and plan for increasing independence as children acquire skills.

The most important difference between adult–child interaction with typically developing children and adult–child interaction with children with disabilities is the manner in which interactions take place. Facilitating self-control, for example, is an important practice for adults who work with all children. In the original context, Bredekamp's (1987) use of *self-control* meant control of behavior during times of stress or conflict. The term has a broader meaning when applied to some children with disabilities. For example, expectations are different when the child is functioning below chronological age level. Self-control in all aspects of development may never be achieved by a child with physical disabilities or autism. The guideline must be understood in terms of what adults should work toward, adjusting expectations to match each child's developmental level.

Similar adjustments are necessary for Guidelines 2 and 3. Children with communication delays may need more direct intervention than is implied in the phrase "provide many varied opportunities." Children with disabilities or delays may not be able to learn as readily from trial and error as their typically developing peers. More direct intervention may prove necessary to assist them to complete tasks.

This brief overview of DAP as outlined by NAEYC and the examples of modifications that can be made when working with young children with disabilities demonstrate that the NAEYC guidelines have great value and are generally developmentally appropriate for all children, regardless of ability levels. Answering the following questions will help you make more effective adaptations in the play activities of children with special needs.

- What role should I play?

- Is there a place for direct teaching in my classroom?

- How can I make sure the play environment is developmentally and individually appropriate?

- How can I adapt play to provide a means for practicing newly acquired skills?

FULLY INCLUDING CHILDREN WITH SPECIAL NEEDS

In 1975, the Education for All Handicapped Children Act (PL 94-142) established the right to free appropriate public education for all children with disabilities. Subsequent legislation further evolved these services for children with disabilities (Guralnick, 2001). Of note, IDEA '97 (PL 105-17) mandated that the first placement option taken into account for children with disabilities younger than 5 years of age be the natural environment. Therefore, all professionals (e.g., special education teachers and therapists, preschool and Head Start teachers, child care professionals, early childhood administrators) have an incentive to fully include children with special needs in environments with typically developing children.

A varied legal framework is evolving to facilitate inclusion at the preschool level; an example is the series of local interagency agreements between school districts and Head Start agencies that have been written or revised nationwide to work out details concerning who will serve children with disabilities, who will provide what services, how parents will be involved, and other matters (Guralnick, 2001; Hanson & Widerstrom, 1993). Most children with developmental delays or disabilities in the United States will be served in general early childhood classrooms, where play is already a primary context for learning.

The advantages are numerous for children who spend time in general early childhood classrooms. Typically developing peers can act as role models for children with delays or disabilities, and they can also offer leadership for group play, take greater initiative in planning and carrying out play activities, and be counted on to plan more elaborate and often more creative play sequences than their peers with disabilities.

For further reading on inclusion, consider the following suggested resources:

Cavallaro, C.C., & Haney, M. (1999). *Preschool inclusion.* Baltimore: Paul H. Brookes Publishing Co.

Cook, R., Tessier, A., & Klein, D. (2000). *Adapting early childhood curricula for children in inclusive settings* (5th ed.). New York: Charles E. Merrill.

Guralnick, M.J. (Ed.). (2001). *Early childhood inclusion: Focus on change.* Baltimore: Paul H. Brookes Publishing Co.

Hanson, M.J., & Zercher, C. (2001). The impact of cultural and linguistic diversity in inclusive preschool environments. In M.J. Guralnick (Ed.), *Early childhood inclusion: Focus on change* (pp. 413–432). Baltimore: Paul H. Brookes Publishing Co.

Peck, C.A., Odom, S.L., & Bricker, D.D. (1993). *Integrating young children with disabilities into community programs.* Baltimore: Paul H. Brookes Publishing Co. [out of print]

Pretti-Frontczak, K., & Bricker, D. (2004). *An activity-based approach to early intervention* (3rd ed.). Baltimore: Paul H. Brookes Publishing Co.

Sandall, S.R., & Schwartz, I.S. (with Joesph, G.E., Chou, H.-Y., Horn, E.M., Lieber, J., Odom, S.L., & Wolery, R.) (2002). *Building blocks for teaching preschoolers with special needs.* Baltimore: Paul H. Brookes Publishing Co.

Wolfberg, P.L., & Schuler, A.L. (1993). Integrated play groups: A model for promoting social and cognitive dimensions of play in children with autism. *Journal of Autism and Developmental Disorders, 23*(3), 467–489.

THE ROLE OF DIRECT TEACHING

Children with learning difficulties often cannot succeed at school-related tasks if they are left completely on their own. Many are not able to take the initiative to learn exclusively through play. Some lack creative abilities and simply can't think of ideas to carry out in play. As a result, they may wander aimlessly about the classroom, moving from one play area to another during free play. Others have specific skill impairments that respond well to direct teaching.

The adult's role in promoting play varies according to the developmental level and individual needs of each child. The roles typically taken by the adult can be placed on a continuum of increasingly direct involvement in the play activity. Often, the adult is merely an *observer* of a child's play, using the time as an opportunity to notice the child's skill acquisition or to plan a DAP to be carried out later with other children in the play group. In this role, the adult remains on the sidelines and does not interact directly with the children.

Next on the continuum of involvement is the adult as *facilitator* of the child's play. At this stage, the adult interacts with one or several children to assist them in getting started at an activity, to expand their basic play idea, or to act as referee when conflicts arise. For example, an adult may participate briefly in a pretend cooking activity by saying, "Oh, I love pizza. Are you going to make a pizza for Jamie and me to share with you? What a great idea!" Or, "Can we make the tower a little higher? Shall we try adding just one more block?"

At times, it is necessary for the adult to take on the role of *model* for the child. This means participating directly in the play activity, demonstrating a behavior that will expand the play in a new direction or get it going in the first place. For example, Mark may show that he wants to play with a doll but doesn't have any idea how to go about it. He may simply carry the doll around the room. The adult can sit down with Mark, cradle another doll, and say, "Let's feed the babies, shall we? Here's a bottle for your baby, and look, I have a bottle for my baby, too. Watch me feed my baby."

Finally, the adult may take the role of *direct teacher*. This means having in mind a skill that the child needs to acquire or practice and setting up a play situation that will accomplish this. For example, Jacob may need to learn to separate from his mother in the morning to come to preschool. The adult might engage him in conversation on a toy telephone. "Jacob, let's pretend to call Mommy on the telephone to tell her you're sad about leaving her. I'll be Mommy, and you be Jacob. Okay? Hello, Jacob, this is Mommy. Are you feeling sad this morning? I miss you, too. I'll see you soon, though, right after preschool. Tell me what you're doing in school this morning." Perhaps Shelley needs practice pedaling her tricycle. It may be necessary for the adult to place Shelley's feet on the pedals and hold them there while Shelley rides a few feet.

PRACTICING NEW SKILLS THROUGH PLAY

One of the most effective ways for young children with special needs to practice using newly acquired skills is in a play format. Because children enjoy play so much, they never mind repeating activities carried out in play, and, in fact, they usually repeat their play activities spontaneously, often appearing as if they are practicing skills on their own. It seems quite natural for adults to set up the learning environment in ways that make it interesting and fun for children spontaneously to repeat activities that they have been taught in more structured situations. The play activities suggested in this chapter are found in nearly all early childhood education classrooms. Therefore, they are developmentally appropriate for young children with disabilities. Now, let's explore how to plan objectives for children with disabilities in Chapter 4.

II

Planning and Writing Goals and Objectives for Children with Disabilities

A Planning Matrix for Play

Young children who are eligible for special education or related services due to identified special learning or developmental needs will have individualized education programs (IEPs). Eligible children younger than the age of 3 years will have individualized family service plans (IFSPs). These written plans are developed by a team and address the unique needs of the young child and his or her family. IEPs and IFSPs are similar in that they include goals and objectives (or outcomes) that have been identified by the team as important for meeting the child's needs. Other similarities and differences in the two plans are displayed in Table 4.1.

The challenge for teachers in an early childhood program is to integrate the child's educational goals and objectives into the ongoing program. Ideally, the teacher should participate in the development of the child's IEP or IFSP to ensure that the educational needs at school have been considered when identifying goals, objectives, and intervention strategies for the child. Teacher participation in the development of the IEP or IFSP is important because the teacher is one of the main people who will implement the program and monitor the child's progress. If you are a teacher who does not already participate in IEP or IFSP meetings for your students, talk with your director about ways you can become involved.

INDIVIDUALIZED EDUCATION PROGRAM

The IEP has been called a "blueprint." This name is a bit misleading because the IEP is not an exact or detailed plan. Rather, it provides the major guideposts or benchmarks for progress. It provides the direction and the plan of action. The IEP includes the most important goals and objectives for a child based on the collective opinion of the IEP team, including the child's parents, and multidisciplinary assessment of the child. The identified goals and objectives are considered critical for the child to learn or accomplish during the coming year. During the school year, important needs and corresponding learning objectives that do not appear on the child's IEP may become apparent. Thankfully, an IEP is not set in stone. The child's teacher or parents can call a review meeting to add or change goals and objectives to better meet the child's changing needs.

An example of an IEP for Serena is found in Figure 4.1. Serena is a 4-year-old girl who attends the preschool program at the neighborhood community center. Serena's teacher and the preschool director referred her to the school district's Child Find office because they had observed delays in Serena's language and concept development and because Serena had difficulty playing with her classmates. Assessment results showed that Serena had significant developmental delays and that she was eligible for special education. The team decided that Serena should remain in the preschool and that the school district would provide a visiting teacher (also called an itinerant teacher or consulting teacher) who would help Serena, her classroom teacher, and her parents.

Table 4.1. Comparison of individualized education programs (IEPs) and individualized family service plans (IFSPs)

IEP (for a child 3 years or older)	IFSP (for a child younger than 3 years)
A plan for the child	A plan for the family
Includes a statement of the child's present levels of educational performance	Includes a statement of the child's present levels of development
May include family goals	Includes a statement of the family's resources, priorities, and concerns; may include family outcomes
Includes annual goals and related short-term objectives for the child	Includes expected outcomes for the child and family
Includes a statement of special education and related services needed by the child	Includes a statement of the early intervention services needed by the child and family
Includes a description of the extent to which the child will participate in general education	Includes a statement of the extent to which services will be provided in natural environments
Service coordination is not required	Service coordination required; includes the name of the service coordinator
Transition plan is not required	Includes a transition plan outlining the steps to be taken to support transition to Part B (preschool) services
Reviewed annually	Reviewed every 6 months

One way to assist Serena in learning the critical skills and behaviors identified on her IEP would be for her visiting teacher to remove her from the classroom on the visitation days and provide Serena with special teaching and practice. It is generally agreed, however, that although this method may be effective in helping a child learn specific skills, it may not automatically improve the child's ability to use the learned skills in the classroom with teachers, assistants, or classmates. Because of this *lack of generalization*, the practice of removing a child from the classroom is not the most effective way of providing special help for many children.

Serena's IEP shows that her planning team thought it was important for her to learn to talk and play with the children and adults in her preschool program. Therefore, the visiting teacher and Serena's classroom teacher need to work together to figure out ways for Serena to get the special instruction and practice that she needs in her natural environments—her classroom, her home, and the playground.

PLANNING MATRIX

You may know children who don't take advantage of the materials and experiences that you provide for them. You may also know children who need more time or practice to learn the things that most preschoolers learn easily. How can you plan for the special instruction and practice that these children need? How can you plan for this instruction to happen in the early childhood classroom? What are some ways for this instruction and practice to occur during play?

INDIVIDUALIZED EDUCATION PROGRAM

Student identification information

School _The Learning Tree_   Address _193 Broom Street_

Telephone _____   _Newton, Maryland_

Student name _Serena James_   Student identification number _____

Date of birth _1-27-01_   Grade _Prekindergarten_

Parent/guardian/surrogate parent(s) _Frank and Marcia James_

Telephone _____   Address _314 Green Street_

                                                     Newton, Maryland

IEP status

Initial date _2-8-04_   Annual review date _____   Date revised _____

Temporary/placement date _____

      Principal _____

      Parent _____

Date of IEP meeting _2-8-04_   IEP initiation date _2-9-04_   IEP ending date _2-9-05_

                       IEP initiation date _____   IEP ending date _____

                       IEP initiation date _____   IEP ending date _____

Record of formal assessment

Aptitude		Achievement		Developmental/other	
Instrument	Date	Instrument	Date	Instrument	Date
				Battelle	1-18-04
				PLS	1-21-04

Disability _Developmental delay_

Figure 4.1. Sample individualized education program (IEP).

Goals and objectives

Area of need(s): _Social_

Present levels of performance: _Plays alone, watches others, needs adult's help to share_

Annual goal: _Serena will demonstrate cooperative play with other children._

Unless otherwise noted, all objectives are in order of sequential mastery as established by objective criteria.

Schedule of evaluation of progress

Objectives and criteria	Start date	Date/ objective progress	Date/ objective progress	Date/ objective progress
1. During free-choice time, Serena will play near other children (within 3 feet) for at least half of the play period on 3 different days.	2-9-04			
2. During group activities, Serena will share or exchange objects or toys with other children engaged in the same activity several times (more than 8) during the week.	2-9-04			
3. During free-choice time, Serena will use socially appropriate verbal or nonverbal strategies to join other children in cooperative play at least 4 times during the week.	2-9-04			

Goals and objectives

Area of need(s): _Communication_

Present levels of performance: _Uses 1- or 2-word phrases, answers but doesn't initiate, talks with adults but not children_

Annual goal: _Serena will expand her verbal communication skills._

Unless otherwise noted, all objectives are in order of sequential mastery as established by objective criteria.

Schedule of evaluation of progress

Objectives and criteria	Start date	Date/ objective progress	Date/ objective progress	Date/ objective progress
1. During free-choice time, Serena will use words or phrases to make requests of others at least 3 times on 3 different days.	2-9-04			
2. During free-choice time, Serena will use words or phrases to obtain information from others at least 3 times on 3 different days.	2-9-04			
3. In a variety of settings, Serena will respond to other children's conversations and take at least 2 conversational turns with words or phrases and will do this consistently.	2-9-04			

(continued)

Figure 4.1. *(continued)*

Goals and objectives

Area of need(s): *Cognition*

Present levels of performance: *Doesn't yet sort or categorize, knows color "red"*

Annual goal: *Serena will expand her knowledge of concepts.*

Unless otherwise noted, all objectives are in order of sequential mastery as established by objective criteria.

Schedule of evaluation of progress

Objectives and criteria	Start date	Date/ objective progress	Date/ objective progress	Date/ objective progress
1. During play times, Serena will group objects or toys that are functionally related (e.g., cups and saucers) several times (more than 8) during the week.	2-9-04			
2. During play times, Serena will sort objects into groups according to some physical attribute (e.g., color, size) several times (more than 8) during the week.	2-9-04			
3. In teacher-led activities, Serena will follow directions, answer questions, or identify objects using at least 8 different color words and will do this consistently.	2-9-04			

Setting

Instructions

The following represents a continuum of service delivery. Beginning with the general education setting, each setting must be considered until an appropriate placement has been determined. An explanation, or rationale, of how goals and objectives on the IEP could or could not be achieved in each location must be documented. Once a placement decision has been made, it is not necessary to address more restrictive placements.

The following placement(s), with accompanying rationale, was (were) considered for the provision of services identified in this IEP:

General education setting
Serena will continue at The Learning Tree Preschool. The consulting teacher will meet with Serena, her teacher, and her parents to meet Serena's learning needs.

Services provided both in separate special education classes and in general education settings

Self-contained special education programming in an inclusive setting

Segregated setting

_X_ The child's welfare and meeting of goals within the IEP were considered during discussion of placement.

Placement and parental agreement

This IEP (will)/will not (indicate one) be provided at the school or setting that would otherwise be attended if not requiring an IEP.

I (agree)/disagree (indicate one) with the placement decision as note above and discussed in the meeting.

Maria James   *Frank James*   2-8-04

Parent/guardian/surrogate parent signature(s)   Date

Participants attending meeting

Name	Title	Signature	Date
Roberta O'Neal	Administrator/designee	*Roberta O'Neil*	2-8-04
Maria James	Mother	*Maria James*	2-8-04
Frank James	Father	*Frank James*	2-8-04
Melinda Rose	Teacher	*Melinda Rose*	2-8-04
Stephanie Watson	Special educator	*Stephanie Watson*	2-8-04
Marcella Clark	Speech-language pathologist	*Marcella Clark*	2-8-04

This section requires an "administrator/designee" signature. This individual is required to attend each IEP meeting in order that a commitment of funds and services may be made during the IEP meeting.

Parental participation

1. I acknowledge that I have received a copy of the Procedural Safeguards. My due process rights under those Procedural Safeguards have been explained to me.

2. I (agree)/disagree (indicate one) with the IEP as found in this document.

Maria James   *Frank James*   2-8-04

Parent/guardian/surrogate parent signature(s)   Date

INDIVIDUAL PLAY PLANNING MATRIX

Susan Sandall, Ph.D.

Child's name *Serena*

	Objective *Language: Use words or phrases to make requests*	Objective *Social: Play near other children*	Objective *Cognitive: Group together objects that are functionally related*
Arrival/free choice	• *Practice*		
Circle	• *Teacher* • *Picture board of activities* • *Model*		
Free choice	• *Teacher* • *Art table, missing items* • *Wait time*	• *Peers* • *Any area* • *Encourage, reinforce*	• *Adults, peers* • *Housekeeping* • *Prompt*
Outside		• *Peers* • *Sandbox, climber* • *Encourage, reinforce*	
Bathroom			
Snack	• *Adult* • *Second helping* • *Verbal prompt*		
Story			• *Practice*
Small groups		• *Adults, peers* • *Any area* • *Group with children with similar interests*	
Music			• *Adults, peers* • *Muscial instruments* • *Prompt*

Figure 4.2. Planning matrix for an individual child.

One way to plan is to use a planning matrix, an example of which is found in Figure 4.2. A matrix helps members of the team ensure that special instruction will occur. It also helps identify times when the child will have opportunities to practice new and emerging skills. Furthermore, the matrix format helps the team members plan for generalization by arranging for instruction and practice at a variety of times of the day, during a variety of events or activities, and with a variety of people and materials. The matrix is not a lesson plan or activity plan. You will continue to write lesson or activity plans that include the purpose of the activity, procedures, and materials. The planning matrix ensures that adequate learning opportunities are provided during routines and activities throughout the day. Some people call this *embedding instruction*. There are several benefits of embedding instruction, including these:

1. Integration of learning experiences within usual routines and activities highlights for the child the meaning or use of the learning objectives.

2. Integration of these planned experiences within routines increases the probability that instruction will occur.

3. Use of child-initiated learning experiences capitalizes on the child's attention and motivation.

4. Learning opportunities are distributed throughout the day.

It may also be necessary to make other changes to the learning environment, depending on the child's or children's needs. Changes include reorganizing the physical space, using adaptive equipment, and modifying some learning centers and activities. Some of these adaptations are discussed in later chapters. Even when more complicated changes are necessary, a matrix is a useful planning tool.

To fill out the matrix for Serena in Figure 4.2, Serena's teacher first reviewed the usual schedule of events and activities printed on the left side of the matrix. Then, with Serena's visiting teacher, she wrote Serena's current educational objectives across the top. These objectives can be taken directly from the IEP or, in some cases, they will be subobjectives of the IEP objective, because an IEP objective may have several smaller or enabling objectives. Sometimes, help will be provided in small steps that are also learning objectives; they can be used on the planning matrix.

Looking again at the sample matrix, it is apparent that Serena's preschool teacher and visiting teacher tried to find the best match between the amount and type of instruction that Serena needs and the ongoing activities of the classroom. The preschool teacher shared her knowledge of Serena and also her knowledge of the other children in the classroom and their needs and interests. She also knows how much help she has at various times of the day, how much equipment is available, how her schedule is influenced by the other classrooms, when she has a chance to spend individual time with Serena, and when she must supervise all of the children.

The visiting teacher brings her knowledge of techniques for individualizing instruction, the nature and needs of children with disabilities or developmental delays, and specialized teaching methods and materials. She might also have access to additional resources and equipment. She brings her knowledge of Serena's unique strengths and needs. Building on a child's strengths is an important consideration. Children learn best when they are interested, so in planning or individualizing for Serena (or any other child), the teachers will utilize her strengths, interests, and curiosity to help her learn new things.

Working together, both teachers figure out the best times for Serena to work on her learning objectives. In the cells of the matrix that correspond to these times, they write the names of the people involved, the materials, and the strategies to be used. They also note times when Serena might practice the skill. If a skill or objective cannot be addressed at a given time or in a certain activity, the cell is left blank.

The example in Figure 4.2 is for use with one child. If you are planning for several children with special needs, you will need to make a matrix for each child. Alternatively, you can expand the spaces for children's names and objectives across the top of the matrix. Some teachers simply place Xs in the spaces of the matrix that correspond to times for instruction and use their lesson plans for detailing the procedures and materials. When planning for several children, you will need to attend carefully to the children's objectives and to the use of time in order to ensure that instruction can realistically occur. For example, snack time might be a very good time for language intervention (children can make requests, describe their actions, and so forth), but if you have minimal assistance during this time of the day, or if the snack group includes a child who needs a great deal of help with eating, language instruction might not be possible at this time. In this case, you would need to select other times of the day for language-learning opportunities.

Another example of a planning matrix is found in Figure 4.3. In this example, the plan is for use with several children who will participate in a selected activity in the dramatic play area. The group play planning matrix is used to ensure that opportunities are provided for multiple objectives and multiple children to be served within the same activity. To complete this matrix format, write the names of the children with special needs down the left side of the matrix. The columns are labeled by developmental domain. Within the matrix cells, write the objective that is targeted for instruction for a child within the particular activity area.

This matrix will be useful for planning for the play centers and activities that are available during free choice or small-group time. You might develop matrices for block play, the sand table, the housekeeping area, manipulatives, the computer area, and so forth. New matrices will be written or updated for new activities, as well as when a child accomplishes the targeted learning objectives.

This chapter describes a set of procedures to help transfer a child's IEP goals and objectives to the real-world setting of the classroom. For additional readings on translating learning goals to classroom activities in inclusive settings, the following references are recommended:

GROUP PLAY PLANNING MATRIX
Susan Sandall, Ph.D.

Activity _Dramatic play area—fast-food restaurant_

Child's name	Goal area *Communication*	Goal area *Social*	Goal area *Cognition*
Serena	Will use words or phrases to make requests (example: to place order)	Will play near (within 3 feet) of other children	Will group objects (2 or more) that are functionally related (example: place burger and fries in bag)
Willie			Will recall events that occur on the same day (example: tell teacher about play at end of free choice)
Josh	Will ask wh- questions (example: "What do you want?")	Will take on role during play (example: cashier, cook)	

Figure 4.3.   Planning matrix for a small group.

Allen, K.E., & Schwartz, I.S. (1996). *The exceptional child: Inclusion in early childhood education.* Albany, NY: Delmar Publishers.

Cavallaro, C.C., & Haney, M. (1999). *Preschool inclusion.* Baltimore: Paul H. Brookes Publishing Co.

Cook, R., Tessier, A., & Klein, D. (2000). *Adapting early childhood curricula for children in inclusive settings* (5th ed.). New York: Charles E. Merrill.

Pretti-Frontczak, K., & Bricker, D. (2004). *An activity-based approach to early intervention* (3rd ed.). Baltimore: Paul H. Brookes Publishing Co.

Sandall, S.R., & Schwartz, I.S. (with Joseph, G.E., Chou, H.-Y., Horn, E.M., Lieber, J., Odom, S.L., & Wolery, R.). (2002). *Building blocks for teaching preschoolers with special needs.* Baltimore: Paul H. Brookes Publishing Co.

The planning matrix presented in this chapter helps team members match the child's learning needs with the resources (time, people, and activities) in the classroom. The following chapters will present more specific strategies for providing instruction and practice opportunities during play. In Chapter 5, you will learn how to individualize goals for play.

5

Individualizing Goals for Play

Adapting activities for children with a range of abilities and interests is the heart of early childhood education. In any early childhood group, there are children who approach activities differently, have preferences for some toys while avoiding others, or take a little longer to learn a new skill. You adapt for individual children when you give them choices, provide different ways for them to explore and use their skills, or simplify an instruction. Although you are familiar with these kinds of adjustments, you may not know how to plan or modify activities for children with disabilities.

Many early childhood classes are diversifying to include children with a much wider range of abilities and special needs than before. You may find that you need to figure out ways to adapt easel painting for a child with a visual impairment or to make the climbing structure accessible for a child with minimal movement and control of his or her legs. Including children with disabilities or other special needs in an early childhood program may mean having to adapt or modify some activities you currently use. This chapter describes some of the ways you can make modifications for children with special needs. Planning will help to ensure that every child can participate in the activities at some level.

The starting place for planning activities for a child with special needs is the child's individualized education program (IEP) or individualized family service plan (IFSP). Your choice of activities and modifications should correspond to the goals and objectives listed on the IEP or IFSP. These goals and objectives will help you select and design appropriate activities and match play opportunities with the child's interests and abilities. Ongoing observation of the child will help you continue to match the child's changing interests and abilities.

The word *match* here does not refer to an exact match. Activities should be in tune with the child's interests and current abilities, yet present a little bit of a challenge so that the child can play and practice within his or her current range of abilities and also try something new. For example, one of the objectives developed for Serena is "Serena will use words or phrases to make requests." From observations, Serena's teacher knows that Serena enjoys and plays comfortably in the art center, particularly with the collage materials. Serena's teacher develops a plan to join her at the art table more frequently and to bring a clear box with feathers and scraps of fabric. The teacher then waits for Serena to notice and request these materials. If Serena's request is just a single word ("Feather?"), the teacher models a multiword request ("Want yellow feather.") and waits for Serena to respond. The teacher plans to use this lesson for several days. Of course, if the other children notice the new materials, they can ask for and use them as well, providing Serena with a model of requesting. What the teacher has done is to match Serena's interests and abilities and challenge her a bit.

STRATEGIES FOR INDIVIDUALIZING PLAY ACTIVITIES

You may already have many methods and strategies that you use to meet the interests and needs of the children with whom you work. In this section, other ways of modifying play activities for children with special needs are offered. Although these methods are organized by type of special need, remember that every child is unique. For example, a method that is listed under visual challenges might work just as well—or even better—for a child with a cognitive delay. Children will show you through their responses whether the modification was effective.

Children with Cognitive Delays or Learning Challenges

Children who have difficulty with learning, memory, or problem solving or whose cognitive development is below that expected for their chronological age are sometimes referred to as having a cognitive delay or cognitive impairment. A preschool-age child with such difficulties or delays may have a learning disability or mental retardation. Some helpful modifications and special strategies when working with children with cognitive delays or learning difficulties include these:

- Use real materials and experiences in addition to or rather than using abstract or symbolic materials. Introduce abstract materials only after a child has experienced the task with concrete materials. For example, a visit to a farm to see a real cow or to an airport to see an airplane should be made before a child is introduced to play objects and pictures that *represent* the cow or airplane. Later, you can introduce the most abstract level: the words *cow* and *airplane*, which are symbols for the real object.

- Provide meaningful repetition. A child with cognitive delays or difficulties generally needs more practice than other children.

- Give clear instructions, and repeat if necessary. Highlight the important words in the instructions.

- Provide additional cues. Use gestures and picture cues, but if the child seems to have trouble focusing his or her attention with so many cues, use only the ones that he or she can focus on most easily. Model the action or activity for the child.

- Break down complicated or complex tasks into smaller parts. Help the child learn some of the parts to ensure success at the task. Then, add more components.

- Provide encouragement when the child tries. Don't restrict your praise to completed tasks or projects. Encourage effort and persistence (e.g., "My, Louise, you are working very hard to stack those blocks. Keep trying. I know you can do it.")

- Think of ways to provide assistance other than through direct help from an adult. Suggestions include help from another child, a simpler instruction, more immediate feedback, and the like.

- Provide structure and consistency (without being rigid). This will help the child be more independent.

- Plan your transitions. Some children will need longer than average preparation time. Others need clear signals that one activity is ending and another one is beginning. A reasonably consistent schedule will help children know what to expect.

- Allow plenty of time for trying and for practice. Learning and practice times should be scattered throughout the day and within different kinds of play activities.

Suggested readings on children with cognitive delays or learning challenges and instructional models include

Batshaw, M.L. (Ed.). (2002). *Children with disabilities* (5th ed.). Baltimore: Paul H. Brookes Publishing Co.

Kamii, C., & DeVries, R. (1993). *Physical knowledge in preschool education: Implications of Piaget's theory.* (Reissue ed.). New York: Teachers College Press.

Wolfberg, P.L., & Schuler, A.L. (1993). Integrated Play Groups: A model for promoting social and cognitive dimensions of play in children with autism. *Journal of Autism and Developmental Disorders, 23*(3), 467–489.

Children with Communication Challenges

Many children who are identified for special education and related services during the early childhood years have communication challenges. *Communication* is a broad term that refers to the exchange of thoughts and ideas, feelings, emotions, and preferences. Children with delays in this domain may have greater difficulty speaking clearly, making themselves understood, putting words together, or understanding others. Some children with communication challenges use augmentative and alternative communication (AAC) systems, such as sign language, communication boards, or computer devices. Speech-language pathologists guide the other team members in helping a child with communication delays or difficulties play and learn more effectively within the classroom, playground, and other places where young children typically spend their time. Some useful modifications when working with children with communication needs include these:

- Be a good conversational partner. Listen. Give the child frequent chances to take a turn. Acknowledge the child's communicative attempts, including nonverbal communication attempts.

- If the child uses an AAC system, learn and use the system.

- Position yourself so the child can see your face when you're speaking.

- Ask open-ended questions and questions that help expand the child's thinking. Try to avoid asking questions that the child can answer with a simple yes or no.

- Remember, too, that there's much more to a conversation than just asking questions. Make comments. Repeat and expand on what the child says.

- Add new information slowly and clearly.

Provide lots of opportunities to communicate, both with adults and other children. Support children's efforts to talk, draw, or write by engaging them in activities they find meaningful and fun, and be sure to participate with enthusiasm yourself. Also provide lots of opportunities for the child to practice individual objectives.

Suggested readings on children with communication challenges include the following:

Cook, R., Tessier, A., & Klein, D. (2000). *Adapting early childhood curricula for children in inclusive settings* (5th ed.). New York: Charles E. Merrill.

Dickinson, D.K., & Tabors, P.O. (Eds.). (2001). *Beginning literacy with language: Young children learning at home and school.* Baltimore: Paul H. Brookes Publishing Co.

Notari-Syverson, A., O'Connor, R.E., & Vadasy, P.F. (1998). *Ladders to literacy: A preschool activity book.* Baltimore: Paul H. Brookes Publishing Co.

Children with Motor or Physical Disabilities

Children with motor or physical disabilities may have medical diagnoses such as cerebral palsy, spina bifida, or muscular dystrophy. Some children have delays in their motor development; others have differences in their ability to use their joints, bones, or muscles. Specialists such as physical and occupational therapists help these children, and the children's team members plan ways to help the children move and play. Therapists can also help make or provide adaptive equipment and demonstrate ways to position, hold, or carry children with physical needs.

The following general modifications can serve as guidelines for working with children with motor or physical disabilities. These children tend to have unique abilities and movement patterns, however, so an occupational or physical therapist should always be consulted. In Appendix C you will find guidelines for positioning and handling young children with physical disabilities and strategies for adapting play materials.

- Provide ample time for the child to get to activities, materials, and places.

- Adapt materials and toys by stabilizing or enlarging them. For example, paintbrush handles and colored markers could be enlarged for easier grasping. You can also change the movement that is required to activate a toy. Some of these adaptations are very simple, such as taping the toy to the table so the toy won't slide away.

- Learn about and use adaptive equipment so the child doesn't have to use energy sitting or standing and can use that energy to play. Ask about inexpensive solutions if elaborate adaptive equipment isn't consistently available. For example, a child's feet should always be firmly supported when sitting. A large telephone book or a stack of smaller ones placed under the child's feet might act as a footrest.

- Remember that having a motor delay doesn't imply that a child has a cognitive delay.

- Encourage independence in the way that activities are presented, but at the same time don't discourage the child by making the activity more work than fun.

- Invite the children to think of creative ways to accommodate movement, accessibility, and other disabilities. For example, one group of children made a tray out of cardboard and attached it to a boy's walker so he could move toys from place to place.

Additional readings on children with motor and physical disabilities and instructional models include the following:

Batshaw, M.L. (Ed.). (2002). *Children with disabilities* (5th ed.). Baltimore: Paul H. Brookes Publishing Co.

Blackman, J.A. (Ed.). (1997). *Medical aspects of developmental disabilities in children birth to three.* Gaithersburg, MD: Aspen Publishers.

Cook, R., Tessier, A., & Klein, D. (2000). *Adapting early childhood curricula for children in inclusive settings* (5th ed.). New York: Charles E. Merrill.

Nickel, R.E., & Widerstrom, A.H. (1997). Developmental disorders in infancy. In A.H. Widerstrom, B.A. Mowder, & S.R. Sandall, *Infant development and risk: An introduction* (2nd ed., pp. 89–121). Baltimore: Paul H. Brookes Publishing Co. [out of print]

Sandall, S.R., & Schwartz, I.S. (with Joseph, G.E., Chou, H.-Y., Horn, E.M., Lieber, J., Odom, S.L., & Wolery, R.). (2002). *Building blocks for teaching preschoolers with special needs.* Baltimore: Paul H. Brookes Publishing Co.

Children with Hearing Impairments

Hearing disabilities range from mild losses to profound deafness. A number of specialists (including audiologists, speech-language pathologists, and deaf educators) work with children with hearing impairments to assess their capacity for hearing, to determine treatment and teaching methods, and to establish communication approaches. Some ways to help children with hearing disabilities include

- Learn about the adaptive aids the child uses. For example, learn how to check whether hearing aids are turned on and the batteries are charged, and learn how to change batteries if needed.

- Eliminate excess noise and other auditory distractions from the environment. Hearing aids amplify all sounds, not only speech.

- Get the child's visual attention before giving instructions or starting an activity.

- Position yourself where the child can see your face when you speak.

- Speak clearly, and use gestures as you speak. Try to speak normally, but be prepared to repeat, rephrase, or demonstrate to help the child understand.

- Use other forms of communication to help the child understand—such as pictures, printed words, and objects.

- Get feedback from the child to be sure that he or she understands your message.

- Learn and use the child's communication system.

- Provide the child with lots of opportunities to communicate.

- Involve other children. Young children are usually fascinated by AAC systems such as sign language and will want to learn to use them.

Some recommended readings on children with hearing impairments are

Batshaw, M.L. (Ed.). (2002). *Children with disabilities* (5th ed.). Baltimore: Paul H. Brookes Publishing Co.

Bodner-Johnson, B., & Sass-Lehrer, M. (Eds.). (2003). *The young deaf or hard of hearing child: A family-centered approach to early education.* Baltimore: Paul H. Brookes Publishing Co.

Cook, R., Tessier, A., & Klein, D. (2000). *Adapting early childhood curricula for children in inclusive settings* (5th ed.). New York: Charles E. Merrill.

Children with Visual Challenges

Young children with visual impairments may be partially sighted or blind. Few individuals are totally blind, and most young children with a diagnosis of visual disabilities will have some vision. These children will need to learn to use what vision they have in the most effective ways. Vision specialists and orientation and mobility specialists help children use their vision and learn ways to be as independent as possible. Some ways that early childhood team members can help young children with visual challenges include the following:

- Learn what the child can see and how to position objects so the child can see them most easily.

- Encourage children who have glasses to wear them consistently. This seems to be particularly important when a child first gets glasses.

- Be aware of lighting conditions. Arrange the environment so that lighting and positioning help the child.

- Try to keep the physical environment stable. If you do need to change the room arrangement, do so with thought and planning, possibly in several stages. Explain what changes have been made, help the child learn the new arrangements, and give practice time before making more changes. Keep pathways clear.

- Use the child's name when giving directions or when initiating a conversation.

- Give clear and specific directions. Help the child learn directional language such as *forward, next to,* and *to the left.*

- Describe and label demonstrations, objects, or events that the child isn't able to see.

- Remember that the child cannot see gestures. Use words in addition to gestures.

- Use pictures and picture books that are bold and uncluttered.

- Try to use high-contrast colors in visual images. Black and white isn't always best. Try black and yellow or black and orange.

- Use auditory or tactile cues.

- Plan activities for all children that strengthen all of their senses.

- Help the other children understand visual impairment by providing sensory experiences and involving them in adapting toys, activities, and games.

You will find additional suggestions for including children with hearing and visual impairments in Appendix C. Additional readings include

Batshaw, M.L. (Ed.). (2002). *Children with disabilities* (5th ed.). Baltimore: Paul H. Brookes Publishing Co.

Cook, R., Tessier, A., & Klein, D. (2000). *Adapting early childhood curricula for children in inclusive settings* (5th ed.). New York: Charles E. Merrill.

Children with Health or Medical Needs

Young children with health challenges may have chronic health concerns such as asthma, cystic fibrosis, diabetes, seizure disorders, acquired immunodeficiency syndrome (AIDS), and cancer. These children may or may not be eligible for special education and related services, but their medical needs may affect their classroom experience. Inclusion of a child with health or medical needs requires coordination among many care providers to ensure that the child's specific health problem is cared for, that the child's general health is maintained, and that the child can participate as fully and independently as possible in the early childhood program. Some methods for including children with health or medical needs include these:

- Be sure that health information remains current and complete (within legal guidelines). Get resources so you can read and learn about the specific health condition. Parents often belong to support groups and have very up-to-date information.

- Work with the other care providers to plan the child's program. Health providers should know what the classroom program is like so they can make reasonable suggestions. Teachers need to know warning signs; possible side effects of the illness; and the medications, physical restrictions, and so forth that the condition requires.

- Be sure that classroom emergency procedures are up to date and known by classroom aides and children. Have procedures for health emergencies such as seizures just as you do for fires, earthquakes, and other natural emergencies.

- Encourage the child to be as independent as possible.

- When planning classroom activities, think about the child's physical limitations and the possibility of fatigue, and plan accordingly. You don't necessarily have to eliminate an activity, but you may need to plan for partial participation.

- Have procedures for dealing with the possibility of multiple or lengthy absences.

- Practice good hygiene. Wash your hands, and teach the children to wash theirs as well. Always wear gloves when handling food; changing diapers; wiping runny noses; and cleaning up bodily fluids, such as blood.

Suggested readings on children with health or medical needs include

Batshaw, M.L. (Ed.). (2002). *Children with disabilities* (5th ed.). Baltimore: Paul H. Brookes Publishing Co.

Blackman, J.A. (Ed.). (1997). *Medical aspects of developmental disabilities in children birth to three.* Gaithersburg, MD: Aspen Publishers.

Cook, R., Tessier, A., & Klein, D. (2000). *Adapting early childhood curricula for children in inclusive settings.* (5th ed.). New York: Charles E. Merrill.

Nickel, R.E., & Widerstrom, A.H. (1997). Developmental disorders in infancy. In A.H. Widerstrom, B.A. Mowder, & S.R. Sandall, *Infant development and risk: An introduction* (2nd ed., pp. 89–121). Baltimore: Paul H. Brookes Publishing Co. [out of print]

Children with Challenging Behaviors

Learning to get along with others is an important developmental task of early childhood; however, children with challenging behaviors, especially children who are aggressive, often have difficulty getting along with others. Their behaviors can disrupt a classroom and interfere with their learning as well as the play and learning of other children. Children with challenging behaviors may or may not be eligible for special education and related services; regardless, they will need assistance from their teachers to promote their social development. Here are some strategies that may help:

- Provide a warm, inviting, and *consistent* atmosphere.

- Have a few simple but important classroom rules. Have clear consequences for violating rules, and follow through on them.

- Have a regular schedule. This helps children feel secure.

- Use the physical environment to help children learn how to behave in areas of the room. Have soft, cuddly pillows and chairs in the book area to set the stage for quiet play. You will spend less time stating and restating instructions if you use the environment to provide guidance.

- Think prevention. Anticipate problems and plan to avoid them. Use positive behavior support. This means looking at the antecedents of the challenging behavior to figure out what caused the behavior and how to prevent the behavior from recurring. If, for example, transitions bring on problems of self-control, revise your schedule or procedures to minimize the number of transitions the child must make (Division for Early Childhood, 2000a, 2000b; Lucyshyn, Dunlap, & Albin, 2002; Sandall & Otrosky, 1999).

- Reduce waiting or unoccupied time. Don't require children to wait their turn during group activities, including circle time.

- Have appropriate expectations, especially for group times. If children get restless or fidgety during circle time, think about shortening the time and the number of tasks you do during group times.

- Use positive guidance techniques. Be consistent in your expectations of children's behaviors. Use carefully planned consequences for individual behaviors, remembering to emphasize the positive behaviors and ignore, if possible, the negative ones (Division for Early Childhood, 2000a).

- Be a model of appropriate social behaviors. Use a quiet voice when indoors. Use words to solve problems and express feelings.

- What appears to be inappropriate social behavior may be a child's only way of expressing wants, needs, or feelings. This is particularly true for children with delays in verbal language. Acknowledge these children's attempts to communicate. Work with other team members to help them learn more effective ways to express themselves.

- Be a friend. Children need consistent, caring adults.

Some additional readings on children with challenging behaviors are

Bell, S.H., Carr, V., Denno, D., Johnson, L.J., & Phillips, L.R. (2004). *Challenging behaviors in early childhood settings: Creating a place for all children.* Baltimore: Paul H. Brookes Publishing Co.

Cook, R., Tessier, A., & Klein, D. (2000). *Adapting early childhood curricula for children in inclusive settings* (5th ed.). New York: Charles E. Merrill.

Division for Early Childhood. (2000). Concept paper on the identification of and intervention with challenging behavior. In S.R. Sandall, M. McLean, & B. Smith (Eds.), *DEC recommended practices in early intervention/early childhood special education* (p. 156). Reston, VA: Council for Exceptional Children.

Division for Early Childhood. (2000). Position on interventions for challenging behavior. In S.R. Sandall, M. McLean, & B. Smith (Eds.), *DEC recommended practices in early intervention/early childhood special education* (p. 154). Reston, VA: Council for Exceptional Children.

Hanson, M.J., & Beckman, P.J. (Eds.). (2001). *Me, too! series: On my best behavior.* Baltimore: Paul H. Brookes Publishing Co.

Child's name _Serena_   Domain _Cognition_

Settings _Housekeeping/free choice_

IEP objective _Serena will expand her knowledge of concepts._

Objective

During play times, Serena will group objects or toys that are functionally related (e.g., cups and saucers) several times (more than 8) during the week.

Materials

In the housekeeping area, group objects and toys that go together. Examples include cups and saucers, pots and lids, keys and pocketbooks.

Procedures

When Serena chooses the housekeeping area, join her there when possible. As she plays, insert conversational prompts to help her put functionally related toys together. Examples include, "You have a cup, I need a cup for my saucer," or "Let's put the lids on these pots." Model categorization occasionally as part of participation in play.

When Serena puts objects together, comment on it. ("You put a cup on each of the saucers.")

Evaluation procedures

Use anecdotal notes to record when Serena groups toys on her own. Review the notes at least once a week to determine whether changes are needed.

Figure 5.1. Sample individual lesson plan.

ACTIVITY PLANS

Individualizing for play requires you to be keenly aware of each child's interests, abilities, and objectives. Sometimes there seems to be too much to remember. Successful interventionists have figured out ways to keep track of individual needs and interests. Some ideas for planning are presented here and in subsequent chapters. You will find an example of a lesson plan for Serena in Figure 5.1.

Including children with disabilities and other special needs in the early childhood classroom enriches the learning experience for everyone. You can work with the child's specialists and family in order to meet the child's individual needs. Additional planning and perhaps some special procedures may be necessary to help meet the child's needs, but there are potential rewards for everyone.

Additional resources on activity plans include

Dau, E. (Ed.). (1999). *Child's play: Revisiting play in early childhood settings.* Baltimore: Paul H. Brookes Publishing Co.

Pretti-Frontczak, K., & Bricker, D. (2004). *An activity-based approach to early intervention* (3rd ed.). Baltimore: Paul H. Brookes Publishing Co.

Sandall, S.R., & Schwartz, I.S. (with Joseph, G.E., Chou, H.-Y., Horn, E.M., Lieber, J., Odom, S.L., & Wolery, R.). (2002). *Building blocks for teaching preschoolers with special needs.* Baltimore: Paul H. Brookes Publishing Co.

DEVELOPMENTAL PLAY SEQUENCES

Early childhood teachers and therapists use many sources of information to help them individualize for children. The child's IEP or IFSP is one source of information, and the teaching strategies described in this chapter are another. But, of course, your team's and your knowledge of early childhood development is a critical resource.

Chapters 6–13 each cover a particular type of play, and in each chapter, you will find a developmental sequence for that type of play. These sequences illustrate how typically developing children progress from simple to more complex levels of play. The sequences from all of the play areas are summarized in Table 5.1 to give you an overall picture of play in the preschool classroom. Some types of play, such as block play, are quite straightforward and need little explanation. Other types of play (e.g., creative play) are more complex and require some explanation. Short descriptions are included for items that are not easily defined or measured.

As you read Chapters 6–13, the link between developmental sequences and the typical play activities and play centers in an early childhood program will become obvious. You will see how a child's developmental level determines his or her level of participation in an activity or center. Knowing the child's developmental level (as well as the child's interests) will help your early intervention team do the best possible job of planning play opportunities that are appropriate to the child's abilities. Using a developmental framework will help the team plan activities and centers that allow children to participate and learn at various levels and at individual paces.

The sequences have been converted to a Developmental Sequences of Play Checklist (found in Appendix D) that you may wish to use for determining at what level a child is performing play-related tasks typical of the preschool environment. Then, you can design learning goals for a certain play area that match a child's level of play development. Let's begin by examining play in the block area, in Chapter 6.

Table 5.1. Summary of developmental sequences for play

Developmental sequence of block play

    Level 1: Picks up a block and puts it in mouth

    Level 2: Bangs two blocks together

    Level 3: Stacks one block on top of the other

    Level 4: Uses blocks to stand for other objects

    Level 5: Builds simple structures with blocks

    Level 6: Builds complex structures with blocks

Developmental sequence of sand and water play

    Level 1: *Sensorimotor exploration*—Children use touch, taste, or vision to explore the sand or water.

    Level 2: *Simple exploration*—Children begin to explore and experiment in simple ways. For example, they pour water from one container to another for the pure pleasure of it, without noticing any changes in volume or appearance.

    Level 3: *Beginning conservation*—Children begin to understand conservation and carry out various experiments involving the filling and emptying of different-sized containers. For example, Kayzeena might use a large pitcher of water to fill several small containers, or Maria might compare the size of her pile of sand with her neighbor's.

    Level 4: *Beginning symbolic play*—Children use the sand or water symbolically to engage in imaginary play. Examples are building towers or walls of sand and pretending to sail a boat in the water.

    Level 5: *Full conservation*—Children demonstrate understanding of the basic concept of conservation. That is, they can predict whether the amount of liquid being poured from one container to another will (or will not) fit in the new container without overflowing and spilling.

Developmental sequence of pretend play skills

    Level 1: Substitutes one object for another (e.g., using a stick for a doll)

    Level 2: Uses toys in simple play routines (e.g., feeding a doll with a pretend baby bottle) during solitary or parallel play

    Level 3: Engages in more complex play routines (e.g., dressing up to play Mommy or Daddy) that have a beginning, middle, and end and involve one or two children in associative play

    Level 4: Engages in pretend play with several children taking different roles; participates in complex play routines with one or two children taking the lead and others following in cooperative play

Developmental sequence of play with manipulatives

    Level 1: Puts together simple one- or two-piece puzzles (with large, thick wooden pieces) with some assistance; strings large beads on a shoelace with some assistance; stacks two or three 1-inch cubes in a tower

    Level 2: Completes more complex puzzles (smaller, more numerous pieces); fits together interlocking pieces like those on Lego plastic building blocks; builds towers, houses, and other structures with small blocks

    Level 3: Works independently on manipulative tasks; engages in independent problem solving with materials

(continued)

Table 5.1   *(continued)*

Developmental sequences of common outdoor activities

Playground vehicles

    Level 1: Sits in a wagon while someone pulls it

    Level 2: Rides a tricycle or truck without pedals (may need to be pushed)

    Level 3: Rides a tricycle with pedals (with or without assistance)

    Level 4: Pulls someone in a wagon

    Level 5: Can do all activities independently

Swings and slides

    Level 1: With assistance, swings in a swing with a safety bar

    Level 2: Goes down a slide with assistance

    Level 3: With assistance, swings in a swing without a safety bar

    Level 4: Swings and slides with limited assistance (to start and stop)

    Level 5: Can swing and slide independently

Ball skills

    Level 1: Rolls a ball to an adult or another child sitting on the floor

    Level 2: Throws a large ball with both hands

    Level 3: Attempts to kick a ball (sometimes accurate)

    Level 4: Attempts to catch a ball with both hands (sometimes accurate)

    Level 5: Throws a ball with one hand

    Level 6: Kicks a ball to adult or another child

    Level 7: Catches a ball

Developmental sequence of rhythm skills

    Level 1: Bangs or shakes an object to mark time with music

    Level 2: Bounces in place to music

    Level 3: Uses both hands to play a rhythm instrument (tambourine, drum, or cymbals)

    Level 4: Marches to music, keeping time with both feet

    Level 5: Dances simple steps to music

    Level 6: Leads dancing or rhythm activity

Developmental sequence of music skills

    Level 1: Listens to adults singing a song

    Level 2: Sings some of the words during group singing

    Level 3: Sings the whole song during group singing

Level 4: Sings a song alone

Level 5: Sings a song with accompanying finger-play

Level 6: Makes up songs and sings them alone

Developmental sequence of creative skills

Level 1: *Sensorimotor exploration*—Children explore materials by feeling, looking, and tasting. They get pleasure from smearing things like paint or pudding across the table, feeling runny materials flow through their fingers, and tasting everything that comes into their hands. This is truly the messy stage of creative exploring.

Level 2: *Simple use of materials*—Children begin to use materials in a purposeful way; however, they primarily imitate the work of others, either adults or peers. Children do not yet come up with their own ideas.

Level 3: *Simple creative play*—Children begin to put their own ideas into the creative activity. They explore the materials with the idea of developing a finished product. The activity usually involves a single material such as paint, glue, pudding, shaving cream, or crayons. Children attempt to represent familiar objects in their creative works, a first step in using symbols.

Level 4: *Complex creative play*—Children elaborate on the creative idea, using increasingly complex ideas. More varied materials are used and perhaps more than one medium, such as several colors of paint or glue plus tissue paper. The creative work represents reality in some way, but there is less emphasis than at Level 3 on the representation (e.g., making a house look like a house). At Level 4 there is usually fantasy involved. For example, children might illustrate with colored drawings stories they have made up or paint pictures of their dreams. Older children may paint what comes to mind when they listen to certain music. These activities overlap very well with the emerging literacy skills that are seen at Level 4 (See Chapter 14).

Developmental sequence of literacy

Level 1: *Awareness of print*—Children understand the purpose of print, that words have meaning and are arranged on pages in an orderly way, and that books are read from left to right and right side up.

Level 2: *Awareness of the relationship between oral and written language*—Children realize that print is just speech written down.

Level 3: *Knowledge of letters, their names, and their sounds*—Children learn to associate the letter and its sound with its symbols. For example, they learn to recognize their name in print and understand that it is made up of certain letters with specific sounds.

Level 4: *Phonological awareness*—Children have the ability manipulate the sounds of language and understand that some are spoken and others are written.

Level 5: *Developing vocabulary, both oral and written*—Children learn to use words and sentences in their daily activities.

Level 6: *Development of narrative skills and discourse*—Children are able to recount real events in their lives and retell stories from books. They learn the basic rules of oral conversation, such as turn taking and initiating topics.

III

Let's Play

Embedding Techniques and
Learning Goals in Play Activities

6

Block Play

How High Is Our Tower?

The block center is an important part of the preschool classroom. Nearly all children enjoy playing with blocks, so the block area can be a highly effective play and learning center. Block play is a wonderful way to develop both large and small muscle skills, such as grasping and placing objects; lifting, carrying, and balancing objects; and eye–hand coordination. Blocks also provide excellent opportunities for creative play.

There are many kinds and sizes of blocks with a range of prices and qualities. The large wooden ones are the most expensive, and many programs with tight budgets have purchased the less expensive hollow ones made of pasteboard. Ideally, a preschool classroom should have a supply of many kinds of blocks—large and small, painted and varnished, and all shapes (e.g., square, oblong).

As you observe children of varying abilities in the block area, you will see that blocks can be used in a variety of ways. Some children will explore and manipulate the blocks and carry them from place to place; others will make piles or stacks of blocks or start to arrange them on the floor. You will see children constructing simple roadways and towers and fences. They may include props in their constructions as well. More advanced children will make elaborate structures, incorporate a variety of props, and dramatize their play with blocks. Subsequently, you may observe typically developing children using blocks to stand for objects in their play—for example, riding on them and pretending they are trains, motor scooters, or horses.

You play an important role in organizing the block center, observing the children, and promoting their learning. As in the other learning centers, the arrangement of space and materials in the block area will have an impact on how the children behave and what they learn. Some children will play independently with the blocks, whereas others will play cooperatively with a group of children, sharing ideas and building materials. The block center should be set up in an area where there is plenty of room for several children to play at one time because it is a popular area. In addition, the center should be removed from the middle of classroom activities so that block creations can be saved without getting in the way.

Various environmental cues will also help support appropriate social behavior in the block area. For example, if the area is defined on three sides, it helps delimit the boundaries for children. A floor covering such as indoor/outdoor carpeting makes the space more comfortable and also reduces the likelihood of accidentally toppled towers.

BENEFITS FOR CHILDREN WITH SPECIAL NEEDS

Blocks are especially beneficial for children with special needs because they can be used in very simple ways (e.g., stacking) or more complex ways (e.g., imaginary play) depending on the developmental ability level of the child. Children can play alone or with others. Fine motor, language, cognitive, or social goals can be embedded in block activities as well. Examples of these goals are provided later in the chapter. Furthermore, blocks promote active learning. Regardless of developmental level, children who get involved with blocks are acting and creating opportunities for learning. For children with significant developmental delays, your role in maximizing these opportunities is very important.

Naturally occurring learning opportunities include opportunities to explore the sensory characteristics of the blocks and building materials. As the child moves and manipulates the blocks, more challenging "problems" occur that need to be examined—how to get blocks from one place to another, where to find more of the same kind of block, or where to locate props to extend an experience. Learning opportunities that arise from the child's play may be especially productive because they are child-initiated and build on the child's interests. For children with developmental disabilities, the simple process of stacking and knocking down blocks or taking turns with stacking the blocks can establish some interactions with teachers and peers.

Many young children with identified special needs or disabilities have difficulty expressing themselves in words. Because block play does not require good verbal skills, the block area is often a place where children with language disabilities can capitalize on their strengths. If the block center is interesting and comfortable for a child with language disabilities, you can then take advantage of potential language learning opportunities within it. The child naturally has something to communicate about—a shared topic—and interactions with the materials and other children provide reasons to communicate. You can then use these situations to help the child communicate and convey messages in more conventional ways.

Children with behavior or emotional difficulties may also find the block area a comfortable center in the classroom. To ensure that these children use the area productively, you will need to provide sufficient space, sufficient materials, and clear guidelines for expected behaviors. Start by having group discussions about the rules for block area behavior. Have some of the typically developing children help in drawing up a list of rules to be posted in the block area. Emphasize that children must follow the rules or leave the area.

DIFFICULTIES FOR CHILDREN WITH SPECIAL NEEDS

The benefits of the block center and block play will occur only if a child takes advantage of the center. Thus, the center needs to be attractive and inviting. A particular concern for children with special needs is accessibility. You may need to view the area from a child's perspective to see whether all children can get to the area, reach and remove the blocks, find a space to play, and move about without interfering with other children's play.

If your group includes children with physical or sensory disabilities, some changes to the usual organization of the block center may be required. Examine the blocks to ensure that the children can indeed hold and manipulate them, construct with them, and put them away at the end of the play period.

Difficulties may also occur in this area of the classroom when children have discrepancies between their motor skills and cognitive skills. For example, children might get frustrated if they have a plan for building a tower or fort but do not have the physical skills to carry out the plan. It is important to be alert to this possibility and to have a plan for dealing with it. For example, you might sit beside the child and help him or her balance the blocks, even putting your hand over the child's hand to guide him or her. If a tower falls, get the child to laugh with you instead of expressing anger. You might also ask a peer to join the two of you, then quietly back away.

Children with special needs may need help thinking of creative uses for blocks. They may need help, too, in learning to use blocks for building everything from simple towers to more complex houses. Playing with typically developing children may give children with special needs the models they need for creative play with blocks. At the next play opportunity, children with special needs may be able to repeat the creative activity on their own. For example, a child with cognitive challenges may not discover independently that three large blocks stacked one on top of another make a very simple but effective table on which an imaginary meal can be shared with a friend. If the friend suggests this activity, however, and leads the way through the activity, preparing the "food" and "eating" it, the child with special needs will usually join in.

Some children may not extend or move on in their play. For example, you may notice that one child takes the blocks from the shelf and makes a pile day after day. Another child may build the same roadway every day. The first step is to observe the play very carefully because such children may indeed be demonstrating some very subtle but important changes in their play. For other children, though, you will need to use additional prompts to encourage them to expand their play.

Some ways to overcome these possible difficulties are presented, but remember that the block center does not present tremendous obstacles for most children. If you plan for learning opportunities across all developmental domains in a variety of play centers in the classroom, the child who opts not to play in the block center will have many other ways to learn and practice building, balancing, and playing creatively.

DEVELOPMENTAL SEQUENCES

Children will benefit from the block center only if their teachers and therapists write appropriate objectives for them and appreciate the developmental richness of the block center. Some developmental objectives that children can work on in the block center are listed next. This list is not exhaustive; it is meant to highlight the range of developmental objectives that can be addressed at the block center.

When describing the level of block play appropriate for a particular child, consider the child's fine motor skills, cognitive ability to pretend with objects, and social skills, especially how well he or she can join in a cooperative activity. Numerous developmental checklists are available that you can use to guide your observations and identify a child's current level and range of abilities. Using this information in your planning will ensure appropriate opportunities and challenges for the children.

1. Physical development

   - Sits with good balance and plays with blocks
   - Gets into and out of sitting position
   - Is able to start and stop walking
   - Squats in play
   - Walks while carrying objects
   - Reaches for and grasps blocks
   - Grasps objects with thumb opposed
   - Releases a block into a container
   - Stacks one block on top of another
   - Stacks multiple blocks
   - Places objects with control (e.g., in, on, under, and between other objects)

2. Cognitive development

   - Explores characteristics of objects
   - Combines objects in play
   - Links actions in simple combinations (e.g., places blocks in a truck, then pushes the truck)
   - Uses blocks to represent other objects
   - Matches objects
   - Classifies and sorts objects by shape, function, color, and size
   - Makes and reproduces patterns
   - Demonstrates an understanding of length and weight
   - Demonstrates an understanding of stability and balance
   - Experiments with cause and effect
   - Makes predictions
   - Solves problems

3. Social development

   - Plays independently
   - Plays alongside other children
   - Joins others in play

- Shares toys with other children
- Expresses ideas and feelings with other children
- Cooperates in group projects
- Demonstrates positive self-concept

Developmental Sequence of Block Play

Level 1: Picks up a block and puts it in mouth

Level 2: Bangs two blocks together

Level 3: Stacks one block on top of the other

Level 4: Uses blocks to stand for other objects

Level 5: Builds simple structures with blocks

Level 6: Builds complex structures with blocks

ADAPTATIONS AND MODIFICATIONS

Before concerning yourself with specific adaptations and modifications for individual children's needs, it is important to be sure that you have set the stage for children to use the block center easily and productively as possible. Here are some important questions to consider:

- Is the center large enough to accommodate children playing alone, children playing together, and children with special equipment?

- Is the space well defined, both the total space and a child's own area? (Some teachers use tape to help define the space; others have children use individual pieces of cardboard to build on.)

- Is the center near other active and noisy activities so that it doesn't interfere with quiet play areas?

- Are there are enough blocks for the number of children? (You can never have too many blocks, but children must also learn to share.)

- Are props and accessories matched to the children's interests and abilities?

- Are the blocks displayed and organized to maximize interest and accessibility and to help children clean up at the end of playtime? (You might label the shelves with printed signs, outlines, drawings, or photographs.)

- Are the props and accessories also displayed and organized for greatest interest and accessibility?

To ensure that the blocks are accessible for young children with special needs, get down on the floor, and examine the block center from the child's perspective. If your group includes children who are not yet crawling or walking, lie on the floor to find out whether these children can see the blocks and props and get to them in some way. The carpeting in this area should have a flat weave (e.g., indoor/outdoor carpeting) and should be firmly secured to the floor to assist children who use wheelchairs, walkers, or other equipment. Define a "no building" zone next to the block storage area so that the blocks remain accessible during playtime.

If your group includes children who have difficulty holding and manipulating blocks, experiment with blocks of different sizes or textures. Magnetic blocks, cardboard blocks, or lightweight blocks may be useful options for some children. Cardboard blocks are not as durable as wooden blocks, but they can be made from milk cartons rather than purchased commercially to reduce the expense.

PLANNING ACTIVITIES WITHIN THE CENTER

Your plans for using the block center will depend in part on your observations of the children and your goals for the center. Some teachers and therapists plan to incorporate a certain theme in the block center, whereas others leave the children's activity open ended. If props and accessories that support the theme are available, then the children can choose whether to incorporate them in their play.

Beyond setting the stage for learning opportunities, your role in this center is to support and facilitate the children's play and learning while not interfering much in their play. A very effective strategy for supporting children's learning in this center, as in most others, is to talk about what children are making or building. Many teachers find this much easier to do with children who are making complex plans and building elaborate structures. It can be more difficult to interact with and reinforce a child who is rubbing the blocks together, piling them, or arranging them in very simple ways. You may have difficulty thinking of comments or descriptions for simple arrangements or constructions of blocks—it takes practice! Some ways to interact include talking about the physical characteristics of the child's chosen block (e.g., "That's a long block"), the number of blocks (e.g., "You've got three blocks"), or similarities and differences in the blocks (e.g., "The blocks in your tower are all the same size").

When interacting with children who seem hesitant to play, your use of comments rather than questions may encourage them. Comments give children vocabulary and information and demonstrate your interest in their activity. Comments don't put the child on the spot by requiring him or her to answer you. In contrast, questions are often used to help extend and integrate the child's learning (e.g., "How will the people in this building get to their cars?").

There are a number of ways to facilitate children's learning in the block center:

- *Join in*—Get down on the floor, and join the child's play. You can try doing what the child is doing as a way of beginning the interaction. Sometimes, your simple presence may provide enough support for a child to solve a problem.

- *Reduce frustration*—Offer choices or suggestions if the child is frustrated. Some children become frustrated when their physical skills aren't keeping pace with their building ideas. For example, one youngster was big for his age and a little awkward. His towers and buildings often crashed to the floor, which often resulted in his yelling and screaming. His teacher joined him at the beginning of his play and took turns with him by handing him blocks. This slowed him down and helped him practice more controlled placement of the blocks. The teacher also provided words of encouragement and assistance by stabilizing the blocks when needed.

- *Encourage creativity*—Incorporate pictures to encourage creativity in a child who builds the same thing day after day. Bring in different accessories or props to inspire new ideas. Help children incorporate ideas from field trips or neighborhood walks. You might take photographs on your outing and display them in the block center. Some children may need another kind of model.

- *Expand on the child's play*—Play near the child, and follow the child's lead by playing with the blocks in a similar way. Then, make a very small change in the building, and wait for the child to continue. The child may or may not imitate your model, but what you have done is to help the child see the "in-between" steps to making something new or different. You can try this on several occasions to help extend the child's play repertoire.

EMBEDDING LEARNING GOALS IN BLOCK PLAY

Using the block center to work on specific learning goals for a particular child (i.e., *target child*) is simple and enjoyable. First, make sure there is plenty of room for the target child and a friend to play without being inhibited by larger groups of children working at more complex levels. Then, gather a supply of the blocks needed for the activity. At first, join the two children, and lead the way in carrying out the activity. The learning objectives most easily embedded in block play are fine motor, cognitive (planning, creating, problem-solving), and social goals (being a productive member of a group). Some examples of activities to address fine motor learning objectives follow:

Objective—The child will pick up objects using thumb and one or several fingers and release them with accurate placement.

Developmental age: 1 to 2½ years

1. Help the child to build a tower of five or six blocks (or more if appropriate). Allow the child to knock it down, then rebuild it. Choose small 1-inch blocks for older children and larger blocks for younger children. Children get better at this activity with repetition. Each time the tower is rebuilt, ask the child to

pick up and place more of the blocks on top. Encourage use of thumb and forefinger for picking up. If necessary, put your hand over the child's at first to provide support in picking up the blocks and placing them on the tower. Make sure a friend is involved in watching and taking turns with the target child.

2. Encourage the child to make a train using small wooden or plastic blocks placed in a line and hooked together. Ask the child to tell you where the train is going, who is riding on it, and who is the engineer. Help the child move the train around in a circle on the carpet, making sure the first block (engine) is held using thumb and fingers.

Developmental age: 3 to 6 years

1. Have children build a house or a fantasy structure using many large wooden blocks. This works best if a group of children decide to build together. One child usually becomes the leader and gives orders to the others. You can introduce the target child into the group and then stay to monitor the child's participation. Suggest ways to contribute to the structure. For example, you might say, "Let's put this block here. It will be part of this wall, all right?" Comment on and reinforce the child's building attempts. For example, you might say, "Good idea, Raymond. Putting that block on top of the door will make it much stronger."

2. Pair a child with disabilities with a typically developing child. Encourage both children to construct a tower using blocks of various sizes and shapes. See how high they can make it without it falling down. Using large blocks, try to build a tower as tall as the target child.

The following examples will get you started with work on cognitive goals:

Objective—The child will increase the ability to solve problems involving spatial relations.

Developmental age: 3 to 6 years

1. While the child is building a structure with large blocks, sit nearby and observe. When an impasse is reached—that is, when something doesn't work right—encourage the child to think of another way. For example, if the pile falls over because it has too many blocks in it, ask the child to think of a way to better balance the structure. If a block is wedged into a structure so tightly that it can't be moved, suggest that the child think of a way to fit the blocks together better. Ask questions such as, "How can we make this airplane big enough for three people?" or "Which block can I put up here so it won't fall down?"

2. Define a space about 2 feet square on the floor of the block area, and mark it off with boundaries of some kind. Ask the target child to join you in building a house using small wooden blocks. Ask the child to show you where the liv-

ing room, kitchen, and bedroom will be. Ask the child to build the walls with blocks, then design each room with furniture. Encourage creativity in using small blocks for chairs and tables, but also add play furniture to the house, and finish it with flowers, toy people, and other props.

As you can see, there are many possibilities for embedding techniques and learning goals in block play. Next, let's explore the possibilities available in sand and water play, in Chapter 7.

7

Sand and Water Play

Mud Pies Are Delicious!

Sand and water play are basic elements of early childhood education. Many children play with sand before they enter preschool, either at home or in public playgrounds. Children with disabilities often experience sand and water play in infant intervention programs. As a result, sand and water play areas are usually comfortable places for all children. In addition, these play areas lend themselves very well to parallel play, the level of play often demonstrated by preschool children with developmental delays or disabilities.

WATER TABLE

The water table is always popular in preschool classrooms—at least with the children! Some adults feel it is too much trouble to keep the water table filled with clean water or that it isn't good for children to get wet while playing at the water table, especially if they get their clothes wet (which they usually do). This attitude is unfortunate, for it denies the children an important learning experience. It really is worth the effort to maintain a clean, sanitary water table and to have dry clothing available when necessary in order to allow all the children many opportunities for water play.

For maximum efficiency, it is important to have plastic coverall aprons available for all children at the water table. If your center is located in a moderate climate, take the water table outdoors both for emptying or filling it and for the children's water play. This is the main advantage of a portable water table.

At the water table, children can experiment on many levels. They can explore how water looks and feels and what it is like to splash it, pour it, or rub it onto tables or the ground. They can watch to see how a few drops of food coloring will change the appearance of the water but not its feel (or even its taste!). The water table really is a wonderful place to learn through investigating. Even children who function on a fairly low developmental level can enjoy playing independently at the water table. All children seem to find water fascinating. You can capitalize on their pleasure by embedding learning goals in water play.

SAND AREA

Like the water table, the sand table or outdoor sand area is a very popular play spot. Sand offers children different experiences than water does. It feels heavier (though it may not be) and pours differently. It can be gathered in the hand and allowed to trickle out through the fingers. Small toys can be buried in sand and hidden. Spilled sand may be easier than water to clean up, and usually doesn't get clothes dirty. The sand doesn't need to be changed as often as water does, either, which may explain its higher popularity rating with teachers.

If possible, every preschool classroom should have both sand and water tables available. Children work on the concept of object permanence by burying and finding objects in the sand. They learn number concepts about quantity and size from sand and water play (e.g., "How many toys can we find in the sand?") and begin to understand conservation of liquid and volume from their filling and dumping activities. They learn how different textures feel and how adding water to sand or color to water changes the appearance. They also enjoy playing together at the sand or water table, talking about what they are doing, or observing each other, so social and language skills are practiced. Children with delays or disabilities can often watch more advanced children for ideas about how to play with sand and water. Children with limited verbal abilities may not talk much themselves, but they can listen to their peers at the sand and water areas. Adults can join in unobtrusively when the need arises, for most tables can accommodate several people at once.

BENEFITS FOR CHILDREN WITH DISABILITIES

Because children with special needs may experience delays in the development of their social skills and may have difficulty playing with peers, a common learning goal is for them to learn to play successfully with others. Unwillingness to share materials is a problem sometimes encountered. Although sharing is something preschool teachers work on with all children, children with delays may not be as ready to share as typically developing children. Sharing should not be expected of children who are developmentally below age 3.

It is also true that children with delays are less successful in small-group play, often due to aggressive, nonsocial behaviors. They may be forced out of a playgroup because their behavior antagonizes their peers. The sand and water tables are good situations for working on social learning goals because the activities tend to provide their own structure. Children stand side by side, so there are few territorial battles. If enough duplicates of materials are available, sharing is not necessary. Routine activities such as water play, filling and dumping containers, and pouring from one container to another are quite natural for most children, making it easy for children with disabilities to be successful in these play areas. Children with delays can engage in parallel play and feel as if they are participating with the group.

Please note that some children may find sand and water play uncomfortable. Children with tactile defensiveness, for example, do not like to touch or be touched by unfamiliar materials. Often, these children have neurological problems. Children with poor sensory integration may dislike wearing clothes, taking baths, or tasting food because such sensory experiences are unpleasant. It's a good idea to consult an occupational therapist who specializes in sensory integration; he or she can offer suggestions for alternative classroom activities or accommodations for these children.

DEVELOPMENTAL SEQUENCE OF SAND AND WATER PLAY

Here are some of the skills that can be practiced during sand and water play:

Level 1: *Sensorimotor exploration*—Children use touch, taste, or vision to explore the sand or water.

Level 2: *Simple exploration*—Children begin to explore and experiment in simple ways. For example, they pour water from one container to another for the pure pleasure of it, without noticing any changes in volume or appearance.

Level 3: *Beginning conservation*—Children begin to understand conservation and carry out various experiments involving the filling and emptying of different-sized containers. For example, Kayzeena might use a large pitcher of water to fill several small containers, or Maria might compare the size of her pile of sand with her neighbor's.

Level 4: *Beginning symbolic play*—At this level, children use the sand or water symbolically to engage in imaginary play. Examples are building towers or walls of sand and pretending to sail a boat in the water.

Level 5: *Full conservation*—Children demonstrate an understanding of the basic concept of conservation. That is, they can predict whether the amount of liquid being poured from one container to another will (or will not) fit in the new container without overflowing and spilling.

ADAPTATIONS AND MODIFICATIONS

The sand and water tables accommodate various developmental levels without major modifications. Some suggestions for making these play areas more accessible to children with special needs follow:

1. Limit the number of objects in the table. For sand, have only two shovels and two pails so that one other child can play with the target child and they both will have their own equipment. In the water table, have only one or two containers for filling and pouring. Children with developmental delays often prefer to use their hands to explore; they may not be ready to use tools yet. Independent play, then, can be with the hands only. If an adult facilitates the play by offering suggestions and modeling the use of tools (e.g., buckets, shovels, measuring cups, spoons), such items can be introduced into both the water and sand tables.

2. Periodically introduce innovations into the sand and water tables. Children enjoy having the water colored blue, green, or red (or some combination) with food coloring. They also enjoy tables filled with rice, beans, or other dry materials instead of sand.

3. Pair the target child with a typically developing child who can model ways to engage in sand or water play at higher and more complex levels. Encourage

the two to talk together about what they are doing. For example, you can say, "Jimmy, will you show Derek how you mixed the sand and water together to make that cake? I think he would like to learn how to make mud cakes." Or, "Derek, which of these is bigger, the blue cup or the red bucket? Let's see how much sand we can put into the red bucket. What do you think, Jimmy?"

4. Introduce the sand or water table gradually to children with special needs. If there is a new material, such as rice or beans, in the table, allow the children time to get used to it. This is especially important for children with tactile defensiveness. Some children find tranquility at the water table and spend time alone there, enjoying the feeling of the water on their hands and arms. They should be allowed to do this as long as it isn't their only activity for the day.

EMBEDDING LEARNING GOALS IN SAND AND WATER PLAY

This section includes suggested activities you can do to embed learning goals in sand and water play.

Objective—The child will understand the meaning of *big* and *biggest*, and *small* and *smallest*.

Developmental age: 3 to 6 years

1. Provide containers of various sizes for filling and dumping the water or sand. Cups, measuring spoons, pitchers, and buckets will provide enough variety and allow more than one child at a time to participate in the play. As the children use the containers, sit next to them, and comment on their play, calling their attention to the differences in the containers' sizes. Be sure to use the words *big* and *small*.

2. Play a simple game with the target child and one or two other children. Have each child choose a container and fill it with sand. Then, ask each child in turn to dump out the sand. Ask which child has the biggest pile of sand. Then, ask which child has the biggest container. Repeat the activity with the *small* and *smallest* containers. If the children seem to understand the concepts of *big/small* and *biggest/smallest,* try some comparisons. Ask questions such as, "Whose container is bigger than Sarah's?" and "Is my cup smaller than your bucket?"

3. For more advanced or older children, you may try introducing the idea of conservation. Choose containers that hold the same volume of liquid but are different shapes. Fill both containers at the water table, then ask the child which has more water or whether they are both the same. Pour the water back and forth several times between the two containers to demonstrate that although they look different, the containers really hold the same amount. Note, how-

ever, that conservation is a difficult concept not usually understood by typically developing children until age 7 or older. Therefore, preschool children cannot be expected to understand it. It should be used solely as a means for exploring the ideas of *big* and *small*.

Objective—The child will pour from one container to another without spilling.

Developmental age: 1½ to 4 years

Allow the child to explore the materials independently at the water table first. Children will often spontaneously begin filling containers and emptying them. If this doesn't happen, begin by encouraging the child to fill a container with water then dump it out. Next, suggest that the child try pouring from one big pitcher into another. This should be done while standing at the table so any spilled water falls back into the table. As pouring becomes more accurate, allow the child to try pouring from bigger to smaller containers. At first, you will have to assist by holding the small container. Next, you can have the child hold the container while you steady it with your hand. When the child can pour fairly steadily, move to the snack table, and try pouring juice from a pitcher into a cup.

Objective—The child will play with two peers, sharing materials, without being forced to leave the playgroup.

Developmental age: 2 to 4 years

1. Set up the water or sand table with enough duplicate equipment for three children, plus yourself. Sit or kneel next to the target child, and invite one or two other children to join you. Hand each child a container. Take a similar container, and model filling it and pouring the contents into another container. Talk about what you are doing. Then, observe and prompt the target child to imitate your actions. As the child fills the container, imitate the action, commenting on what the child is doing and drawing the other children's attention to it.

2. Another suggestion is to encourage the target child to imitate peers in water or sand play. To do this, imitate the peers' actions yourself, and comment on what they are doing. Then, suggest that the child imitate an action. For example, you can say, "Look, Henry. Jill is building a road for her car. Let's do that, too."

Sand and water play is a favorite activity of many children. Another area of play that is enjoyable and contains many opportunities to embed learning opportunities is pretend play, which is discussed in Chapter 8.

8

Pretend Play

I'll Be the Mommy, and You Be the Daddy

The housekeeping area is the easiest place in the classroom for children to engage in pretend play. When equipped with small tables and chairs; a toy stove and refrigerator; miniature dishes, pots, and pans; empty food cartons; and other realistic play materials, the housekeeping area enables children to pretend to be grown-ups, an activity that nearly all preschool-age children really enjoy. Pretend play can be enhanced by including a dress-up corner containing grown-up clothes in the classroom.

The importance of engaging in pretend play is well recognized by early childhood professionals. It represents an important step in the development of certain cognitive and language skills, for as Piaget (1962) has pointed out, pretend play helps children learn to represent things, a cognitive ability that is directly related to language development. In other words, children learn that one thing can stand for or represent another. For example, a small block can represent a truck. The child might move the block across the floor, saying, "Vroom! Vroom! Here comes my fast truck! Look out, everybody!" To become good speakers, readers, and writers, children must learn that words represent ideas or facts—that is, they stand for something else. The understandings children gain from pretend play in which objects substitute for real things help them achieve abstract thinking skills and language skills.

Children with special needs often have difficulty engaging in pretend play. Research on the play of children with disabilities has shown that children with developmental delays engage in less pretend play than typically developing children, and they have more trouble initiating it (Widerstrom, 1986). Sometimes, they lack the creative ability to come up with ideas for pretend play. They may get stuck and act out the same play scene over and over. Their creative play is less elaborate than that of typical peers, and their play ideas are less fully developed. Children with autism have perhaps the most difficulty with pretend play and rarely engage in it spontaneously. Research has shown, however, that children with autism can be taught to play and that they can learn through pretend play (Cavallaro & Haney, 1999; Rogers, 1988; Wolfberg & Schuler, 1993).

Research on the play of children with disabilities indicates that two factors can make a difference in the quality of these children's pretend play. First, it helps to place typically developing children in groups with children with disabilities. Typically developing children can act as models, think up more complex ideas to carry out, and take the initiative in pretend play. Second, it is often necessary for the adult to teach children with disabilities to engage in pretend play, using instructional strategies that include modeling, prompting, rewarding, and repetition. These strategies are illustrated later in the chapter in examples of how to embed learning goals in pretend play activities.

DEVELOPMENTAL SEQUENCE OF PRETEND PLAY SKILLS

Level 1: Substitutes one object for another (e.g., using a stick for a doll)

Level 2: Uses toys in simple play routines (e.g., feeding a doll with a pretend baby bottle) during solitary or parallel play

Level 3: Engages in more complex play routines (e.g., dressing up to play Mommy or Daddy) that have a beginning, middle, and end and involve one or two children in associative play

Level 4: Engages in pretend play with several children taking different roles; participates in complex play routines with one or two children taking the lead and others following in cooperative play.

ADAPTATIONS AND MODIFICATIONS

You may wish to consider the following adaptations to both the furniture and equipment in the pretend play area:

- Make sure there is enough open space in the play area for a child using a wheelchair or walker. Furniture should include a sink, stove, and refrigerator, but should also include a table, chairs, and a shelf or bookcase. Choose a low table that can be reached comfortably by a child in an adaptive chair, and keep one side of the table clear so it is accessible for a child who uses a wheelchair. The pretend play area can also be used to play restaurant or post office.

- Stock the kitchen with large, easy-to-grip spoons, forks, and knives and large plastic plates, bowls, and cups. Full-size cutlery is easier for children with fine motor difficulties to handle than the tiny ones. Use empty cereal boxes, soup tins, and other actual food containers. Make sure you have a variety of sizes of everything. This variety is important for working on goals such as seriation (big cup, bigger cup) and also for making the equipment more available to children with motor difficulties.

- Brooms and other cleaning equipment should be sturdy, heavy enough for stability, and of medium size. Include small brushes and a dustpan, a bucket, and a scrub brush. Sometimes trial and error is the best way to choose play equipment for a particular child with a disability.

- Most children like to wear aprons in the housekeeping area. Be sure to include some chef outfits, including tall chef hats. Both boys and girls enjoy wearing these for pretend cooking activities. Wearing a costume similar to those worn by peers can make a child with special needs feel a part of the group. It can give a big psychological boost to any child who has trouble gaining group entry.

- For the dress-up area, you may want to consider clothing that is adapted to make it easier for children with motor difficulties to dress and undress independently. Hook-and-loop fasteners (e.g., Velcro) should be used instead of laces or zippers on shoes, dresses, skirts, and pants. Expand necklines on pullover clothing.

- The pretend play area can easily be linked to literacy and other activities by expanding it beyond simple housekeeping or cooking activities. A dress-up area can provide props for chefs, waiters in a pretend restaurant, or firefighter outfits in a pretend firehouse. A pretend post office can be set up so children can "write" letters and mail them. Children can pretend to buy things at a grocery store, acting as cashier or customer. The pretend play area can also be set up to support current learning skills and content, such as animals in a pet store or zoo.

EMBEDDING LEARNING GOALS IN PRETEND PLAY

There are many ways that learning goals can be embedded in pretend play.

Objective—The child will pick up objects using thumb and one or several fingers and release them with accurate placement.

Developmental age: 2 to 4 years

Set up a tea party in the kitchen area, using real cups and saucers and a plate of fruit or crackers or popcorn. The cups should be filled with a liquid the children can pretend is tea, poured from the teapot by you or another child. Encourage the target child to drink the tea from the cup, picking up and replacing the cup in the saucer. Ask a child to pass the plate of food, and monitor the target child's use of thumb and finger grasp.

Objective—The child will increase receptive and expressive vocabulary of words associated with dressing and undressing, eating, and other self-help routines.

Developmental age: 1 to 2½ years

Developmentally young children enjoy dressing up with peers and watching the other children play. They may not wish to participate fully in the pretend activities going on in the housekeeping area and may feel happier on the sidelines. Dressing up in Mom's or Dad's clothes is fun and can be a great opportunity to work on receptive language goals. Describe for the child what's happening as the play activity proceeds. Provide a running commentary as long as you can maintain the child's attention. Calling attention to details of dress on both the target child and other children can increase receptive vocabulary.

Developmental age: 3 to 5 years

As the children begin a dress-up activity, ask what the target child is wearing and who he or she is pretending to be. Ask leading questions about the play activity, being careful not to intrude too much into the play or distract the child from full participation. Sometimes you can ask questions during the activity (e.g., "Where are we going? To visit Carlos's grandmother? Will you show us the way, Carlos?"), but other times questions are best left until the activity is finished, which requires the child to recall what happened (e.g., "Where did we go? Did we visit Grandmother?" "Did you enjoy seeing Grandmother this morning? What did we have to eat at Grandmother's house?" "We only pretended, but it was fun, wasn't it?").

Objective—The child will practice daily routines in the housekeeping area.

Developmental age: 1 to 2 years

Engage the child with a peer in simple daily routines, such as having a tea party, cooking and eating food, or sweeping the kitchen. These play activities will introduce the child to simple pretend play. Later, a doll can be included to give the child opportunities to further extend the symbolic play.

Pretend play is an excellent activity for small groups or individual children. Playing with manipulatives, (e.g., pop-apart beads, puzzles) is also a great way for children to play with each other or by themselves. Chapter 9 describes how to achieve learning goals though manipulative play.

Manipulative Play

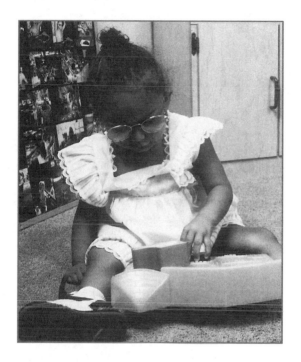

Real Materials Are Best

Although not all preschool classrooms have a specific area for manipulative materials, there are some benefits to creating one. Manipulative materials such as puzzles, beads to string, and interlocking blocks or other items all promote development of fine motor and prewriting skills. They also provide practice in problem solving and can be useful for creative activities. Children usually love manipulative materials and often want to do their favorite puzzle several times each time they pull it off the shelf. Typically developing children as young as 18 months of age enjoy putting puzzles together. Sometimes, they can work on two or three at the same time! Pop-apart beads and stringing beads are popular toys often found at home, as are Lego plastic building blocks. Thus, toddlers and preschoolers are usually very familiar with manipulative materials because they have played with them at home before starting school. Because their confidence level is high, children with special needs often perform very well with manipulatives and can experience feelings of true success when using them.

Manipulatives are useful for play in small groups where children can cooperate (e.g., working together on a puzzle), but they are also ideal for individual or solitary play. Some materials are self-correcting (e.g., inlay puzzles, pop-apart beads, Montessori materials), allowing a child to work alone or with minimal adult assistance. Other materials are free-flowing and creative; there are no right or wrong ways to use them. This flexibility makes manipulative materials highly suitable for fine motor or problem-solving goals.

DEVELOPMENTAL SEQUENCE OF PLAY WITH MANIPULATIVES

Level 1: Puts together simple one- or two-piece puzzles (with large, thick wooden pieces) with some assistance; strings large beads on shoelace with some assistance; stacks two or three 1-inch cubes in a tower

Level 2: Completes more complex puzzles (smaller, more numerous pieces); fits together interlocking pieces like those on Lego plastic building blocks; builds towers, houses, and other structures with small blocks

Level 3: Works independently on manipulative tasks; engages in independent problem solving with materials

ADAPTATIONS AND MODIFICATIONS

It is not necessary to make major adaptations in manipulative materials for the child with disabilities. Most preschool classrooms already have enough suitable materials for children who cannot handle very small objects or very heavy, awkward ones. It is really just a matter of identifying the best size, shape, and number of objects for a particular child to use. Keep in mind that the materials must be engaging for the child and at the appropriate developmental level. Then, choose materials that are easy to handle. This means, for example, choosing 1-inch beads instead of smaller ones that are more difficult to pick up and manipulate. Choosing a large paintbrush or crayon that is easier to hold is another example. The following suggestions may help the child with disabilities to play successfully with manipulatives:

1. Limit the number of objects on the table (or immediate play area) at any one time. This makes the environment less visually distracting for a child with attention problems and less complex for a child with developmental delays.

2. Place the objects the child is working with on a placemat or a small piece of fabric. This creates a visual boundary for the task that children with developmental delays often find helpful. This technique was first used by Montessori to define the child's work space, and it is still a useful concept.

3. Pair the target child with a typically developing child who can model how to engage in manipulative play at higher and more complex levels. Encourage the two to talk together about what they are doing. Call the target child's attention to the possibilities demonstrated by the other child.

EMBEDDING LEARNING GOALS IN MANIPULATIVE PLAY

There are many ways to embed learning goals in manipulative play. Consider the following examples.

Objective—The child will understand the meaning of *big* and *biggest*, *small* and *smallest*.

Developmental age: 3 to 6 years

1. Use beads of various sizes and a thick string. Tie a knot at the end of the string, and put a large bead on the string. Then, help the child find another big bead to add to the string, giving as much physical assistance as necessary. Comment to the child, "We now have two big beads on our string. Shall we add another big bead, or shall we find a small bead next?" Encourage the child to string as many beads as possible onto the string and tell you whether each bead is small or big. When the string is full, ask the child to show you the smallest and biggest beads on the string. After the child has gone through these steps with you, invite another child to join in, and encourage both children to carry out the game while you act as a facilitator.

2. Make a simple matching game for practicing *big* and *small* (or other opposites) by cutting out large and small pictures of everyday objects and people, then pasting them onto large cardboard playing boards and laminating them. Each board should be divided into six or eight squares, allowing for three or four large and small versions of the same object. For example, a big girl and a little girl, big and small houses, big and small cars, and big and small dogs could fill

Big items

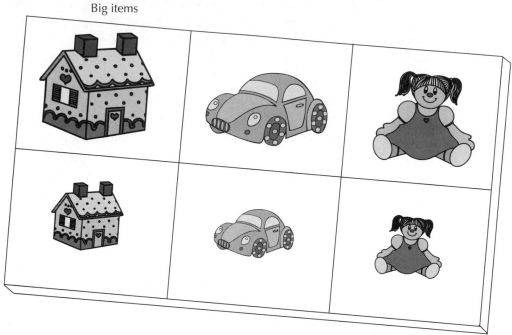

Small items

Version 1: A simple matching board like the one illustrated here can be used to practice concepts such as *big* and *small*. Cut out pictures of large and small objects, and paste them on a piece of cardboard as illustrated. Cover the board with clear plastic shelf paper or laminate the board to preserve it. Young children can point to big or small pictures and name the objects.

Version 2: Version 2 of this game is appropriate for older or more advanced children. This version involves a set of hand-held cards that match the objects on the board. Children can choose two or three cards each and then take turns matching them to pictures on the board.

Paste the set of *large* pictures on a thick piece of cardboard as shown in the illustration. Paste each *small* picture on a card that is large enough for children to hold easily. Laminate all the pieces or cover with clear plastic shelf paper.

Figure 9.1. Directions for making a laminated matching board.

one board. Having four or five boards allows several children to play together, using either duplicate gameboards or different gameboards. This makes it possible for a child and adult to play simple games (like having the child show you specific big and small objects), or for several children to play more complex games (e.g., lotto) together. Figure 9.1 illustrates how to make simple matching boards.

Objective—The child will understand the concepts *my/mine* and *your/yours*.

Developmental age: 1 to 3 years

Sit beside the child with a pile of small objects that can be easily handled and can be sorted by an obvious visual parameter such as color, size, or shape. You might use, for example, tokens, beads, small blocks, interlocking blocks, or miniature cars. Provide two empty coffee cans or other similar containers for sorting the objects. Take one of the containers, explaining, "This can is mine." Give the child the other container, saying, "This can is yours."

Begin by picking up one of the objects while explaining and demonstrating how to sort the items. For example, you can say, "All of the blue ones are mine. The red ones are yours. Let's put our [beads, blocks, toys] into our cans. This blue bead is mine. I'm going to put this blue bead into my can. This red one is yours. Can you put it into your can?"

Continue until all the objects have been sorted, then dump everything out of the cans and begin again. If you are targeting the concepts *mine* and *yours*, make sure that the child already can reliably sort objects based on whatever parameter you choose. This game is also good for teaching classification by color, size, or shape for children who have not mastered this skill.

As you can see, manipulative play can be used to teach important concepts such as size and possession. Next, let's explore ways to achieve learning goals through outdoor games and play, in Chapter 10.

10

Outdoor Games and Play

See How Fast I Can Go!

Outdoor play is necessary for all children. Even children who live in cold climates like to go outdoors as often as possible. Young children like to play with dirt, mud, water, and other appealing materials and are interested in the textures of things, how they look and smell, and how they taste. They also like to poke, dig, splash, and pat. Older children enjoy pretend play outdoors using natural materials they find, such as leaves, sticks, mud, and rocks, and they might decide to run and climb or lie on the ground and look at the sky.

Outdoor play can be much less structured than indoor play. Play limited to playground equipment such slides, swings, and tricycles isn't as much fun for children as being able to explore the great outdoors on their own. Such informal exploration is important for cognitive development. The gross motor activity developed through children's running, climbing, jumping, and balancing is also important.

Children with special needs are usually less able to enjoy outdoor play on their own. Many have physical disabilities that prevent easy movement. Adults tend to overly protect such children and sometimes restrict them from participating in outdoor play. Children with special needs may be unable to keep up with their typically developing peers, so they may be left out of group outdoor play activities; however, children with special needs have much to gain from outdoor play. They, too, learn through exploring and satisfying their curiosity. They like to be with other children and to do the same things they do. Learning to swing, go down a slide, or climb on a jungle gym can greatly increase their confidence and self-esteem. Fine and gross motor skills can be improved through outdoor play activities. Cognitive and language skills can be improved, too, while playing in the sand or water, gathering leaves or small stones, using sticks in pretend play, and participating in similar games.

Children with physical disabilities may need a special buddy or an adult aide assigned to them to help them participate and keep up with the other children, especially if they use a wheelchair or walker outdoors. Children with cognitive or language delays also might do better outdoors with a buddy to help them keep up with the group in such activities as swinging, throwing and catching a ball, or going on a nature walk.

If the early childhood program includes children with special needs, there should be special education specialists available to assist in setting learning goals and devising ways to achieve these goals during indoor and outdoor play. Although a child's learning goals were developed by the transdisciplinary team and included in the child's individualized education program (IEP), the adults working in the classroom have the responsibility of working on the goals and objectives. Physical therapists, occupational therapists, early childhood special educators, and/or inclusion support specialists work collaboratively with the early childhood teacher in the classroom and elsewhere (e.g., at the child's home, outdoors in the play area, on nature outings) to achieve learning goals. The early childhood teacher can participate fully in this process, but specialists take the lead in adapting activities to include individual goals and objectives. Collaboration is therefore essential, and the responsibilty for planning and monitoring progess is a group process.

DEVELOPMENTAL SEQUENCES OF COMMON OUTDOOR ACTIVITIES

Following is a list of developmental squences for the common outdoor actvities of playing with playground vehicles, using swings or slides, and playing with balls.

Playground vehicles

Level 1: Sits in a wagon while someone pulls it

Level 2: Rides a tricycle or truck without pedals (may need to be pushed)

Level 3: Rides a tricycle with pedals (with or without assistance)

Level 4: Pulls someone in a wagon

Level 5: Can do all activities independently

Swings and slides

Level 1: With assistance, swings in a swing with a safety bar

Level 2: Goes down a slide with assistance

Level 3: With assistance, swings in a swing without a safety bar

Level 4: Swings and slides with limited assistance (to start and stop)

Level 5: Can swing and slide independently

Ball skills

Level 1: Rolls a ball to an adult or another child sitting on the floor

Level 2: Throws a large ball with both hands

Level 3: Attempts to kick a ball (sometimes accurate)

Level 4: Attempts to catch a ball with both hands (sometimes accurate)

Level 5: Throws a ball with one hand

Level 6: Kicks a ball to an adult or another child

Level 7: Catches a ball

ADAPTATIONS AND MODIFICATIONS

Outdoor play equipment can be adapted quite easily for children with physical disabilities. For example, adding toe guards to a tricycle results in more stable pedaling. Handlebars can be equipped with larger hand grips. The back and sides of a swing can be padded to give extra trunk support, and wagons can be padded for the same reason. In addition to the play equipment described so far, the outdoor play area should contain pull toys; large and small balls for rolling, kicking, or throwing; buckets and shovels for the sand area; aprons or smocks for the water table; and any special toys the children like to use outdoors (e.g., favorite trucks).

A child with special needs will be able to play outdoors most productively in a small group of one or two other children who serve as role models and an adult who keeps things on track by providing prompts. For example, two children (i.e., one typically developing, one with disabilities) ride in the wagon. The teacher asks a third child to help pull the wagon, saying, "Come on, Sarah. These two kids are too heavy for me to pull alone. Can you help me?" Other activities include riding tricycles together; you can guide the tricycle of the child with special needs. Children can also take turns on the slide. You may need to talk the child to the top of the slide and wait for him or her at the bottom. You can also talk about taking turns on the slide. Ball play is also good for a group of two or three children. One child can roll the ball while you assist the child with disabilities in kicking the ball to another child.

EMBEDDING LEARNING GOALS IN OUTDOOR PLAY

Outdoor play can be a wonderful time to embed learning goals because of the variety of activities that can be encouraged. Consider the following suggestions.

Objective—The child will demonstrate eye–hand coordination adequate for simple motor tasks.

Developmental age: 3 to 5 years

Choose an area of the playground that is out of the way of other children. The target child can either sit on the ground or stand. Roll a large ball to the child, and ask him or her to roll it back. Then, ask another child to join you, and gradually withdraw from the game. If the target child has the motor skills, the pair can try rolling the ball while squatting, then standing. Allow the typically developing child to throw the ball if desired. After several sessions, encourage the target child to throw the ball rather than rolling it. Be sure to prompt the child when necessary, and praise both children for keeping the game going.

Modify the game by progressively decreasing the size of the ball and increasing the distance between the two players. A game of catch can be simplified at the beginning by using a beanbag instead of a ball. In this case, the two children should stand fairly close together. Throwing is easy; catching takes some time to master.

Objective—The child will develop head and trunk control necessary to maintain seated posture while using playground equipment.

Developmental age: 6 to 12 months

1. Take the child for a ride in a wagon that has been built up on three sides with boards or padding.

2. Sit on a swing, holding the child in your lap, then swing gently back and forth. Support the child's head and trunk with your body. Gradually move the child

forward in your lap until his or her head is no longer resting on you. Support the child's trunk with both of your hands. Assist the child in trying to keep his or her head erect by supporting the child's trunk in as upright a position as possible.

3. If the child is not too heavy and if you can manage it, take the child down the slide with you, getting assistance from another adult. Place the child in front of you, supporting the child's trunk with your body as you slide down the slide together. Do all of these activities during regular outdoor play time when all of the children are playing outdoors. This will help the target child to feel a part of the group, even though he or she cannot participate in more demanding activities.

Developmental age: 1 to 2 years

Activities such as rolling on the ground, walking on hands and feet like an elephant, crawling under and over things, or swinging in a swing help develop the balance and head and trunk control that typically replace primitive reflexes during the first 2 years of life. Such activities can all be practiced in the outdoor play area as a natural part of children's play. Physical and occupational therapists may occasionally set up an obstacle course that requires these skills in order to challenge all of the children to expand their gross motor skills. Children with developmental delays will probably need adult assistance in negotiating an obstacle course, but they gain a strong sense of competence from such an experience.

In addition to outdoor games and play, children love music and rhythm activities. Singing songs, clapping to a beat, and dancing to music are all fun activities that provide opportunities to embed learning goals. Chapter 11 explores music and rhythm play.

11

Play with Music and Rhythm

Beating Our Drums and Tooting Our Horns

Music has an important place in children's lives. Children love to listen to songs from the time they are very young. Later, they like to sing along and, as with favorite stories, they like to sing the same songs over and over—just think of the songs and finger-plays that are so popular for circle time in nearly every preschool! Children learn many things from music including how to express themselves through movement and rhythm, how to sing a song from memory, and how to join others in an enjoyable activity. They can use music as a way to be creative, and a music group can be an early and simple way for children to participate in a cooperative activity with others.

Children with special needs can gain specific benefits from music because musical activities are varied and allow participation at several levels. A child with motor problems may not be able to dance but can shake a tambourine, perhaps with assistance, during rhythm activities. A child with communication disorders may have a limited ability to sing a song but can beat a drum or move to the music with enthusiasm. Musical activities allow all children to participate at their own levels. This participation fosters social development and self-esteem.

Besides the social benefits, music and rhythm activities allow for practice of cognitive skills (e.g., auditory memory, sequencing), language skills (e.g., singing the words to songs), and motor skills (e.g., movement, playing rhythm instruments), and these skills can be practiced in an enjoyable way with other children. Music is one of the easiest ways to integrate the child with special needs into regular classroom activities.

The music area should be located at one end of the classroom, away from the center of activity. This will ensure that music and rhythm activities will not disturb nonparticipants working or playing in other groups. Store rhythm instruments on nearby shelves for easy access by children without adult assistance, and be sure to have plenty of drums, shakers, and clackers for children with special needs. Your instrument collection should also include cymbals, bells, sticks for banging, and tambourines. The piano, record player, audiotape player, and/or compact disc player should be in the same area. You should also provide headsets for children who want to listen to music by themselves.

DEVELOPMENTAL SEQUENCES OF RHYTHM SKILLS

Level 1: Bangs or shakes an object to mark time with music

Level 2: Bounces in place to music

Level 3: Uses both hands to play rhythm instrument (tambourine, drum, or cymbals)

Level 4: Marches to music, keeping time with both feet

Level 5: Dances simple steps to music

Level 6: Leads dancing or rhythm activity

DEVELOPMENTAL SEQUENCE OF MUSIC SKILLS

Level 1: Listens to adults singing a song

Level 2: Sings some of the words during group singing

Level 3: Sings the whole song during group singing

Level 4: Sings a song alone

Level 5: Sings a song with accompanying finger-play

Level 6: Makes up songs and sings them alone

ADAPTATIONS AND MODIFICATIONS

Music and rhythm activities probably need less modification than other play activities because they tend to be informal and flexible and don't have any real performance standards to which children must adhere. Music activities can be scattered throughout the day, with children participating or not as they choose. Children with special needs may be reluctant to plunge into a musical activity independently, however, so you should be alert for any signs of interest they might show and be ready to help them join in. All of the encouragement they need may be for you to hand them instruments and demonstrate how to use them. Other children may need assistance to play an instrument or may even need to be held on your lap while you play the instrument. Be sure to adapt each child's participation only to the extent that is truly needed. Back away as soon as possible.

In setting up the center, make certain that instruments are kept where children with motor difficulties can easily reach them. Low, open shelves are best. Outlining the place for each instrument with paint (using a stencil) makes it easy for all the children in the class to put instruments away properly and gives them opportunities to categorize objects—an important cognitive skill—as they store all of the drums together, all of the tambourines together, all of the clackers together, and so forth.

EMBEDDING LEARNING GOALS IN MUSIC PLAY

Music play is a wonderful place to embed children's learning goals.

Objective—The child will learn the meanings of opposites such as *loud* and *soft*, *big* and *little*, *slow* and *fast*, and *start* and *stop*. The child will listen for the beginning and ending of music.

Developmental age: 1 to 5 years

1. In a play activity using rhythm instruments, ask each child to choose an instrument that can make a loud noise or a soft noise. Gather a group of three or four children around the piano or record player and play a few bars loudly, then softly. As the children listen, ask them to play their own instruments loudly, softly, as loudly as they can, and very, very softly. Repeat the activity, having children play fast and slow music, then choose big and little instruments. The activity can be varied by leading the children on a parade around the classroom with the "band" playing loudly or softly and walking fast or slow. The children can listen to the recorded music to practice starting and stopping on cue. Tell them to listen for when the music starts and stops so they can do the same with their instruments. This activity is especially good for children with lower functioning or who are difficult to engage.

2. With the target child and a friend playing together, use several instruments to practice loud and soft. The children can try out their favorites to find the loud ones and the soft ones. Prompt the target child to say the words *loud* and *soft* appropriately. Do the same for *big* and *little* and for *fast* and *slow*. As other children approach the music area during playtime, ask them to join the target child in finding the loud instruments.

Objective—The child will achieve trunk stability and control of the upper body and head.

Developmental age: 6 to 18 months

For children with motor disabilities, music and rhythm activities offer enjoyable and easy ways to practice muscle control. There are many ways to give these children opportunities to participate with the group while working on motor goals; examples are sitting and holding an instrument, walking (with support) or wheeling around the room to music, or standing (with support) to sing or play a song. You can encourage typically developing children to form a group for marching, dancing to music, or playing instruments, and use your hands to provide whatever support the child with motor disabilities needs for stability. If necessary, move the child around the room with the other children to give a sense of participation. Monitor trunk and head stability at all times, and ask the physical or occupational therapist how to position the child for maximum trunk stability.

Objective—The child will learn to participate with enjoyment in small-group activities and take a leadership role with peers.

Developmental age: 2 to 6 years

1. Set up a rhythm activity with a small group of children, handing out drums, triangles, tambourines, and other instruments. Seat the target child next to you with a drum. Take a drum yourself, and begin to beat it, setting a slow

tempo. Ask the children to follow your lead as you drum fast, then slow, then fast again. Once the target child can follow your tempo, ask this child to set the beat for the group (e.g., explaining, "We'll follow you"). Watch and imitate the child beating the drum. Remind the other children to follow the target child's lead (e.g., "Let's watch what Catherine does and follow her"). At the end of the activity, praise the child (e.g, "You're a good leader, Catherine. We all enjoyed playing together this morning with you leading us").

2. Choose a time when the children are playing instruments or marching to music. Ask the target child to join in with you, and suggest to all the children that they begin following your lead. Gradually shift the leadership from yourself to the target child (e.g., "Now let's follow Robert this time. Oh, look! He's going into the block area. Shall we follow him? Let's go, everyone! Here we come, Robert!").

Children love to play with the many instruments available in the music and rhythm area. They love to use music to express themselves. Another good way for children to express their thoughts and feelings is through play with creative materials. Chapter 12 explains some ways children can learn goals while getting messy with glue and paint!

12

Play with Creative Materials

Getting Messy with Glue and Paint

Creative play means interacting with various materials in a free, exploring, and uninhibited way. Children like to use certain materials in a free, creative way from the very beginning of their play experiences. Many children have played with materials such as glue, crayons, fingerpaints, food coloring, and flour-and-water paste at home, so they are familiar with them before they enter preschool. Some people think that children with disabilities or delays are not capable of creative activities, but this is certainly not true, as many early interventionists can attest. The level of enjoyment can be high, for there are no rules and no rights or wrongs, and children can freely explore visually, tactually, and emotionally.

Some adults may have unrealistic expectations of young children, holding them to traditional standards of creative expression. The familiar horror story of the preschool teacher who has every child cut out the same spring daffodil, color or paint it green and yellow, then paste it together "just so" to make a "pretty" bulletin board for parents to see, doesn't have to be true. For children of any ability level to really explore with creative materials, an adult must be willing to allow them some freedom to be messy, to carry out their own ideas, and sometimes even to produce things that the adult finds unattractive. Therefore, the first requirement for successful creative play is an adult willing to give up control!

Another aspect that is important for all children is that creative play can be very satisfying either in a group or alone. As a result, it is easier to carry over to home than some other types of play that require special materials, a large physical space, or several children playing together. Creative materials are limited only by the imaginations of those using them. Children can have lots of fun exploring creatively with materials they find around the house, such as magazine pictures, food coloring, flour-and-water paste, old beads or buttons, pasta, yarn, fabric scraps, boxes, and dried flowers. Parents can be enlisted to promote creative play at home with their children, especially if they are aware of their children's learning goals.

A third benefit of creative play, especially art activities and storytelling, is the relationship to emergent literacy. As children explore creative materials and discuss their creations, they begin to use language as a tool for communicating their feelings and opinions. They may use crayons, markers, and so forth to scribble on paper and discover that the objects they draw represent the actual object. For example, the picture they draw of their family is a symbol for their actual family. When children tell stories about their experiences, their drawings, or other creative work, they begin to use *symbols* (i.e., words) to *represent* real objects and events. As they learn to write their words down, they begin to understand that written words are just another way to use *symbols* to *represent* real objects and events. That is, written words are simply spoken words written down. These creative expressions give children a good foundation for later literacy. See Chapter 13 for a fuller discussion of emergent literacy.

ROLE OF THE ADULT IN CREATIVE PLAY

Children with developmental delays or disabilities sometimes appear to lack imagination. As a result, they may need more guidance from typically developing peers or adults for creative play than for other forms of play. Aside from specific individual learning goals that can be addressed during creative play, there is a general learning goal that all children share during the preschool years: to develop increasingly complex interactions with materials. Children with disabilities often interact with objects or materials in quite stereotypical ways, repeating simple actions over and over without expanding or elaborating on them. For example, a child may paint horizontal lines on a sheet of paper, using the same color, until the sheet is completely filled. Some educators and psychologists label this a *perseverative* behavior that is sometimes associated with autism or attention-deficit/hyperactivity disorder. It may also, however, simply be due to a lack of imagination about what to do next and how to vary the activity.

Even typically developing children vary widely in their imaginative or creative abilities. All children at times need help in exploring new materials and coming up with new ways of working with familiar materials. You must walk a fine line between encouraging and facilitating versus stifling creativity by making rigid demands for conformity. It may be important for some children to learn to follow directions or manipulate materials in a certain way—and this may justify lock-step art activities such as the daffodil display mentioned previously—but such events should not be mistaken for lessons in creativity.

Here are steps to successfully facilitating creative play:

1. Have in mind the learning goals you wish the child to work on. These might include fine motor skills, visualizing, spatial relationships, or whole-arm movements. They might also include communication skills such as describing the creative experience, describing the product, or communicating wants or needs.

2. Collect enough materials for several variations of an activity. For a pasting or gluing activity, for example, have pictures cut out from magazines, strips of colored tissue paper, pieces of string, plastic buttons of various sizes and colors, and so forth. For fingerpainting, supply a variety of objects that can be used to make designs in the paint, such as small pieces of sponge, terry-cloth mittens, and blocks of wood.

3. Get everybody started. Seat two or three children together at a table or help them get easels ready for painting. Then, demonstrate some activities that can be carried out with the available materials. Explain to the children what you are doing, then suggest they take over while you watch.

4. Remain close by without interfering. Comment on what the children are doing. For example, you can say, "What a great idea, Jonathan! That purple color really looks nice with the red, doesn't it?" If some children are reluctant to plunge into the activity, encourage them to get started. "Look, watch what I do, and try it. Then, I'll watch what you do, and I'll try what you do." Imitating what children do gives them confidence in their own ideas and sends a message that what they are doing is important and valuable.

5. Encourage children to talk about what they are doing, what's easy or difficult, and what they plan to do next. This encourages them to think about what

they are doing, something important in all types of play. There is a fine line here, however. Asking too many questions can be intrusive, and children may resent being quizzed while they are trying to work.

6. Take a facilitating role at cleanup time as well. Get as much cooperation as you can without being too controlling. Sometimes adults must take on most of the burden of cleanup, just to keep things running smoothly and avoid becoming bogged down in control issues.

DEVELOPMENTAL SEQUENCE OF CREATIVE SKILLS

Level 1: *Sensorimotor exploration*—Children explore materials by feeling, looking, and tasting. They get pleasure from smearing things like paint or pudding across the table, feeling runny materials flow through their fingers, and tasting everything that comes into their hands. This is truly the messy stage of creative exploring.

Level 2: *Simple use of materials*—Children begin to use materials in a purposeful way; however, they primarily imitate the work of others, either adults or peers. Children do not yet come up with their own ideas.

Level 3: *Simple creative play*—Children begin to put their own ideas into the creative activity. They explore the materials with the idea of developing a finished product. The activity usually involves a single material such as paint, glue, pudding, shaving cream, or crayons. Children attempt to represent familiar objects in their creative works, a first step in using symbols.

Level 4: *Complex creative play*—Children elaborate on the creative idea, using increasingly complex ideas. More varied materials are used and perhaps more than one medium, such as several colors of paint or glue plus tissue paper. The creative work represents reality in some way, but there is less emphasis than at Level 3 on the representation (e.g., making a house look like a house). At Level 4 there is usually fantasy involved. For example, children might illustrate with colored drawings stories they have made up or paint pictures of their dreams. Older children may paint what comes to mind when they listen to certain music. These activities overlap very well with the emerging literacy skills seen at Level 4 (Chapter 14).

EMBEDDING LEARNING GOALS IN CREATIVE PLAY

Embedding learning goals in creative play is a great idea. Consider the following suggestions as a starting point for the many possibilities you can create.

Objective—The child will understand the meaning of *big* and *biggest*, and *small* and *smallest*.

Developmental age: 3 to 6 years

1. Approach a group of children who are playing with uncooked macaroni and gluing it on sheets of construction paper. Ask the target child to help you sort

the pieces of macaroni into piles of big and little pieces. Talk about the process as you go along. When everyone has glued some pieces, ask the group questions such as, "Who has the smallest pieces (or entire picture) of macaroni?" and "Whose pieces are the biggest?"

2. Let children who want to explore tactually paint with shaving cream on flat pieces of mirror. Demonstrate how to move the whole arm in a circle to make a big circle on the mirror. Then, make small circles using an index finger or thumb. Comment on what the children do. For example, you can say, "Oh, look! Jackie has made the biggest circle using her arm. You've made the smallest one with your finger, Mohammed. Shall we try to make a really big one this time?"

3. Set up a large block of modeling clay in the classroom. It will arrive in a large, dry block that needs to be moistened by adding water. As it softens, children can pull off pieces and mold them into different shapes. Talk to the target child about his or her work using terms such as *big* and *small*.

Objective—The child will recognize circles, squares, and triangles and distinguish among them.

Developmental age: 3 to 6 years

Make faces on plain rice cakes spread with cream cheese topped with pieces of raw vegetables cut in square and triangular shapes. For example, the eyes might be carrot triangles, and the mouth, a square-shaped piece of tomato. Other vegetables could include celery, green peppers, broccoli, or zucchini slices. Triangle shapes work well for cheeks or mouths; circles or squares make good eyes. Label the shapes as the activity proceeds. Let children eat the faces they make immediately or save the faces for snack.

Objective—The child with sensory integration disorder will become comfortable using objects of various textures, thus reducing tactile defensiveness.

Developmental age: 2 to 6 years

1. Allow the child to participate at his or her own pace. Set up a "texture table" with many different materials, from silk to sandpaper, and encourage children to feel them, rub them on arms or legs, and describe them. For example, you can say, "Look, this feels soft! This one is scratchy, isn't it?"

2. Introduce liquids to the "texture table." Add thick liquids (e.g., honey) and thinner ones (e.g., paint, pudding, milk), and use the same approaches mentioned in the previous example for reticent children.

As mentioned previously, play with creative materials is linked to literacy—an important skill for all children. Chapter 13 explores ways to encourage children's language and literacy development.

13

Emergent Literacy

Please Read Me a Story

Language development is one of the most important achievements of young children during the preschool years, and it is closely related to literacy development. Because language and literacy development occur simultaneously, it is doubly necessary to include a multitude of activities and interactions in the preschool curriculum that foster early literacy (Notari-Syverson, O'Connor, & Vadasy, 1998). These activities, often referred to as *preliteracy* events (Cook, Tessier, & Klein, 2000), have in common that they promote various forms of symbolic representation. Speaking, drawing pictures, listening to stories read aloud, singing songs, and finger-plays are some examples.

Engaging in these activities helps children to develop an understanding of how one object may represent another. This understanding of symbols is crucial for the development of all forms of language and cognition. For emergent reading, children also need to develop a rich vocabulary and skills in auditory processing and phonological awareness, such as sound discrimination and rhyming. Being read to from an early age is of paramount importance as is handling books and pretending to read them.

As children develop skills of communication—first nonverbal (pointing, crying, grabbing an adult's hand) and then verbal (speaking, singing simple songs)—they learn to develop social relationships. These early social interactions with parents and siblings and later interactions with teachers and peers give children opportunities to practice communications that lay the groundwork for later reading and writing. Research has shown that there is a direct relationship between several developmental domains (e.g., fine motor skills, visual skills, cognitive representation, oral language) and the development of reading and writing (Cook et al., 2000). As Cook and colleagues noted, it is particularly important to provide children with socially useful experiences such as writing a letter or making a grocery list.

PARENTS' ROLE

Parents need to understand that emergent literacy begins very early in the infant's life. Singing songs to the baby, reading bedtime stories, and making trips to the library to choose books are activities that all parents can do to foster their children's emergent literacy skills. Many of these activities are a natural part of the developing parent–infant relationship (Widerstrom, 1986).

Parents' attitudes toward literacy also greatly affect children's motivation to read and write. Parents can either present reading as a source of enjoyment or as a set of skills to be learned (Espinosa & Burns, 2003). The first perspective appears to be more successful because children react to their parents' enthusiasm for reading and have more motivation to read later on. Another important aspect is parents' awareness of their children's desire to read. According to Espinosa and Burns, "Parents who believe their children are interested in reading are more likely to provide abundant print-related experiences than parents who do not perceive such interest" (2003, p. 51).

TEACHERS' ROLE

Once children enter school, their school experiences build on what they have already learned from their parents. Research shows that emergent literacy is better fostered in some classrooms than in others (Dickinson & Tabors, 2001). In the Home–School Study of Language and Literacy Development reported by Dickinson and Tabors and their contributors, researchers found that teachers who emphasized a child development approach to curriculum and adult–child interactions had classrooms that fostered language and literacy development. These teachers believed that the primary focus of preschool should be the child's social and emotional development. In contrast, those teachers who took a more academic approach believed that the preschool curriculum should emphasize specific skill development. They used didactic methods that resulted in lower levels of development of language and literacy for the children at preschool age and again at the end of kindergarten (Dickinson & Tabors, 2001).

This study showed that classroom practices that support literacy development depend mainly on the teacher. Although class size and number of children learning English as a second language were factors, they did not make the differences that the teacher's pedagogical style made. Positive practices for encouraging emergent literacy included the following (Dickinson & Tabors, 2001):

- Support children's learning throughout the day in informal situations by using varied vocabulary, challenging children to think, and stimulating their curiosity and imagination.

- Be conscious of the important role children can play in supporting each other's language development. Reinforce children's use of novel words, and provide children ample opportunities for dramatic play together.

- Be available for many conversations with children on an informal basis, during free play, mealtimes, and so forth. Be aware that oral language fosters emergent literacy.

Sandall and Schwartz (2002) developed a checklist of important elements for teachers to use to support emergent literacy. Consider the following activities to promote literacy skills in your classroom.

- Create a comfortable place in the classroom where adults and children can sit together.

- Have about five books available per child, and replace these with different books frequently.

- Create a book repair box for students to place books that are accidentally damaged, and show children that books can be repaired with glue, tape, and other materials.

- Add books made by the class to the story area.

- Encourage parents to get involved in literacy activities.

- Have some books available for children to take home with them.

- Play letter and sound games throughout the day.

Further suggestions for teachers who wish to promote emergent literacy are found in *Beginning Literacy with Language: Young Children Learning at Home and School* (Dickinson & Tabors, 2001, pp. 201–203). These suggestions can help teachers plan their daily program around book reading and discussion.

CREATING LITERACY-RICH ENVIRONMENTS

Storybooks are an excellent way to expose children to print. Because children's books usually contain simple sentences and restricted vocabulary, story reading is ideal for the language learning of children with disabilities (Notari-Syverson et al., 1998). Story reading also engages children in new types of oral discourse and provides conversational topics for their interactions with adults. It expands children's vocabulary and teaches them narrative skills such as story structure and narrative form and can foster reading comprehension. When a child with disabilities is actively engaged in a book, the reader can encourage the child to make predictions about what will happen next in the story, ask questions about why the events in the story took place as they did, and ask the child to summarize what happened in the story (Espinosa & Burns, 2003).

In addition to fiction books, nonfiction books are wonderful for children to have in the classroom and at home. Show children that nonfiction books are used to look up information to answer their questions. Nonfiction books also encourage children to develop interests and expand on classroom themes (Ritchie, James-Szanton, & Howes, 2003). Try placing nonfiction books relevant to the class theme around the room for children to explore throughout the day.

Children need to be taught how to handle books (Sandall & Schwartz, 2002). They should learn how to hold a book, turn the pages without ripping them, and place the books back on the shelf when they are finished reading them. Highlighting words with a finger as you read shows children that books are read left to right and top to bottom.

Besides reading stories, it is important to surround children with other printed materials outside of the book area. Menus and recipes in the housekeeping area show that printed materials have a practical purpose. Object labels around the room help children understand that words are symbols for objects, and these labels also help children expand their sight-word vocabulary (Ritchie et al., 2003). Books, writing materials, and paper placed around the room allow children to have access to these items throughout the day. Finally, creating nametags and sign-in sheets helps children recognize their names and practice writing their names or placing a stamp next to their names when they arrive at school (Ritchie et al., 2003). All of these activities expose children to different ways print is used.

EARLY LITERACY GOALS AND OBJECTIVES

When designing goals and objectives for students that target emergent literacy, consider the following important foundations for reading and writing: awareness of print, relationship of print to oral language, letter knowledge, and phonological awareness (Smith & Dickinson, 2002). Awareness of print means that children understand the purpose of print—that words convey meaning—and recognize what words look like and how they are arranged on a page. When children understand the relationship of print to oral language, they realize that oral language corresponds with written language, and they know that similarities and differences exist between the two modes of communication. Letter knowledge involves knowing the names and sounds of letters as well as recognizing the symbols used for the letter. Finally, phonological awareness is the ability to manipulate the sounds of language and to separate sounds in spoken words from those in written words.

Another set of skills to consider when creating literacy goals and objectives is the child's vocabulary, narrative skills, and literate discourse. Notari-Syverson and colleagues provided the following explanations of these areas:

- *Vocabulary*—the use of words and sentences. These objectives refer to the child's use of one-word and two-word utterances to label objects, people, and events and to express a variety of semantic intentions, such as agent–object, agent–action, location, and possession. The use of adult forms (statements, questions, commands) is also addressed.

- *Narrative skills*—recounting real events and stories from books. Objectives include relating events with a beginning, middle and end; labeling pictures in books and commenting on them; and telling stories that link events based on pictures, using conversational language.

- *Literate discourse*—includes fairly complex skills such as maintaining social interactions during two or more turns, initiating and maintaining a topic, and generalizing experiences to other settings. Also, this category includes the expression of feelings and motivations, as well as the use of metalinguistic words to refer to the use of language.

CULTURAL DIFFERENCES IN EARLY LITERACY DEVELOPMENT

Children from different cultures do not approach literacy the same way. As Espinosa and Burns stated, "All cultural groups share attitudes and beliefs about the uses and values of literacy and have preferred literacy practices" (2003, p. 53). For example, some researchers have reported differences in adult–child interactions among several groups, including white middle-class parents or caregivers, white working-class families, and rural non-white families (Hanson & Zercher, 2001). Middle-class white parents were found to use more varied verbal language with their children and to read stories to them more often. It is important not to confuse racial or ethnic differences with socioeconomic status because many non-white, middle-class parents and caregivers also expose their children to more preliteracy experiences than working-class families.

Children will learn best when there is continuity between the literacy culture of their home and school (Espinosa & Burns, 2003). Therefore, it helps to learn as much as you can about your students' backgrounds and early learning and socialization environments. For some excellent suggestions on strategies for facilitating emergent literacy, please consult Cook et al. (2000, pp. 378–383).

DEVELOPMENTAL SEQUENCE OF LITERACY

Level 1: *Awareness of print*—Children understand the purpose of print, that words have meaning and are arranged on pages in an orderly way, and that books are read from left to right and right side up.

Level 2: *Awareness of the relationship between oral and written language*—Children realize that print is just speech written down.

Level 3: *Knowledge of letters, their names, and their sounds*—Children learn to associate the letter and its sound with the symbol. For example, they learn to recognize their name in print and understand that it is made up of certain letters with specific sounds.

Level 4: *Phonological awareness*—Children have the ability to manipulate the sounds of language and understand that some are spoken and others are written.

Level 5: *Developing vocabulary, both oral and written*—Children learn to use words and sentences in their daily activities.

Level 6: *Development of narrative skills and discourse*—Children are able to recount real events in their lives and retell stories from books. They learn the basic rules of oral conversation, such as turn taking and initiating topics.

ADAPTATIONS AND MODIFICATIONS

There are many ways to adapt or modify literacy activities to include children with disabilities. First, you can place a child with disabilities on your lap or next to you while you read stories. Ask the child to turn the pages of the book at the appropriate times (Bricker, 2002). You may want to consider looking at the same books many times so that the child can eventually get the book, hold it, and turn the pages by him- or herself as you read the story. Another option is to make storybooks from the child's artwork. Use these books to encourage the child to make up a story or to hold the book and pretend to read.

If a child with disabilities is easily distracted or tends to distract other children, make sure the story area is away from other centers and in a quiet place (Sandall & Schwartz, 2002). Place comfortable chairs or cushions so that children will want stay in the story area, and consider limiting the number of children who can use the area at one time. Modifications for physical disabilities include providing a small table and chairs as an alternative to sitting on the floor and attaching Styrofoam on page corners to make them easier to turn.

Adding books on audiotape or compact disk to the story area will allow children to listen to stories with headphones while peers read books in the same area. Use simple button labels (e.g., *stop* and *go*) to operate the tape or compact disc player so that children do not have to ask for assistance to use them. Many books on tape include a storybook for children to follow along and may even include a signal to tell children when it is time to turn the page. You can also help children record their favorite stories on audiotape to listen to later (Ritchie et al., 2003).

It is also a good idea to use older children as role models. Invite older siblings—especially siblings of children with disabilities—and children from higher grades into the classroom to read. An older student can take turns reading from the same book as a child with disabilities. Younger children love to imitate older children, so older children are an excellent way to motivate younger ones to read!

Finally, work with children's preferences to excite their interest in books. If a child has a favorite subject, such as trains, place books on that subject around the classroom. Perhaps you can place books that make noises in the story area or add toys or puppets related to the stories to help prolong the child's interest.

EMBEDDING LEARNING GOALS IN LITERACY ACTIVIES

Consider the following suggestions for embedding learning goals in literacy activities.

Objective—The child will demonstrate eye–hand coordination adequate for simple motor tasks.

Developmental age: 3 to 5 years

Create a nursery rhyme rebus (i.e., a sentence made up primarily of pictures). Ask children to sing the nursery rhyme that is listed on the rebus. Demonstrate pointing to each picture as the children sing about it. Next, ask the target child to use the pointer to emphasize the pictures as they are sung. Allow other children to take turns using the pointer. For example, you can say, "Let's sing 'Three Blind Mice' again. This time, Bobby, why don't you take the pointer and point to the pictures as we sing about them. Then, we'll let Lin try."

Objective—The child will recognize circles, squares, and triangles and distinguish among them.

Developmental age: 4 to 6 years

Invite the target child and a friend to join you in the book area. Allow each child to pick out a book for you to read. As you read the story, pause periodically and ask the children what shapes they see. For example, you can say, "Do you see any squares on this page? I see three squares. Can you find them?" Try to encourage both children to participate equally. You may direct questions to each child separately. For example, you can say, "Wow! That dinosaur has some big teeth! Angelo, what shape are the dinosaur's teeth? That's right, triangles! The dinosaur also has some big eyes. James, do you know what shape the dinosaur's eyes are?"

Now that you have learned about embedding learning goals in different types of play activities, you may be wondering what activity you should choose for a particular learning goal. Chapter 14 contains a catalog of play activities organized by skills addressed. The catalog is a quick way to reference information from Chapters 6–13.

14

Catalog of Play Activities

Embedding Learning Goals in Play

Chapters 6–13 have explained how to embed teaching and learning goals in specific play activities. This chapter contains a catalog of play activities that will help you choose activities that are appropriate for particular learning goals. You will learn how specific skills can be addressed during particular play activities.

Included among these listings are activities that have been described throughout the book. They are included again here for ease of location. To use this chapter, first identify which learning goal on the child's IEP you wish to target. Then, locate for that skill the appropriate developmental domain (i.e., cognitive, communication, motor, social, or preliteracy), where you will find suggested play activities that can help the child achieve the learning goal. Although this list is not exhaustive, it is extensive. It represents a starting point for learning to embed learning goals into play activities. As you progress, you will add many other activities to this collection.

The organization of the skills and activities is as logical as possible, but some groupings may overlap, and some skills are included in more than one grouping. Table 14.1, found at the end of this chapter (pages 142–145), lists the specific skills, developmental ages, play area, and page number for each activity. It might be best to start with the table to identify the target skill, then find the corresponding pages for relevant play activities.

COGNITIVE SKILLS

Several types of skills are covered under the cognitive domain. *Classification* involves a variety of skills related to identifying attributes in common among several objects, matching identical or similar objects, and grouping objects. *Seriation* involves ordering objects by size or length. Number concepts are also important cognitive skills for children to learn. Some other significant cognitive skills are time concepts, problem solving, predicting outcomes, and spatial concepts.

Classification

An early-developing cognitive skill, classification involves recognizing objects that belong together. It includes identifying objects' major traits, placing like objects together (i.e., sorting), and knowing which objects are the same and which are different (i.e., matching).

Identifying

The following activities encourage children to identify major traits of objects in the manipulatives area and the pretend play area.

1. *Manipulatives area*—With two or three children seated together at a table, place some objects in front of them, and ask the children to identify the items'

attributes. For example, you can say, "Who can pick up the blue one?" "What color is the car? Can you pick it up?" or "Where is the yellow flower?" Make sure the target child is included in the game by allowing plenty of time for responses. This activity is appropriate for a child with a developmental age of 3–6 years.

2. *Manipulatives area*—Pair two children, one with disabilities and one typically developing. Arrange a group of objects in front of each child. Ask the two children to trade objects with each other, asking for the ones they want and offering the ones they are less fond of. For example, you can say, "Here's a bear. Do you want a bear?" or "I want a horse." Children with fewer verbal skills can use gestures or one-word requests. This activity is appropriate for a child with a developmental age of 3–6 years.

3. *Pretend play area*—During pretend play in the kitchen, identify by name the objects being used. For example, you can say, "Here is the eggbeater. Can you find a bowl to put the eggs in? Where is the bread? Shall we toast it in the toaster?" Encourage the child to imitate these identifying labels. For children who cannot say the names, let them use the objects in functional ways so they have a meaningful experience to associate each name with. This activity is appropriate for a child with a developmental age of 3–6 years.

Sorting

Use the following activities to encourage children to sort objects.

1. *Pretend play area*—On the shelves in the kitchen area, paint circles with the correct size for cups, saucers, and plates. On the wall, paint the outlines for various sizes of saucepans, frying pans, and other kitchen utensils that hang on the wall. Make sure that the hooks are a size and shape that allow for easy hanging of each utensil. During cleanup time, ask several children to replace the dishes, pots, and pans where they belong. (This is also a matching activity.) This activity is appropriate for a child with a developmental age of 2–6 years.

2. *Dress-up area*—Organize a "cleanup crew" for the dress-up area. Children can sort items of clothing into piles of similar shoes, hats, dresses, skirts, jackets, and so forth. Two children should be in charge of putting the objects away on shelves or hanging them on hooks. A child with disabilities can assist as a member of the sorting crew. This activity is appropriate for a child with a developmental age of 3–6 years.

3. *Creative play area*—On beginning a gluing activity, ask the target child to choose just two colors to use that day. Then, assist with sorting the pieces into two piles by color. The same can be done for many other characteristics: size or shape of paper, large versus small objects, tools for paint versus tools for glue, or things that sparkle versus things that do not. This activity is appropriate for a child with a developmental age of 3–6 years.

4. *Manipulatives area*—Sit beside the target child with a pile of small objects that can be easily handled and can be sorted by an obvious visual parameter such as color, size, or shape. You might use, for example, tokens, beads, small blocks, interlocking blocks, or miniature cars. Provide two empty coffee cans or other similar containers for sorting the objects. Take one of the containers while explaining, "This can is mine." Give the child the other container, saying, "This can is yours." Begin by picking up one of the objects while explaining and demonstrating how to sort the items. For example, you can say, "All the blue ones are mine. The red ones are yours. Let's put our [beads, blocks, toys] into our cans. This blue bead is mine. I'm going to put this blue bead into my can. This red one is yours. Can you put it into your can?" Continue until all of the objects have been sorted, then dump everything out of the cans and begin again as long as you still have the child's interest. This activity is appropriate for a child with a developmental age of 1–3 years.

5. *Creative play area*—Cutting out pictures of people from magazines and pasting them on cardboard to make "people posters" is another categorization activity. Children can classify people as big or little by pasting pictures of children on one sheet and pictures of adults on another. This can be a fun and rewarding activity requiring socializing, sharing, and cooperating if the whole group contributes to one set of posters. This activity is appropriate for a child with a developmental age of 2–6 years.

Matching

The following activities address the skill of matching.

1. *Manipulatives area*—The manipulatives area offers many opportunities for embedding fine motor and cognitive goals in play, particularly in matching activities. Whereas lotto games are appropriate for older and higher-functioning preschoolers, younger children and those with delays should be given no more than four objects at a time, two of which are identical. If you use form boards, matching play can be carried out almost independently, even by developmentally young children. (Figure 14.1 illustrates how to make a homemade form board.) The advantage of a form board is that it is self-correcting. Other self-correcting materials good for matching are one-, two-, or three-piece puzzles with backing, Montessori cylinders, and other toys that require direct placement of one piece into another. This activity is appropriate for a child with a developmental age of 1–6 years.

2. *Manipulatives area*—You can make a simple matching game for practicing *big* and *small* (or other opposites) by cutting out large and small pictures of everyday objects and people, then pasting them onto large cardboard playing boards and laminating them. Each board should be divided into six or eight squares, allowing for three or four large and small versions of the same object.

Required materials: 2 sheets unpainted extra-thick cardboard, 10" x 14"

Marker

6 colors of water-based paint and paintbrush

Knife or sharp scissors to cut cardboard

Strong glue to hold cardboard pieces together

5 knobs or large buttons (optional)

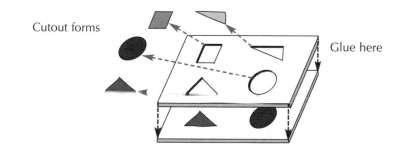

Directions: Draw four or five shapes on one piece of cardboard and cut them out as shown. Paint this piece of cardboard, then glue it on top of the second piece when dry. Paint each cutout form a different color that does not match the color used for the first sheet of cardboard. The shapes in the bottom piece of cardboard that show through the holes in the top piece should be painted to match the corresponding cutout forms. If you wish, you may glue a knob or button on each cutout form to assist the children in grabbing the shapes.

Figure 14.1.   Directions for making a form board.

For example, a big girl and a little girl, big and small houses, big and small cars, and big and small dogs could fill one board. Having four or five boards allows several children to play together, using either duplicate game boards or different game boards. This makes it possible for a child and adult to play simple games (e.g., having the child show you specific big and small objects) or for several children to play more complex games (e.g., lotto) together. See Figure 9.1 for an illustration of a matching board. This activity is appropriate for a child with a developmental age of 3–6 years.

3. *Pretend play area*—A cooking activity such as making soup or pudding can be used to teach matching of sizes and volumes. For example, give all of the children measuring cups to fill with water. Have the children compare the water in their cups, and try to make the amounts equal. For example, you can say, "Does Robert have more water in his cup than you do? Let's try to make the water the same." This activity is appropriate for a child with a developmental age of 3–6 years.

4. *Music area*—Rhythm instruments can form the basis for a discussion of *same* and *different*. Ask one child to play an instrument, then have the other children try to match the sound, rhythm, or pitch. This activity is appropriate for a child with a developmental age of 2–6 years.

Seriation

Seriation involves recognizing the relative size of similar objects in a group. Being able to line up a series of objects from smallest to largest is an example of seriation. Knowing the difference between long and short and being able to identify the longest and the shortest in a series are also seriation skills.

Big, Little, Large, and Small

The following is a list of how you can help children recognize the concepts of *big, little, large,* and *small.*

1. *Creative play area*—Approach a group of children who are playing with uncooked macaroni and gluing it on sheets of construction paper. Ask the target child to help you sort the pieces of macaroni into piles of big and little pieces. Talk about the process as you go along. When everyone has glued some pieces, ask the group questions such as "Who has the smallest pieces (or entire picture) of macaroni?" and "Whose pieces are the biggest?" This activity is appropriate for a child with a developmental age of 3–6 years.

2. *Creative play area*—Let children who want to explore tactually paint with shaving cream on flat pieces of mirror. Demonstrate how to move your whole arm in a circle to make a big circle on the mirror. Then, make small circles using your index finger or thumb. Comment on what the children do. For example, you can say, "Oh, look! Jackie has made the biggest circle using her arm. You've made the smallest one with your finger, Mohammed. Shall we try to make a really big one this time?" This activity is appropriate for a child with a developmental age of 3–6 years.

3. *Creative play area*—Set up a large block of modeling clay in the classroom. It will arrive in a large, dry block that needs to be moistened by adding water. As it softens, children can pull off pieces and mold them into different shapes. Talk to the target child about his or her work, using terms such as *big* and *small.* This activity is appropriate for a child with a developmental age of 3–6 years.

4. *Manipulatives area*—Use beads of various sizes and a thick string. Tie a knot at the end of the string, and put a large bead on the string. Then, help the target child find another big bead to add to the string, giving as much physical assistance as necessary. You can comment, "We now have two big beads on our string. Shall we add another big bead, or shall we find a small bead next?" Encourage the child to string as many beads as possible onto the string, telling you whether each one is small or big. When the string is full, ask the child to show you the smallest and biggest bead on the string. After the child has gone through these steps with you, invite another child to join in, and encourage both children to carry out the game while you act as a facilitator. This activity is appropriate for a child with a developmental age of 3–6 years.

Long, Tall, and Short

Use these activities to help teach children the concept of *long, tall,* and *short.*

1. *Sand or water table*—While two or three children are playing at the water or sand table, ask the target child to label who is tall and who is short. Then, ask the child to compare two children and decide who is taller. Ask the two children to stand side by side so the children can see who really is the taller one. This activity is appropriate for a child with a developmental age of 3–6 years.

2. *Music area*—For a parade around the classroom to music, ask the shorter (younger) children to march at the front of the line and the taller (older) children to march at the back. Use the words *taller* and *shorter* several times to reinforce the concept. Choose three tall children, and line them up in order from tall, to taller, to tallest. Comment to the group on the three children's relative heights; for example, you can say, "Joseph is tall, but Linda is taller. Jill is the tallest." This activity is appropriate for a child with a developmental age of 3–6 years.

Number Concepts

Number concepts involve not only counting (cardinal numbers), but also understanding the relationships among numbers. Ordinal numbers (e.g., first, second, third), and one-to-one correspondence (e.g., there are the same number of blocks in two towers) are important number concepts for children in the preschool age range to learn.

Cardinal Numbers

These activities will help children count and use cardinal numbers.

1. *Block area*—The block area offers many opportunities to use numbers in a meaningful way. Children can say how many blocks they are stacking, use such expressions as "one more," or ask for several blocks at a time. You can also draw attention to the number of blocks children used for specific structures; for example, you can say, "Danny used five blocks to make this bridge." This activity is appropriate for a child with a developmental age of 1½–4 years.

2. *Pretend play area*—During pretend play, ask the target child to set the table for the meal. Ask how many people will be eating, then help the child determine how many plates and utensils are needed for each person. For example, you can say, "How many people will be eating lunch with us today? We will need four plates, then, right? Will you put four plates on the table? Now, how many spoons and forks will we need?" This activity is appropriate for a child with a developmental age of 3–6 years.

3. *Creative play area*—As materials are being handed out for gluing or painting activities, comment on the number of items available to choose from. For

example, you can say, "We have four colors of paper to choose from this morning. Look at these three colors of paint." This activity is appropriate for a child with a developmental age of 2–4 years.

Ordinal Numbers

These activities teach children the concept of ordinal numbers.

1. *Manipulatives area*—Sit nearby as the child puts together a three- or four-piece-puzzle. As the child fits pieces into the frame, label the pieces as the first piece, the second, and the third. Try to elicit the word *first*. This activity is appropriate for a child with a developmental age of 3–6 years.

2. *Pretend play area*—During a cooking activity, ask two or three children to help with measuring, pouring, or stirring in a specified order. For example, you can say, "Maria, will you be the first pourer? Jaime, will you be the second pourer?" This activity is appropriate for a child with a developmental age of 3–6 years.

More or Less

The following is a list of activities you can use to teach the concept of *more* or *less*.

1. *Sand or water table*—Provide containers of various sizes for filling with water or sand and dumping out. Cups, measuring spoons, pitchers, and buckets will provide enough variety and allow several children at a time to participate in the play. As the children use the containers, sit next to them, and comment about how much water or sand each one holds, calling their attention to the differences. Be sure to use the words *more* and *less*. This activity is appropriate for a child with a developmental age of 3–6 years.

2. *Sand or water table*—Play a simple game with the target child and one or two other children. Have each child choose a container, and fill it with sand. Then, ask each child in turn to dump out the sand. Ask which child has the biggest pile of sand. Then, ask which child has the biggest container. Repeat the activity with *small* and *smallest* containers. If the children seem to understand the concepts of *big* and *small* and *biggest* and *smallest*, try some comparisons. Ask questions such as "Whose container is bigger than Sarah's?" and "Is my cup smaller than your bucket?" This activity is appropriate for a child with a developmental age of 3–6 years.

3. *Sand or water table*—For more advanced or older children, you may try introducing the idea of conservation. Use containers that hold the same volume of sand or water but are different shapes. Fill both containers, then ask the children which container has more water (or sand) or whether they are both the same. Pour the contents back and forth several times between the two containers to demonstrate that although they look different, the containers really hold the same amount. Note, however, that conservation is a difficult concept not usually understood by typically developing children until age 7 or older.

Therefore, preschool children cannot be expected to understand it. This activity should be used solely as a means for exploring the ideas of *big* and *small,* and *more* and *less.* This activity is appropriate for a child with a developmental age of 3–6 years.

4. *Pretend play area*—during cooking activity, use the words *more* and *less* when you describe what the children are doing. For example, you can say, "Johnny, you need more water in your pudding bowl." This activity is appropriate for a child with a developmental age of 3–6 years.

One-To-One Correspondence

One-to-one correspondence can be taught in a variety of ways, including the following:

1. *Block area*—As the child builds with large or small blocks, line up a row of several different blocks. Ask the child to help you place a block on top of each one you have laid out. Point out that each block has one on top of it. Help the child recognize that the groups are the same in number. This activity is appropriate for a child with a developmental age of 1½–3 years.

2. *Music area*—During a marching or dancing activity, ask each child to hold hands with the next child. Ask everyone to find a partner. Be sure to assist any child who is without a partner to pair up with a peer or an adult. Point out that everyone has a partner and that there are enough partners for everyone to have one. This activity is appropriate for a child with a developmental age of 1–3 years.

Time Concepts

Preschool children learn to think about the past and future. They know that some events happen before and after other events. They begin to understand that an event may have a sequence: First Event A happens, then Event B happens, and finally Event C happens. They also learn that the past and future are spoken about using different verb tenses.

Before and After

To help children master the concept of *before* and *after,* consider the following examples:

1. *Manipulatives area*—Display for the target child several large beads of different colors to string on a shoelace. Ask the child to choose a bead of a specific color and string that bead on the lace. If necessary, demonstrate how to string the first bead or two, or guide the child's hands. After several beads of different colors have been strung, point out the sequence of colors on the lace. For example, you can say, "Look, first you put a red bead on the lace, then two blue ones, and then a green one. Let's try to copy this pattern. What color bead

comes *before* the blue beads? What color did you put on *after* the blue beads? Let's try to do it again with these beads." This activity is appropriate for a child with a developmental age of 3–6 years.

2. *Outdoor area*—Outdoor play is a good time to emphasize turn-taking because outdoor play equipment is usually in short supply and must be shared. For popular items such as trucks, tricycles, and wagons, it sometimes works to have a portable message board on which a waiting list can be posted. A flannel board works well because children's names or symbols can easily be put on and removed as their turns come up. Use *before* and *after* when commenting about the order in which children can use the various pieces of equipment. Help children to be patient by making statements such as "Your turn is coming very soon, Jeffrey. You will get the red tricycle *after* Sandra. Your turn is *before* George's." This activity is appropriate for a child with a developmental age of 2–6 years.

Past and Future Tenses

When helping children learn about the past and the future, try the following activity.

1. *All areas*—Whenever possible, ask the target child to describe, with your help, what he or she did during play time that day. Ask what the child plans to do tomorrow. This activity is suitable for a child with a developmental age of 2–6 years.

2. *All areas*—The High/Scope Foundation has developed some creative ways to encourage children ages 3–5 to think about the past and the future during the Plan/Do/Review time that is part of the High/Scope curriculum (Hohmann, Banet, & Weikart, 1979). Please check out this resource for some wonderful sample activities.

Spatial Concepts

Spatial concepts at preschool age are centered on the child's own body. As children learn about their bodies in relation to other objects and people in space, they are able to expand their general understanding of spatial relationships. This includes recognizing the relative sizes of objects, what objects can fit inside given spaces, and how objects of varying sizes relate to the size of their own bodies.

Shape Recognition

The following are some examples of how children can be encouraged to recognize shapes in the creative play area and the manipulatives area.

1. *Creative play area*—Make faces on plain rice cakes spread with cream cheese topped with pieces of raw vegetables cut in square and triangular shapes. For example, the eyes might be carrot triangles, and the mouth a square-shaped piece of tomato. Other vegetables could include celery, green peppers, broc-

coli, or zucchini slices. Triangle shapes work well for cheeks or mouths; circles or squares make good eyes. Label the shapes as the activity proceeds. Let children eat the faces they made immediately or save them for snack. This activity is appropriate for a child with a developmental age of 3–6 years.

2. *Manipulatives area*—Use the form board (illustrated in Figure 14.1) to reinforce recognition of squares and circles. This activity is appropriate for a child with a developmental age of 3–6 years.

Spatial Relations

To help children learn about spatial relations, try the following activities.

1. *Block area*—Define a space about 2 feet square on the floor of the block area, and mark it off with boundaries of some kind. Ask the target child to join you in building a house using small wooden blocks. Ask the child to show you where the living room, the kitchen, and the bedroom will be. Ask the child to build the walls with blocks, then design each room with furniture. Encourage creativity in using small blocks for chairs and tables, but also add play furniture to the house, and finish it with flowers, toy people, and other props. This activity is appropriate for a child with a developmental age of 3–6 years.

Body Awareness

Body awareness is an important concept for young children. Consider these examples from the creative play area.

1. *Creative play area*—While children are fingerpainting, ask them to show you how they can use one whole hand (i.e., with flat palm) in the paint, then both hands, then one arm, or just one finger. This activity is appropriate for a child with a developmental age of 1–3 years.

2. *Creative play area*—Children of preschool age and younger like to have someone trace around their bodies. Ask the child to lie on the floor on a large sheet of brown wrapping paper or butcher paper. Trace around the child's head, arms, legs, and torso. Show the child his or her body outline, talking about the arms, legs, head, neck, and so forth. Then, help the child draw in eyes, nose, mouth, hair, and clothing as appropriate. More advanced children like to paint these outlines. This activity is appropriate for a child with a developmental age of 1–4 years.

Problem Solving

Problem-solving skills include trial-and-error methods, experimenting with several solutions, and seeking adult assistance. Consider the following suggestions:

1. *Block area*—While the child is building a structure with large blocks, sit nearby and observe. When an impasse is reached—that is, when something doesn't work right—encourage the child to think of another way. For example, if the

pile falls over because it has too many blocks, ask the child to think of a way to better balance the structure. If a block is wedged into a structure so tightly that it can't be moved, suggest that the child think of a way to fit the blocks together better. Ask questions such as, "How can we make this airplane big enough for three people?" or "Which block can I put up here so it won't fall down?" This activity is appropriate for a child with a developmental age of 3–6 years.

2. *Sand or water table*—Before the activity, move all shovels, pails, or other toys out of reach from the children but in plain sight above or near the table. Accompany the target child and one or two peers to the sand or water table. Wait for the children to comment on the missing toys. Encourage the children to ask for help or to think of alternative toys they can play with at the table. For example, you can say, "The shovels are missing? Where could they be? Oh, they are on the shelf. How can we get them down?" Wait for the children to ask for help or indicate nonverbally that they would like you to get the items. If the children do not ask for the items, you can say, "Well, I guess we have no shovels today. What are some other toys we can play with in the water area?" This activity is appropriate for a child with a developmental age of 2–4 years.

Predicting Outcomes

Being able to predict the outcome of an event, activity, or story is an important and sophisticated cognitive skill. At the preschool level, children begin to predict by guessing what will happen next in a story they are reading or by predicting how soon they will finish a creative task.

1. *Block area*—Invite children to join you in the block area. Encourage them to stack blocks until they fall down. Then, ask the children to make guesses about how many blocks they can stack before the next tower falls down. If the target child cannot participate by stacking the blocks, pair him or her with another child, and encourage him or her to make a guess. Then, count along with the target child as the peer stacks the blocks. For example, you can say, "Wow! What a big tower we built. I wonder how many blocks we can stack this time before the tower falls down again? Jimmy, how many blocks do you think Maria can stack? Five? Let's see. One, two . . ." This activity is appropriate for a child with a developmental age of 3–5 years.

2. *Dress-up area*—Place a box of clothing for various purposes in the dress-up area, such as raincoats and boots, gloves, sunglasses, and sandals. Ask the target child and a peer to join you in the area and put on one or two items from the box. Comment on the children's clothes, and ask them what would happen if they wore the items in certain weather. For example, you can say, "Juan, you are wearing sunglasses. What would happen if you wore sunglasses at night?" "Carrie, what would happen if you wore those shorts on a cold day?" or "Oh no, Keesha. It's very windy outside. What do you think

would happen to your hat if you were to go outside?" This activity is appropriate for a child with a developmental age of 3–5 years.

COMMUNICATION SKILLS

Communication can be nonverbal or verbal. Nonverbal communication includes using gestures or signs, protodeclaratives, and protoimperatives. Verbal communication includes receptive language, labeling familiar objects, increasing utterance length, grammatical forms, language content, pragmatic usage, asking questions, and carrying on a conversation.

Nonverbal Communication

Children with communication or cognitive delays often rely primarily on nonverbal communication, including manual signs, to share their needs and express their points of view.

Using Simple Gestures or Signs

You can help children learn to express themselves with simple gestures or signs. Here are two activities to contemplate.

1. *All areas*—Encouraging use of nonverbal communication during play activities is relatively easy. Sit beside the target child, and ask questions that can be answered by signing or pointing. Do not overdo this practice or the child will soon tune you out. As the child becomes more at ease with you, encourage the use of higher forms such as protoimperatives and protodeclaratives (explained next). This activity is appropriate for a child with a developmental age of 1–2 years.

2. *Creative play area* —As the child works on a creative play activity, ask whether you might show it to another child. Encourage the target child to comment on the work of art nonverbally, by pointing to his or her favorite part, for example. This activity is appropriate for a child with a developmental age of 1–2 years.

Protodeclaratives and Protoimperatives

A *protodeclarative* is an immature and incomplete form of the verbal declarative sentence. It consists of a vocalization (e.g., "Oh!" "Uh!"), eye contact with the listener, and a gesture. Most young children use protodeclaratives and protoimperatives before they begin using words. An efficient means of preverbal communication, protodeclaratives and protoimperatives usually enable children to get their meanings across very well. Like protodeclaratives, *protoimperatives* are immature forms that consist of vocalizing, making eye contact, and pointing to or reaching for an object. Rather than commenting on something, however, the child requests or demands something.

1. *Manipulatives area*—When the child is working with a manipulative activity requiring several pieces—for example, putting beads in a bottle—encourage the child to ask for the next piece. Hold up the piece just out of reach and say, "Would you like this one?" Try to get the child to look at you and point to the bead while vocalizing a request. This activity is appropriate for a child with a developmental age of 1–3 years.

2. *All areas*—Throughout the day, encourage the child to use nonverbal declaratives and imperatives to express thoughts. Respond to and acknowledge this form of communication. Encourage the child to make eye contact when communicating. This activity is appropriate for a child with a developmental age of 1–3 years.

Verbal Communication

For purposes of remediation, spoken language usually is divided into several types, as listed in this section. Learning goals usually focus on increasing the number of words a child can use in one sentence, on teaching grammatical forms and content, or on using language to influence others. The latter area, *pragmatics*, includes such skills as how children interact verbally with adults and peers in conversation and how they use language to get their needs met. (For an introductory overview of typical language acquisition, refer to Chapter 5, "The Development of Language," in Thurman & Widerstrom, 1990.)

Receptive Language

Receptive language entails understanding others' language. The following activities are helpful to promote this skill.

1. *Pretend play area*—Children who are developmentally young enjoy dressing up with peers and watching other children play. Such children may not wish to participate fully in the pretend activities going on in the pretend play area, feeling happier on the sidelines. Dressing up in Mom's or Dad's clothes is fun and can be a great opportunity to work on receptive language goals. Describe for the target child what's happening as the play activity proceeds. Provide a running commentary as long as you can maintain the child's attention. Calling attention to details of dress on both the target child and other children can increase receptive vocabulary. This activity is appropriate for a child with a developmental age of 1–2½ years.

2. *Cooking area*—Ask the target child to be your assistant at the cooking center. Have ready whole bananas, grapes, sliced pears, whole strawberries, and a large bowl of yogurt with two large serving spoons. Also have small cutting boards available, one for each child around the table, as well as aprons, bowls,

and small knives for cutting the bananas and strawberries. As children come to the cooking center, ask the target child to hand out fruit, bowls, and aprons. For example, you can say, "Please give Ronald some fruit to cut up. Then, give him a bowl for his yogurt." Give general instructions to the children, two steps at a time, as in these examples: "First, choose some fruit. Then, cut it up," and "Now, we're ready to spoon some yogurt into the bowl. Then, mix the fruit with the yogurt. Now, it's ready to eat!" This activity is appropriate for a child with a developmental age of 3–6 years.

3. *Music area*—In a play activity using rhythm instruments, ask each child to choose an instrument that can make a loud noise or a soft noise. Gather a group of three or four children around the piano or stereo, and play a few bars loudly, then softly. As the children listen, ask them to play their own instruments loudly, softly, as loudly as they can, and very, very softly. Repeat the activity, having children play fast and slow music, then choose big and little instruments. The activity can be varied by leading the children on a parade around the classroom with the "band" playing loudly or softly and walking fast or slowly. This activity is appropriate for a child with a developmental age of 3–5 years.

4. *Music area*—With the target child and a friend playing together, use several instruments to practice loud and soft. The children can try out their favorites to find the loud ones and the soft ones. Prompt the target child to say the words *loud* and *soft* appropriately. Do the same for *big* and *little* and for *fast* and *slow*. As other children approach the music area during playtime, ask them to join the target child in finding the loud instruments. This activity is appropriate for a child with a developmental age of 3–5 years.

Labeling Familiar Objects

The following activities help children learn to label familiar objects.

1. *Manipulatives area*—Sit beside the target child with a pile of various small objects that are easy to handle and that you know are familiar to the child. You might use, for example, beads, small blocks, dolls and doll furniture, or miniature cars. Provide two empty coffee cans or other similar containers for sorting the objects. Take one of the containers, explaining, "This can is mine." Give the child the other container, saying, "This can is yours." Begin by naming one of the objects, then picking it up and placing it in your can. Then, encourage the child to name whichever object he or she wishes to take. Continue until all of the objects have been sorted, then dump everything out of the cans and begin again. This activity is also useful for teaching the possessive pronouns *mine* and *yours* and for practicing classification. This activity is appropriate for a child with a developmental age of 1–3 years.

2. *Music area*—Allow children to each choose an instrument from the music area. Then, ask all children with drums to raise their hand. Do the same for each instrument. Allow children to play the instruments for a few minutes. Then,

ask questions about the sounds, rhythm, and so forth. You can say, for example, "What instrument was the loudest?" or "Becky played a really interesting rhythm. What instrument is she using to make that nice pattern?" This activity is appropriate for a child with a developmental age of 3–5 years.

Increasing Utterance Length

Increasing utterance length is an important goal for young children. The following activities show how you can encourage children to use longer utterances in the pretend play area and creative play area.

1. *Pretend play area*—As children begin a dress-up activity, ask what the target child is wearing and who he or she is pretending to be. Ask leading questions about the play activity, being careful not to intrude too much into the play or distract the child from full participation. Sometimes you can ask questions during the activity (e.g., "Where are we going? To visit Carlos's grandmother? Will you show us the way, Carlos?"), but other times questions are best left until the activity is finished, which requires the child to recall what happened (e.g., "Where did we go? Did we visit Grandmother?" "Did you enjoy seeing Grandmother this morning? What did we have to eat at Grandmother's house?" "We only pretended, but it was fun, wasn't it?") This activity is appropriate for a child with a developmental age of 3–5 years.

2. *Creative play area*—When children have finished an art activity, they enjoy telling others about their creation. Ask a small group of children, including the target child, to recount their experiences that morning in the creative area. After a few other children have taken turns (to provide models), encourage the target child to talk about his or her artwork. At first, the child may be more comfortable listening, but gradually encourage more active participation. You can ask questions such as these about the child's creative experiences: "How did you make it?" "What did you glue on first?" "Did you decide to paint it blue?" and "It's really beautiful. Do you think Mommy will like it?" This activity is appropriate for a child with a developmental age of 2–6 years.

3. *Pretend play area or creative play area*—Organize a double set of materials, such as beads for stringing; play dishes; or paper, paste, and paint. Place one set of materials beside you at the table, saying to the target child, "These are mine. I have blue paper, some paste, and some paint. Would you like some, too? Tell me what you want." Prompt the use of "I want." As the activity progresses, make comments such as, "My picture is nearly finished now. How is your picture coming?" If necessary, prompt the use of "my picture," "I," and "mine." This activity is appropriate for a child with a developmental age of 3–6 years.

Grammatical Forms

The earliest grammatical forms children begin to use are the 13 morphemes identified by Brown (1973). The first four in order of typical acquisition are *-ing, in,* and *on,* plurals, and possessives. Play activities, especially in the pretend play area, present good opportunities for encouraging the use of these grammatical forms.

1. *Pretend play area*—During a dress-up, cooking, or housecleaning activity, talk with the child about what is going on, using the present progressive tense. For example, you can say, "Jackie is *stirring* a cake. Joe is *wearing* an apron." Plurals can be emphasized during cooking play. For example, you can say, "We need four *bowls* on the table. We need four bowls for *serving* the soup. There are four children." For possessives, concentrate first on *mine* and *yours,* because these are the most interesting for young children. For example, you can say, "Here is *your* bowl. This one is *mine.* We each have a bowl, don't we?" This activity is appropriate for a child with a developmental age of 1½–3 years.

2. *Dress-up area*—As children are playing in the dress-up area, comment on what is taking place using the present progressive tense. For example, you can say, "Maryann is *putting* on a red shirt. Paolo is *wearing* big green sunglasses." Examine all of the items in the dress-up area, calling attention to singular and plural items. For example, "There are three *shirts.* There is only one *hat.*" Finally, encourage children to comment on each other's clothing by saying such things as "Tommy, do you like *Leila's* shirt?" and "Carlie, let's ask Mike what he thinks about *your* shoes. Do you like *his* pants?" This activity is appropriate for a child with a developmental age of 3–6 years.

Language Content

The content of children's early language consists of simple two-word combinations such as agent–action ("Mommy go") or action–object ("Drink milk"). These combinations can be reinforced during play activities and expanded as the child's utterance length increases. Encourage children to expand their spontaneous utterances. For example, you can say, "Where is Mommy going? Mommy is going home, isn't she? Mommy is going home." Or, "Who wants to drink milk? Does dolly want some milk? Right, the dolly is drinking milk. Right. Dolly drinking milk."

Pragmatic Usage

In addition to expanding form and content, it is important that children learn to use language functionally to get their needs met. Children use language in context, and often the context helps the listener understand what they mean. Adults can help children learn language by providing a variety of contexts in which children will want to communicate. This is part of the rationale for a preschool classroom devoted to a variety of play activities.

Asking Questions

Children learn very early to ask questions. Typically developing 2- and 3-year-olds are infamous for asking "why" questions. Two good ways to encourage question asking during play are:

1. Don't do all the talking. If adults anticipate the child's every need for information, there is no reason to ask questions. For example, you might say, "We're taking a bus trip tomorrow." Wait to be asked where, when, and why we are going.

2. Encourage children to use each other as resources. Encourage them to ask each other for answers to questions. For example, you can say, "I'm not sure about that, George. Why don't you ask Juanita? Juanita, George has a question to ask you."

Carrying On a Conversation (Turn Taking)

Turn taking is a vital social skill that preschool children learn through, for example, sharing toys and taking turns in games. Turn-taking skills can be practiced in many play situations. For example, children can practice taking turns making noises in the music area or adding or stirring ingredients to a recipe during a cooking activity. Through sharing conversation, children learn to take turns being the listener and the speaker.

Turn-taking situations may need to be monitored because some children talk too much, while others say little. You should encourage shy children or children with language delays to talk while making sure that more verbal children wait their turn. Pairing a highly verbal child with a less verbal one works surprisingly well, as the verbal child is often more successful at encouraging the other child to talk than an adult is.

MOTOR SKILLS

In this section, you will find activities for gross motor and fine motor skills. *Gross motor* refers to large muscle movements such as walking and jumping. *Fine motor* refers to delicate, controlled movements typically involving the hands and eyes. Also included in this section are self-care skills, such as feeding and dressing oneself.

Gross Motor

Activities to promote the development of gross motor skills most often take place outdoors. Outdoor equipment such as swings, slides, and tricycles are commonly used, but gross motor activities can also be carried out at home and indoors.

Head and Trunk Control

1. *Outdoor area*—Take the child for a ride in a wagon that has been built up on three sides with boards or padding. This activity is appropriate for a child with a developmental age of 6–12 months.

2. *Outdoor area*—Sit on a swing, holding the child in your lap, then swing gently back and forth. Support the child's head and trunk with your body. Gradually move the child forward in your lap until the head is no longer resting on you. Support the child's trunk with both of your hands. Assist the child in trying to keep the head erect by supporting the trunk in as upright a position as possible. This activity is appropriate for a child with a developmental age of 6–12 months.

3. *Outdoor area*—If the child is not too heavy and if you can manage it, take the child down the slide with you, getting assistance from another adult. Place the child in front of you, supporting the child's trunk with your body as you slide down the slide together. Do all of these activities during regular outdoor play time when all of the children are playing outdoors. This will help the target child to feel a part of the group, even though he or she cannot participate in more demanding activities. This activity is appropriate for a child with a developmental age of 6–12 months.

4. *Music area*—For children with motor disabilities, music and rhythm activities offer enjoyable and easy ways to practice muscle control. There are many ways to give these children opportunities to participate with the group while working on motor goals, such as sitting and holding an instrument, walking (with support) or wheeling around the room to music, or standing (with support) to sing or play a song. Encourage typically developing children to form a group for marching, dancing to music, or playing instruments. Use your hands to provide whatever support the child with motor disabilities needs for stability. If necessary, move the child around the room with the other children to give a sense of participation. Monitor trunk and head stability at all times. Ask the physical or occupational therapist how to position the child for maximum trunk stability. This activity is appropriate for a child with a developmental age of 6–18 months.

Balancing

The following activities can promote children's use of balancing.

1. *Outdoor area*—Activities such as rolling on the ground, walking on hands and feet elephant-style, crawling under and over things, or swinging in a swing help develop the righting and equilibrium reactions that typically replace primitive reflexes during the first 2 years of life. Such activities can all be practiced in the outdoor play area as a natural part of children's play. Therapists may occasionally set up an obstacle course that requires these skills in order to challenge all the children to expand their gross motor skills. Children with developmental delays will probably need adult assistance in negotiating an obstacle course, but they gain a strong sense of competence from such an experience. This activity is appropriate for a child with a developmental age of 1–2 years.

2. *Sand or water table*—While two children are playing at the sand and water table, encourage them one at a time to try standing on one foot for a short time, holding onto the table if necessary. For example, you can say, "Maria, can you stand on one foot? It's okay to hold onto the table if you need help." Be sure that the table is sturdy enough for this activity before encouraging the children to stand on one foot. Be sure to stand close to the children in order to steady them if necessary. You can also hold onto the child's waist to aid in balance. Gradually reduce physical assistance as the child gains balance. This activity is appropriate for a child with a developmental age of 1–4 years.

Jumping

Jumping is a fun activity to encourage during outdoor play. Consider the following suggestions.

1. *Outdoor area*—Children can practice jumping down steps outdoors. You can encourage them to jump from the bottom step to the ground. This activity is appropriate for a child with a developmental age of 1½–4 years.

2. *Block area*—An obstacle course can be set up in the block area. Children can use it independently during free play, while therapists or teachers can use it for teaching specific motor skills at other times. Children might practice jumping with both feet over the sides of a block, hopping over the sides of the block on one foot at a time, or jumping over a line taped to the floor. This activity is appropriate for a child with a developmental age of 1½–4 years.

Fine Motor

Fine motor skills are a component of nearly all play activities, and they are probably the easiest goals to embed in play. Handling objects is a natural part of creative and dramatic play, pretend play, music, and sand and water play. Thus, it is not difficult to find ways to work on fine motor goals in the preschool classroom.

Picking up and Placing Objects

Picking up and placing objects is one important fine motor skill. Consider the following suggestions:

1. *Pretend play area*—Set up a tea party in the kitchen area, using real cups and saucers and a plate of fruit or crackers or popcorn. The cups should be filled with a liquid the children can pretend is tea, poured from the teapot by you or another child. Encourage the target child to drink the "tea" from the cup, picking up and replacing the cup in the saucer. Ask a child to pass the plate of food, and monitor the target child's use of thumb and finger grasp. This activity is appropriate for a child with a developmental age of 2–4 years.

2. *Block area*—Help the child to build a tower of five or six blocks (or more if appropriate). Allow the child to knock it down, then rebuild it. Choose small,

1-inch blocks for older children, larger ones for younger children. Children get better at this activity with repetition. Each time the tower is rebuilt, ask the child to pick up and place more of the blocks on top. Encourage use of thumb and forefinger for picking up. If necessary, put your hand over the child's at first to provide support in picking up the blocks and placing them on the tower. Make sure a friend is involved in watching and taking turns with the target child. This activity is appropriate for a child with a developmental age of 1–2½ years.

3. *Block area*—Encourage the child to make a train using small wooden or plastic blocks placed in a line and hooked together. Ask the child to tell you where the train is going, who is riding on it, and who is the engineer. Help the child move the train around in a circle on the carpet, making sure the first block (engine) is held using thumb and fingers. This activity is appropriate for a child with a developmental age of 1–2½ years.

4. *Block area*—Have children build a house or a fantasy structure using many large wooden blocks. This works best if a group of children decide to build together. One child usually becomes the leader and gives orders to the others. You can introduce the target child into the group and then stay to monitor the child's participation. Suggest ways to contribute to the structure. For example, you might say, "Let's put this block here. It will be part of this wall, all right?" Comment on and reinforce the child's building attempts. For example, you can say, "Good idea, Raymond. Putting that block on top of the door will make it much stronger." This activity is appropriate for a child with a developmental age of 3–6 years.

5. *Block area*—Pair a child with disabilities with a typically developing child. Encourage them to construct a tower using blocks of various sizes and shapes. See how high they can make it without it falling down. Using large blocks, let them try to build a tower as tall as the target child. This activity is appropriate for a child with a developmental age of 3–6 years.

Eye–Hand Coordination

The following activities are helpful for improving eye–hand coordination.

1. *Manipulatives area*—Using small implements such as needles can be difficult even for adults. In the preschool classroom, lacing and sewing activities are intended for developing fine motor skills and eye–hand coordination. If you punch large eyelet holes in cardboard, then children can have fun lacing the pieces together. Children can also string beads on thick pieces of lacing. These activities can be done independently or with adult assistance and are appropriate for a child with a developmental age of 1½–4 years.

2. *Outdoor play*—Choose an area of the playground that is out of the way of other children. The target child can either sit on the ground or stand. Roll a large ball to the child, and ask him or her to roll it back. Ask another child to join you

and gradually withdraw from the game. If the target child has adequate motor skills, the pair can try rolling the ball while squatting, then standing. Allow the typically developing child to throw the ball if desired. After several sessions, encourage the target child to throw the ball rather than roll it. Be sure to prompt the child when necessary, and praise both children for keeping the game going. Modify the game by progressively decreasing the size of the ball and increasing the distance between the two players. A game of catch can be simplified at the beginning by using a beanbag instead of a ball. In this case, the two children should stand fairly close together. Throwing is easy; catching takes some time to master. This activity is appropriate for a child with a developmental age of 3–5 years.

Using Pencils, Crayons, and Paintbrushes

Holding implements like crayons and paintbrushes encourages development of a pincer grasp. A child with an immature grasp (e.g., using the whole fist) should be encouraged to color with crayons or paint with a brush. Consider the following activities for helping children use pencils, crayons, and paintbrushes.

1. *Creative play area*—As an alternative to traditional easel painting, encourage the child to color placemats for the lunch or snack table. This activity is appropriate for a child with a developmental age of 2–4 years.

2. *Music area*—Allow children to select instruments and play them for a few minutes. Then, pass out pencils and crayons. Ask the children to draw pictures of their instruments. Tracing the instrument may be an option if the instrument can't be damaged in the process. This activity is appropriate for a child with a developmental age of 4–5 years.

Self-Care

Many common preschool activities give children daily opportunities to practice self-care skills. Dressing, eating, and toileting are usually part of the daily routine and may not need to be embedded in play as much as skills in other developmental domains. Nevertheless, pretend play offers opportunities to practice bathing, dressing, and feeding dolls, an enjoyable way to learn good self-care routines.

Feeding

Feeding is an important self-care skill. Consider the following activities:

1. *Sand or water table*—Allow the child to explore the materials independently at the sand or water table first. Children will often spontaneously begin filling containers and emptying them. If this doesn't happen, begin by encouraging the child to fill a container with water (or sand), then dump it out. Next, suggest that the child try pouring from one big pitcher into another. This should be done while standing at the table so any spillage falls back into the table. As

pouring becomes more accurate, allow the child to try pouring from bigger to smaller containers. At first, you will have to assist by holding the small container. Next, you can have the child hold the container while you steady it with your hand. When the child can pour fairly steadily, move to the snack table, and try pouring juice from a pitcher into a cup. This activity is appropriate for a child with a developmental age of 1½–4 years.

2. *Pretend play area*—Place a tea set in the pretend play area. If desired, fill the teapot with water or another beverage. Put real crackers or other finger foods near the tea set so that children can eat as they drink their "tea." This activity is appropriate for a child with a developmental age of 3–5 years.

Bathing and Washing

The following activities will help children practice the skills associated with bathing and washing:

1. *Creative play area*—After fingerpainting or easel painting, help the child to wash up and clean the paintbrushes and other equipment. As children wash their hands and arms, you can prompt appropriate use of soap and towels and demonstrate how to adjust the water temperature as necessary. Demonstrate how to rub one's hands together to clean them and how to dry one's hands independently. This activity is appropriate for a child with a developmental age of 2–4 years.

2. *Outdoor area*—Setting up a wading pool on a warm day makes for instant fun and is a natural opportunity to practice dressing and undressing skills. The child should be encouraged to try unbuttoning or untying clothing and getting out of pants and shirts. This activity is appropriate for a child with a developmental age of 2–6 years.

SOCIAL SKILLS

Some social skills are especially important for children with disabilities to master. Being able to make and keep friends, be welcomed into playgroups, and resolve disputes without physical aggression are difficult for some children with delays.

Group Entry

Preschool is a time when children learn to play in groups. Group entry is a very important skill. Consider the following activities to help teach group entry skills.

1. *Music area*—Choose a time when the children are playing instruments or marching to music. Ask the target child to join in with you, and suggest to all of the children that they begin following your lead. Gradually shift the leadership from you to the target child (e.g., "Now let's follow Robert this time.

Oh, look! He's going into the block area. Shall we follow him? Let's go, every-one! Here we come, Robert!"). This activity is appropriate for a child with a developmental age of 1½–4 years.

2. *Creative play area*—Approach a group of children who are preparing to glue uncooked macaroni on sheets of construction paper. Ask the target child and one or two other children to help you sort the pieces of macaroni into piles of big and little pieces. Talk about the process as you go along. Then, assign the target child to distribute handfuls of big and little pieces to children who request them. This activity is appropriate for a child with a developmental age of 2–6 years.

3. *All areas*—To demonstrate how to initiate a successful play overture, place yourself close to the target child, perhaps taking the child in your lap or hold-ing one hand. Approach the potential friend in a quiet, friendly manner, speaking directly to the friend. As the child looks on, model polite, positive, indirect statements that indicate that you are willing to take a secondary role in the play activity. This activity is appropriate for a child with a developmen-tal age of 2–6 years.

Sharing Play Activities with Peers

The following activities encourage children to share play activities with peers.

1. *Music area*—Set up a rhythm activity with a small group of children, handing out drums, triangles, tambourines, and other instruments. Seat the target child next to you with a drum. Take a drum yourself, and begin to beat it, setting a slow tempo. Ask the children to follow your lead as you drum fast, then slowly, then fast again. Once the target child can follow your tempo, ask him or her to set the beat for the group, explaining, "We'll follow you." Watch and imitate the child beating the drum. Remind the other children to follow the target child's lead. For example, you can say, "Let's watch what Catherine does and follow her." At the end of the activity, praise the child. You can say, "You're a good leader, Catherine. We all enjoyed playing together this morning with you leading us." This activity is appropriate for a child with a developmental age of 2–6 years.

2. *Manipulatives area*—Use beads of various sizes and a thick string. Tie a knot at the end of the string, and put a large bead on the string. Then, help the target child find another big bead to add to the string, giving as much physical assis-tance as necessary. You can comment, "We now have two big beads on our string. Shall we add another big bead, or shall we find a small bead next?" Encourage the child to string as many beads as possible onto the string, telling you whether each one is small or big. When the string is full, ask the child to show you the smallest bead on the string and the biggest. After the child has gone through these steps with you, invite another child to join in and encour-age both children to carry out the game while you act as a facilitator. This activ-ity is appropriate for a child with a developmental age of 3–6 years.

3. *Sand or water table*—To work on this goal, set up the water or sand table with enough duplicate equipment for three children, plus yourself. Sit or kneel next to the target child, and invite one or two other children to join you. Hand each child a container. Take a similar container, and model filling it and pouring the contents into another container. Talk about what you are doing. Then, observe and prompt the target child to imitate your actions. As the child fills the container, you should imitate the action, commenting on what the child is doing and drawing the other children's attention to it. This activity is appropriate for a child with a developmental age of 2–4 years.

4. *Sand or water table*—As a group of children are engaged in water or sand play, imitate their actions yourself, and comment on what they are doing. Then, encourage the target child to imitate something one of the other children is doing. For example, you can say, "Look, Henry. Jill is building a road for her car. Let's do that, too." This activity is appropriate for a child with a developmental age of 3–6 years.

5. *Creative play area*—Cutting out pictures of people from magazines and pasting them on cardboard to make "people posters" is another great group activity. The children can classify people as big or little by pasting pictures of children on one sheet and pictures of adults on another. This can be a fun and rewarding activity requiring socializing, sharing, and cooperating if the whole group contributes to one set of posters. This activity is appropriate for a child with a developmental age of 1½–4 years.

Peaceful Conflict Resolution

Play activities offer many opportunities for adults to facilitate peaceful resolution of disputes. Many preschool children, particularly children with delays or disabilities, are not able to settle disagreements verbally and resort to getting what they want by grabbing, hitting, or shouting. Such aggressive behavior tends to exclude these children from group activities and isolates them in play. You can intervene indirectly to referee disputes. Gently lead children who have conflicts to peaceful solutions by:

• Making it clear that you are on the child's side and that you sympathize with the problem.

• Holding children who are very angry, letting them know you are doing this to keep them safe.

• Helping children to explain their feelings and what they want. You may have to model the words for the children at first, gradually letting them take over.

You can also help children to learn about their emotions. For example, in the creative play area, you can encourage children to create pictures of an incident when someone took a toy or other favorite object away from them and made them upset. Allow children to share and talk about their creations. Afterwards, discuss better ways the situation could have been resolved. For example, you can say, "Mei-ling, you felt angry when your mom gave your doll to your sister. Was there another way for your sister to get a turn with the doll without your feelings getting hurt?" or "Mark, a boy on the playground grabbed your basketball from you. What could he have done instead to ask for the ball? Could he have asked to join your game?" (See Ritchie, 2003, for more information.) This activity is appropriate for a child with a developmental age of 3–6 years.

PRELITERACY SKILLS

At the preschool level, children are exposed to activities that help them get ready to read and enjoy books. All children should be included in literacy activities in order to develop positive attitudes toward reading and writing in preparation for learning to read and write (Thurman & Widerstrom, 1990). Literacy skills are important for school success, so it is essential that preliteracy activities in preschool include all children. Some common ways children acquire preliteracy skills are listening to stories, telling stories, looking at picture books and pretending to read, and participating in flannel board storytelling.

Listening to Stories

Children love to listen to stories. This activity is fun, but it also allows children to learn new vocabulary and develop an appreciation for books. A good idea is to create a story area with a collection of picture books that children can browse through on their own. Make sure the books can be reached by all children, especially those with disabilities. Encourage an interest in reading by making sure to read to children every day for a short period. Be sure to allow them to choose the stories you read, even if they choose to read the same favorites every day. Consider the following activities as well.

1. *Story area*—When a typically developing child picks up a book and pretends to read it, ask him or her to "read" the story to you and the target child. You can also read to a small group of children who choose to join your impromptu "story hour." This activity is appropriate for a child with a developmental age of 1½–6 years.

2. *Story area*—Ask the target child to choose a story to listen to during story time. In preparation, the two of you should browse through a selection of books together as you comment about each one to help the child identify favorite books. This activity is appropriate for a child with a developmental age of 1½–6 years.

3. *Music area*—Place books about instruments and famous musicians in the music area. You can also include storybooks based on songs or anything you think might be appropriate. Before children choose instruments, tell them that you

are going to read a book to them, and explain the significance. For example, you can say, "Today I am going to read a book to you about a boy who loves to play the drums. After we read this book, we are all going to choose instruments to play!" After the children play their instruments, ask them what they like about their instrument. This activity is appropriate for a child with a developmental age of 3–6 years.

Telling Stories

Telling stories is a wonderful way for children to develop their oral language skills, which are closely connected to reading comprehension (Espinosa & Burns, 2003). The following activities encourage children to tell stories.

1. *Story area*—In the story area, ask a child who is looking at books to share the experience with the target child. Gather another typically developing child into the group and encourage storytelling or pretend "reading." Ask the target child to join in at whatever level is realistic, whether just listening or taking a turn telling the story from the pictures in the book. For example, you can say, "Let's read together, shall we? Sharon would like to read this book to us. It's about a raccoon who lives in the park. Can you read us the story from the pictures, Sharon?" This activity is appropriate for a child with a developmental age of 3–6 years.

2. *Story area*—During playtime, organize a small group of children to help tell a story about what happened in the classroom on the previous day (or earlier in the morning). Begin by saying something like this: "Remember when we made the clay yesterday? What did we do? Jan, do you remember how we made the clay?" Or you might say, "Let's tell a story about our trip to the fire station. Who can start telling the story?" This activity is appropriate for a child with a developmental age of 3–6 years.

3. *Pretend play area*—Observe children playing in the pretend play area. After they have played for a while, approach them, and ask them to tell you what is going on. For example, you can say, "I see you are playing mommy and daddy. Is this your baby? What is your family doing?" When necessary, prompt them with questions related to your observations. For example, you can say, "Lisa, I saw you mixing the pot. What were you making? Cookies? How do you make cookies?" or "Benito, I saw you rocking the baby. Was the baby crying? What happened to make the baby cry?" This activity is appropriate for a child with a developmental age of 2–5 years.

Looking at Picture Books and Pretending to Read

The following activities encourage children to look at picture books and pretend to read.

1. *Story area*—In the story area, encourage the target child to look at picture books. Be sure to have some wordless picture books in which the story is told through pictures. Ask the child to "read" the story to you. This activity is appropriate for a child with a developmental age of 1½–6 years.

2. *Dress-up area*—Place clothing from various occupations and corresponding books in the dress-up area. For example, place helmets and coats with books on firefighting or white coats and stethoscopes with stories about going to the doctor. Allow the target child to dress up in the clothes. Then, allow the child to choose between two or more relevant books. Encourage the child to "read" the story to you. This activity is appropriate for a child with a developmental age of 4–6 years.

Participating in Flannel Board Storytelling

Preschoolers like to listen to stories. Some of them are able to tell stories, too. Many are beginning to understand the connection between written and spoken words, learning that reading is just "talking written down." Children with delays often do not understand this connection yet, but they like to participate in flannel-board activities in which flannel pieces that correspond to a story are placed on a flannel board. The following activities allow children to participate in flannel board storytelling.

1. *Story area*—Encourage children to assist you in telling stories at the flannel board, using cutout pictures of animals, people, and the like. As each flannel form is placed on the board, the children can tell the story that goes with it. The target child may participate only as a listener. This activity, more directed than typical play activities, is nevertheless important for preparing children to understand the similarity between reading and telling a story. This activity is appropriate for a child with a developmental age of 1½–6 years.

2. *Story area*—Move from generic flannel cutouts and made-up stories to cutouts that represent the children's favorite storybook characters. In this way, the connection between reading books and storytelling becomes more explicit. Finally, for children nearing 6 years of age, you might introduce the experience story chart. On the chart, you will write a storyteller's words *exactly* as the child says them. This step completes the transition from storytelling to reading for those children who are developmentally ready to make this leap. Children who are not ready to dictate story charts can still participate in the small group and develop an understanding that reading is important. This activity is appropriate for a child with a developmental age of 3–6 years.

3. *Music area*—Us the flannel board to accompany children's songs. For example, have felt pieces to illustrate "Old McDonald" or "The Farmer in the Dell." At first, you should put up each piece (e.g., cow) as it comes up in the song. Later,

children can take turns doing this. This activity is appropriate for a child with a developmental age of 1½–6 years.

As you practice embedding the children's learning goals in play activities, you will become more aware of how specific types of learning occur. This will make you a better planner of individualized learning activities and less willing to allow learning to happen by chance.

Table 14.1. Index of play activities

Skill category	Specific skill	Activity number	Play area	Developmental age	Page
Cognitive					
Classification	Identifying	1	Manipulatives	3–6 years	114
		2	Manipulatives	3–6 years	115
		3	Pretend play	3–6 years	115
	Sorting	1	Pretend play	2–6 years	115
		2	Dress-up	3–6 years	115
		3	Creative play	3–6 years	115
		4	Manipulatives	1–3 years	116
		5	Creative play	2–6 years	116
	Matching	1	Manipulatives	1–6 years	116
		2	Manipulatives	3–6 years	116
		3	Pretend play	3–6 years	117
		4	Music	2–6 years	117
Seriation	*Big, little, large, and small*	1	Creative play	3–6 years	118
		2	Creative play	3–6 years	118
		3	Creative play	3–6 years	118
		4	Manipulatives	3–6 years	118
	Long, tall, and short	1	Sand or water table	3–6 years	119
		2	Music	3–6 years	119
Number concepts	Cardinal numbers	1	Block	1½–4 years	119
		2	Pretend play	3–6 years	119
		3	Creative play	2–4 years	119
	Ordinal numbers	1	Manipulatives	3–6 years	120
		2	Pretend play	3–6 years	120
	More or less	1	Sand or water table	3–6 years	120
		2	Sand or water table	3–6 years	120
		3	Sand or water table	3–6 years	120
		4	Pretend play	3–6 years	121
	One-to-one correspondence	1	Block	1½–3 years	121
		2	Music	1–3 years	121

Category	Subcategory	#	Activity area	Age	Page
Time concepts	Before and after	1	Manipulatives	3–6 years	121
		2	Outdoor	2–6 years	122
	Past and future tenses	1	All	2–6 years	122
		2	All	3–5 years	122
Spatial concepts	Shape recognition	1	Creative play	3–6 years	122
		2	Manipulatives	3–6 years	123
	Spatial relations	1	Block	3–6 years	123
	Body awareness	1	Creative play	1–3 years	123
		2	Creative play	1–4 years	123
Problem solving		1	Block	3–6 years	123
		2	Sand or water table	2–4 years	124
Predicting outcomes		1	Block	3–5 years	124
		2	Dress-up area	3–5 years	124
Communication					
Nonverbal communication	Using simple gestures or signs	1	All	1–2 years	125
		2	Creative play	1–2 years	125
	Protodeclaratives and protoimperatives	1	Manipulatives	1–3 years	126
		2	All	1–3 years	126
Verbal communication	Receptive language	1	Pretend play	1–2½ years	126
		2	Cooking	3–6 years	126
		3	Music	3–5 years	127
		4	Music	3–5 years	127
	Labeling familiar objects	1	Manipulatives	1–3 years	127
		2	Music	3–5 years	127
	Increasing utterance length	1	Pretend play	3–5 years	128
		2	Creative play	2–6 years	128
		3	Pretend play/creative play	3–6 years	128

(continued)

143

Table 14.1. *(continued)*

Skill category	Specific skill	Activity number	Play area	Developmental age	Page
	Grammatical forms	1	Pretend play	1½–3 years	129
		2	Dress-up	3–6 years	129
	Language content *(overview)*	—	—	—	129
	Pragmatic usage *(overview)*	—	—	—	129
	Asking questions *(overview)*	—	—	—	129
	Carrying on a conversation (turn taking) *(overview)*	—	—	—	130
Motor					
Gross motor	Head and trunk control	1	Outdoor	6–12 months	130
		2	Outdoor	6–12 months	131
		3	Outdoor	6–12 months	131
		4	Music	6–18 months	131
	Balancing	1	Outdoor	1–2 years	131
		2	Sand or water table	1–4 years	132
	Jumping	1	Outdoor	1½–4 years	132
		2	Block	1½–4 years	132
Fine motor	Picking up and placing objects	1	Pretend play	2–4 years	132
		2	Block	1–2½ years	132
		3	Block	1–2½ years	133
		4	Block	3–6 years	133
		5	Block	3–6 years	133
	Eye–hand coordination	1	Manipulatives	1½–4 years	133
		2	Outdoor	3–5 years	133
	Using pencils, crayons, and paintbrushes	1	Creative play	2–4 years	134
		2	Music	4–5 years	134
Self-care	Feeding	1	Sand or water table	1½–4 years	134
		2	Pretend play	3–5 years	135

Bathing and washing	1	Creative play	2–4 years	135
	2	Outdoor	2–6 years	135

Social

Group entry	1	Music	1½–4 years	135
	2	Creative play	2–6 years	136
	3	All	2–6 years	136
Sharing play activities with peers	1	Music	2–6 years	136
	2	Manipulatives	3–6 years	136
	3	Sand or water table	2–4 years	137
	4	Sand or water table	3–6 years	137
	5	Creative play	1½–4 years	137
Peaceful conflict resolution (overview)	—	—	3–6 years	137

Preliteracy

Listening to stories	1	Story	1½–6 years	138
	2	Story	1½–6 years	138
	3	Music	3–6 years	138
Telling stories	1	Story	3–6 years	139
	2	Story	3–6 years	139
	3	Pretend play	2–5 years	139
Looking at picture books and pretending to read	1	Story	1½–6 years	140
	2	Dress-up	4–6 years	140
Participating in flannel board storytelling	1	Story	1½–6 years	140
	2	Story	3–6 years	140
	3	Music	1½–6 years	140

IV

Playing Together and Making Friends

15

Big Groups, Little Groups

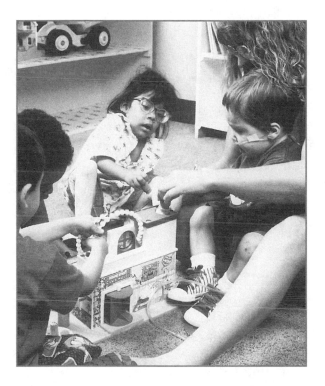

Let's All Learn Together

Because young children should be in environments that are as natural as possible, adults should try not to dominate children's learning environments. It is important to maintain a place where children can learn that is not too different from their home, especially when they first begin to attend school. For very young children, the bridge between home and school is very important. You can help the children in your care make an easy and gradual transition from home to school by helping them avoid painful separations from their parents and disruptions in their familiar routines.

You may need to take extra care in assisting children with special needs to adjust to school. Many of these children participate in infant programs, so they have already made one transition—from home to the center-based infant program—and have experienced a group environment. For children who do not participate in a center-based infant program, preschool will be their first group experience. The stress of this new experience might then be combined with the stress of becoming familiar with a new set of adults. In either case, remember to introduce group activities gradually and to involve parents as much as possible. This helps the child to feel comfortable at school and ready to learn.

CLASSROOM ENVIRONMENT

Your classroom should be a pleasant, relaxed place where children can learn at their own paces. Many children with special needs, however, will require extra direct instruction, which means that less time will be devoted to group activities. For example, a good, balanced daily schedule for a child with disabilities might look like this. The times are approximate and include gaps to allow time for making transitions from one activity to the next:

8:45–9:20	Greeting, talking about the day's plans (big group)
9:30–9:45	Large muscle activity involving movement to music, marching, or dancing (big group)
9:45–10:40	Free play, with adult helping the target child to work on individual learning goals (small or big group)
10:45–11:10	Snack (small or big group)
11:15–11:45	Manipulative, dramatic play, or language activities (small-group activities)
11:45–12:15	Outdoor play using large muscles (This time could be devoted to individual or small-group physical therapy.)
12:15–12:45	Hand washing, lunch, cleanup
1:00–2:00	Quiet-time nap, rest, or story reading (individual according to each child's need for rest)

PLAYING IN A BIG GROUP

Young children first watch others play, then begin to play *beside* another child. They don't play together in real groups until they are 3 or 4 years old. The two stages of true group play—called *associative play* and *cooperative play* (Parten, 1932)—require children to have certain skills in order to participate successfully.

Associative Play

In associative play, all the children in the group do the same thing, for example, filling and pouring at the water table, stacking blocks to make a tower, or riding tricycles on the playground. It is quite easy to help a target child enter an associative playgroup. Simply take the target child by the hand, and lead the way to the play area. Sit beside the child, and explain what is happening and what he or she is expected to do. You may wish to prepare some children for a big-group experience by letting them practice the play activity with you alone or with a small group (one other child) before joining a group.

For example, you can say, "Sammy, I see you have a truck. Can I play with the truck with you? I'm going to load the truck with these red pieces. Can you help me load the truck? Find some more red pieces for your truck. Now, let's show Juanita the truck. Juanita, come and play with us. Sammy has loaded his truck with red pieces. Will you help him find some more? Would you like your own truck to load? Let's find one. Sammy, Juanita wants a truck like yours. We're going to get one so she can play with you."

If you begin like this and gradually increase the number of children in the group, you will soon have an associative playgroup. You must watch carefully to ensure that the playgroup isn't dominated by an aggressive child. You must also keep the playgroup interesting enough for other children to want to participate. When you see that they are getting bored, change the activity or suggest cleaning up and listening to a story.

Cooperative Play

Cooperative play differs from associative play in that the children take different roles, with one or two leading the activity.

Cooperative play is more difficult for all children than associative play, for it usually means excluding someone from the playgroup. Exclusion probably occurs because as children grow older, they begin to develop a sense of self, and their self-identity is based in part on whom they choose to play with and be friends with. Their choice of playmates reflects who they perceive themselves to be as developing people. As toddlers, most children begin to associate with some children more often than others. This occurrence leads gradually to their choosing some children to be their friends and excluding other children from their playgroup. This trend begins with early cooperative play and becomes even more pronounced in middle childhood and adolescence.

Research has shown that children with disabilities are often excluded (Guralnick, 2001). If the exclusion happens early in childhood, a pattern is established that follows the child through elementary school. Therefore, it is important to help the child avoid that experience if possible. In Chapter 16 (see Table 16.2), you will find techniques that you can expand with your own ideas to help children with disabilities avoid being excluded from group play.

Using Play to Prevent Behavior Problems

Play can be a useful format for preventing behavior problems if adults are careful to structure it so that all children follow certain rules. Play can easily be individualized for children who are at different developmental levels, which means all of the children in the group don't have to do the same thing at the same time. This allows for the freedom of expression that automatically prevents some behavior problems. The following list gives some times when behavior problems commonly occur that could be prevented by making the child a member of a playgroup and allowing some freedom.

Sitting Still Too Long

There are many times when children might become disruptive because they are required to sit too long. Consider the following examples:

- *Being required to sit and listen to an adult reading a story.* Make sure that all children can see the book. Choose stories that are short, and allow the class to pick which story you read. Place children with disabilities in a comfortable position on the floor with other children.

- *Being required to sit and listen to an adult giving directions.* Make sure that the directions are not too long and complicated so that all of the children can understand.

- *Having to sit and listen to other children during circle time.* Make sure that one or two children do not dominate a group. All children should have the opportunity to share with the group. Make sure that children with disabilities have a way to signal that they would like a turn (e.g., a switch to activate a recording of a child saying, "I have something to say!")

- *Having to wait too long for a turn at an activity.* Some activities can be arranged so that more than one child can participate at a time. For example, place children in pairs or small groups to make a collaborative art project. Try to have adequate materials available to minimize waiting (e.g., plenty of crayons, multiple copies of preferred books).

- *Having to wait for others to finish snack or lunch before being excused from the table.* Make up a plan for what children should do when they finish lunch before the rest of the class. Perhaps they can quietly look through a book or listen to music with headphones until the next class activity.

Following Adult Directions Too Much of the Time

Children are generally less motivated to do as they're told than to initiate their own activities. Children need opportunities to explore their interests and will be most motivated to learn if the activities evolve from things they are already doing. These situations spell trouble:

- *Having to respond to adults most of the time.* Be alert to subtle initiatives for attention from children with disabilities. These are often lost among more aggressive overtures from typically developing children.

- *Having to wait for a turn to do exactly what every other child in the group is required to do.* Turn taking is usually fine, but limit waiting time by reducing size. Also, vary the activities.

- *Being required to sit through activities that the child perceives as meaningless and unnecessarily repetitive.* In a play-based model, children make most of the choices and don't have to conform to the group.

- *Being unable to make any decisions about what to do or say.* Don't be too directive. Listen to children.

- *Having to listen nearly all of the time and being expected to talk only when repeating what adults say.* Keep quiet when appropriate, and let children talk to each other, not always to adults.

PLAYING IN A SMALL GROUP

Small groups are especially useful for working on specific learning goals in both infant and preschool programs. With only three or four children per adult, special attention can be given to each child's learning goals (Pretti-Frontczak & Bricker, 2004). Examples of how learning goals can be addressed in small groups follow.

Table Top (Manipulatives) Group

Four children and one or two adults are sitting at a table while the children work on individualized fine motor games. James's individualized education program (IEP) goal is to grasp large objects using a palmar grasp. Therefore, the adult gives him some 2-inch cubes to pick up and place in an empty coffee can. He can then dump them out and begin again. Julia is working on her pincer grasp. Her activity consists of picking up small circles cut out of heavy cardboard and putting them into an empty milk carton. Ricardo has difficulty grasping objects, so he is given a wooden puzzle with three large pieces to put together. An adult holds his hand to assist him in picking up each piece and finding its place in the puzzle. Margaret has average fine motor skills, so she is given a more difficult task—stringing beads on a length of string. Once the children finish their assigned fine motor tasks, they are allowed to choose any other activities at the fine motor table that they wish to do—putting together puzzles, stringing beads, using fill-and-dump toys, water painting using paint-with-water books, drawing with colored markers, and similar activities.

Embedding separate activities for each child while they all work as a small group is difficult. It involves becoming familiar with each child's IEP goals, developmental level, and preferred activities, but all effective preschool teachers come to know their children well enough to successfully plan these individualized goals within group lessons.

Language Group

Although language must be addressed in all activities, sometimes there is a need for a more intensive and specific experience for some children. Then, a small group with more specific objectives makes sense (Dickinson & Tabors, 2001). The language group can focus on receptive or expressive language skills. For example, if several children are working on recognizing and naming pictures of familiar objects (also a cognitive skill of representation), the goal can be addressed by having two or three children play a lotto game with an adult. Cutting out pictures of people from magazines and pasting them on cardboard to make "people posters" is another receptive language activity. The children can classify people as big or little by pasting pictures of children on one sheet and pictures of adults on another. This can be a fun and rewarding activity requiring socializing, sharing, and cooperating if the whole group contributes to one set of posters.

Math Group

Math groups can focus on number-related activities and also on activities to develop categorization, seriation, and conservation. Sorting activities, for example, develop the ability to place similar objects in one category. Grouping by color or shape is the least difficult. Individual goals can be embedded into the group activities. For example, Sarah's goal is to sort objects by color, and Moira's goal is to arrange objects in order of size. They can work side by side, each with her own materials.

Cooking Group

A good size for a cooking group is four or five children with two adults. A cooking activity requires everyone to participate in the same activity. Children can take different roles and different levels of responsibility according to their individual needs and abilities, however. If the activity is making instant pudding, each child can take a turn mixing the pudding and milk together. In this case, turn taking is not frustrating for children with short attention spans because the group has only five members. The cooking group differs from the cooking *center* in that the center is designed for children to use independently, when they wish, and for as long as they wish. In the drop-in format of the learning center, the adult is primarily a facilitator, whereas the small group involves primarily adult-directed activities that are done by the group as a whole.

LEARNING CENTERS AND PLAY

Many classrooms for toddlers and preschoolers are organized around learning centers. The classroom is divided into skill areas such as science, manipulatives, cooking, language, computers, and the like. Activities can be initiated by the child or adult directed, depending on each child's skill levels.

The activities available in each learning center are changed regularly. For example, the choice of activities for one day might include planting seeds in the science center, making butter in the cooking center, listening to audiotapes or viewing a videotape in the language center, and making valentines in the fine motor center. Learning centers are valuable because they allow small groups of children to work together semi-independently. An adult can serve as facilitator, allowing some children to work independently and others to receive more adult direction or assistance. Learning goals can quite easily be embedded in learning center activities (Pretti-Frontczak & Bricker, 2004).

Here are some examples of how to work on goals in the learning center:

Goal: Mary will use the pronouns *I, my,* and *mine* when referring to herself.

Learning center activity: Set up a center with a double set of materials such as beads for stringing; play dishes; or paper, paste, and paint. Place one set of materials beside you at the table, saying, "These are mine, Mary. I have blue paper, some paste, and some paint. Would you like some, too? Tell me what you want." Prompt the use of *I want.* As the activity progresses, make comments such as, "My picture is nearly finished now. How is your picture coming, Mary?" If necessary, prompt the use of *my picture, I,* and *mine.*

Goal: Jonathan will follow a two-step direction accurately.

Learning center activity: Ask Jonathan to be your assistant at the cooking center. Have ready whole bananas, grapes, sliced pears, whole strawberries, and a large bowl of yogurt with two large serving spoons. Also have small cutting boards available, one for each child around the table, as well as aprons, bowls, and small plastic knives for cutting the bananas and strawberries. As children come to the cooking center, ask Jonathan to hand out fruit, bowls, and aprons.

For example, you can say, "Please give Ronald some fruit to cut up. Then, give him a bowl for his yogurt." Give general instructions to the children, two steps at a time, as in these examples:

- "First, choose some fruit. Then, cut it up."

- "Now, we're ready to spoon some yogurt into the bowl."

- "Then, mix the fruit with the yogurt. Now, it's ready to eat!"

While this activity requires considerable teacher direction, it fits the learning goal quite well and provides an activity the whole group will enjoy. Any cooking activity can replace snack time because the children eat their creations at the end of the activity.

From the preceding discussion, it is obvious that learning opportunities are present in both big and small groups. Having large and small groups offers teachers and therapists the flexibility to provide high or low structure and to take a more or less directive role, depending on each child's needs. It is important to include both big-group and small-group activities in the daily preschool schedule. Group activities can also be used to promote friendship development. Chapter 16 explores techniques you can use to help children make friends.

16

Learning Social Skills Through Play

Learning how to get along with other children has always been an important part of children's preschool life. Having friends is a natural part of growing up and becoming a successful adult. In many early childhood education programs, children acquire the social skills they need for developing and maintaining friendships through their daily routine of playing and interacting with other children. Teachers don't have to do much formal planning to make this happen, for social development is typically a natural process that children can undertake on their own, given the proper environment.

Although this process is easy for some children, children with disabilities may have trouble making friends on their own. Even when they are in the same classroom as typically developing children, they may be isolated from their peers because they have poor social skills. In the past, this area of development was often overlooked. When special education programs for young children with disabilities first began in the 1970s, they emphasized helping children catch up with their peers in skill development. As a result, the curriculum consisted almost exclusively of activities for cognitive, motor, and language development. Whether these children had friends—especially friends in their own neighborhoods or friends without disabilities—didn't seem very important.

Educators now recognize that having friends is natural and necessary for everyone, and the benefits for children with disabilities are innumerable. Friends are not only fun to play with, but children can learn things from their friends that they can't learn from an adult. Having friends also builds children's self-esteem and confidence. All children profit from improving their social skills.

MAKING FRIENDS IS HARD WORK!

If you take a moment to analyze just what is involved in beginning a new friendship, you'll recognize how complicated it really is. Among other things, it requires taking initiative, making indirect and nonthreatening overtures, reading others' cues, avoiding conflict, identifying common interests, and suggesting joint activities that are mutually enjoyable. Making friends successfully also requires imagination, creativity, and the ability to take another person's point of view. Clearly, these are cognitive as well as social skills. The process is a complex one that we can by no means take for granted.

The following section discusses social and cognitive skills children need for developing friendships and ways to help children with disabilities accomplish this vital part of childhood. This section is intended not only for children who have progressed beyond the parallel play stage and are ready to begin associative play, but also for children with more serious developmental delays who may still be engaging in parallel play or solitary play even though chronologically they would typically be ready for associative play. Table 16.1 reviews the developmental stages of play.

Table 16.1. Types of play

1–3 years: *Unoccupied behavior*—The child engages in random behavior such as watching something of momentary interest, following an adult, or engaging in play with his or her own body.

2–3 years: *Parallel activity*—The child plays independently but chooses an activity that will naturally bring him or her close to other children. The child uses toys similar to those of the nearby children but plays beside the other children rather than interacting with them.

2½–3½ years: *Onlooker*—The child watches others play, often talking to the children being watched, making suggestions or asking questions, but not entering into play. The onlooker may be either a child who lacks the social skills to engage in play with other children or a very skilled child who is using indirect means to enter the play group.

4–5 years: *Solitary independent play*—The child plays alone and independently, with different toys from those the children nearby are using. The child makes no effort to get close to or interact with other children. Solitary play is not necessarily a stage of development. Although common at ages 4 to 5, it can be seen at all levels of development—even adults engage in solitary independent play sometimes. Unless the child engages only in solitary play, there is no cause for concern. If only solitary play is used, some intervention is recommended.

4–6 years: *Associative play*—The child plays with other children in a common activity, forming a group that excludes other children. Each child acts independently without considering the needs of the group. All the children engage in a similar, if not identical, activity, but there is no division of labor.

4–6 years: *Cooperative or organized supplementary play*—The child plays in a group organized for some play purpose (e.g., create a product, perform a drama, compete in a competition, play a game). There is division of labor, with children taking different roles. One or two children dominate, acting as leaders, assigning roles, and excluding some other children from the group.

From Parten, M.B. (1932). Social participation among preschool children. *Journal of Abnormal and Social Psychology, 27,* 243–269; adapted by permission.

Note: Ages given for each category indicate the years during which that type of play is most commonly seen.

MAKING A SOCIAL OVERTURE

One of the most difficult steps in establishing a friendship is making the first move. Even adults may find it difficult, for there is always the risk of rejection. After several rejections, some children will give up making social overtures. In order to prevent this from happening, you should take steps to ensure success. The social overtures that are most likely to be successful are nonthreatening to the potential friend and offer something the child might want or be interested in. Unsuccessful overtures are most often aggressive, taking the form of hitting, yelling, or grabbing a toy away from the potential friend. You can model successful overtures, point out successful overtures as they are being made by other children, or directly help a child to make an overture. In this case, the weight of adult authority can help to ease the way for the child by reducing the risk of rejection.

Modeling Successful Overtures

To demonstrate how to initiate a successful play overture, place yourself close to the target child, perhaps taking the child in your lap or holding one of the child's hands. Approach the potential friend in a quiet, friendly manner, speaking directly to the friend as in the following examples. In these examples, the target child is an onlooker.

Example 1

Adult: Oh, I see you are baking some cookies, James. May I help you? Are these peanut butter cookies? They're my favorite. What can I do to help you make the cookies?

James: Hand me the baking pan.

Adult: Okay. Here's the pan. My goodness, those cookies will be delicious.

Example 2

Adult: Look, I have something to show you. It's a secret. Can you guess what it is? That's right. It's a new puzzle. May I help you put it together?

Example 3

Adult: (stacking blocks) Where is a big one, Maria? Can you find a big one for our tower? Jamie needs some help.

Maria: Here's one.

Adult: Good. If you give it to Jamie, he can put it on the tower.

In these examples, the adult models polite, positive, and indirect statements to show the potential friend that the adult is willing to take a secondary role in the play activity. This lets the potential friend know that there is nothing threatening in the overture, so it is safe to respond to it positively.

Alerting the Child to Successful Overtures by Peers

With this strategy, you might call the child's attention to an initiation or potential initiation by another child. Sometimes this is a true initiation by a potential friend that the target child simply does not recognize; at other times it may be an approach by the potential friend intended not as a play overture, but rather as a simple request for attention. You can often interpret such approaches as play overtures and use them as opportunities to teach the target child to be receptive to play overtures.

Example 1: A typically developing child has run into difficulty completing a puzzle and shows it to you. The target child is nearby.

Adult: Oh, Rebecca, I see you're having some trouble with that puzzle. Let's see what the problem is. Maria, will you help us here? Rebecca is asking us to help her with the puzzle.

Example 2: A child approaches the target child and attempts to get the target child's attention. The target child does not recognize the overture and ignores the potential friend.

Adult: Maria, look what Rebecca has to show you. She would like you to help her dress the dolly. Let's help her dress the dolly.

Assisting Directly with Play Overtures

This strategy involves encouraging the target child to initiate overtures. You will need to guide the child and to lend some moral weight to the overture to lessen the likelihood that it will be rejected by the potential friend. Take as passive a role as possible at the beginning, increasing participation only enough to ensure that the overture is successful. It may be necessary to take any of the following steps, depending on the target child's level of social skills:

1. For children who do not give any evidence of being able to attempt a social overture without assistance or who appear not to understand the purpose of making social overtures, take the initiative. At this level, the child must be walked through the process of initiating the social overture. Take such a child by the hand, and suggest that the child do an activity with a peer, as in these examples:

   "Let's invite Richard to help us do this puzzle."

   "This is Letitia's favorite story, I think. Let's ask her to read it with us."

   "Look. David is feeding his baby with a bottle. Let's see if we can help him. Here's another baby (doll). Shall we feed this baby like David is feeding his baby?"

2. If the child makes overtures but the overtures are too aggressive to be accepted, take direct action. Physically restrain the child from hitting, pushing, or grabbing by taking both of the child's hands. Kneel so you can make eye contact, and explain quietly that playing is more fun and works better without hitting, pushing, or grabbing. Model a more effective overture. For example, you can say, "Let's ask Paul to play with us. Let's do it together. Paul, Amy would like to help you build that tower. May we watch you do it for a few minutes? Then, maybe Amy can help you."

   This response helps the aggressive child to slow down and to understand that he or she must first take a secondary role in the play. It helps the other child to feel less threatened because he or she is reassured that his or her primary role in the play activity will not be usurped by the aggressive child. Typically, aggressive children will need several tries before they can successfully initiate, with adult assistance, a satisfying play overture. To expect quick results is unrealistic.

3. If the target child wishes to initiate play but does not have the necessary social repertoire, or if the child is too shy to make an overture, the adult can support the child's efforts without directly intervening. A statement like this can ease the way: "Eric would like to help bake that cake, Veronica. Will you let him help you? Eric, why don't you turn on the oven for Veronica?

UNDERSTANDING AND PLEASING YOUR CONVERSATION PARTNER

Successful social overtures are nonthreatening and nonaggressive. They are also aimed at pleasing the potential friend (without using bribery, of course). To make successful overtures, children must learn to let go of their own desires, to give and take, and to compromise. The ability to compromise requires sufficient ego strength to be able to consider the needs of others aside from one's own, as well as the cognitive ability to take another's point of view. Piaget called this ability *decentering*, or learning that one is not the center of the universe. Empathy is another component of successful social interaction. All of these components require considerable cognitive skill, emotional maturity, and social experience. No wonder making and keeping friends is so complicated!

Wise teachers will use their observational skills to assist children individually in acquiring these prerequisites to successful social interaction. They will provide experiences that enhance self-esteem by allowing children to feel successful and masterful. In addition, they will encourage the development of empathy in all children by talking about feelings; by showing empathy themselves toward children who are sad, disappointed, or angry; and by acknowledging children who show empathy toward others. They will also use praise for accomplishing small steps. Above all, they will have expectations for *all* the children in their care to develop satisfying friendships with their peers.

Research has shown that children who are popular and who make friends easily are usually good at taking leadership roles. Because social skills overlap a great deal with cognitive skills, it is not surprising that these children tend to be the more able members of the group. Therefore, it follows that learning to take the lead is a skill that will make it easier for children with fewer skills to make friends during play activities.

Becoming a leader is a complex process not well understood by developmental psychologists. At a minimum, it appears to require the imagination to come up with new ideas, the willingness to risk rejection of one's ideas, and the ability to tune into the play partner's opinions and needs. Again, these are sophisticated skills that are not easily acquired; witness the small number of children who grow up to be leaders in their communities. Nevertheless, you can provide valuable support to children as they attempt to learn and practice leadership roles. Many times, the moral weight of an adult can at least create an opportunity for a child to try out a leadership role with peers that would not have been available without an adult's insistence.

Parten (1932) found that some children were always excluded from associative and cooperative playgroups. To Parten, this exclusion was a necessary descriptor of the higher levels of group play, a conclusion that is reflected in her definitions (see Table 16.1). Although little attention has been given to this phenomenon in the play literature, it is an important consideration for children with delays, for they are often the ones excluded from the group. Parten observed that children with disabilities are usually excluded from playgroups by children who take leadership roles. What purpose this serves developmentally is open to speculation, but exclusive groups are certainly quite characteristic of adult social interaction. It seems important, therefore, to ensure that children with disabilities or delays gain membership in associative and cooperative playgroups.

Children who lack the ability to successfully enter playgroups on their own require support from adults. Although these children usually take secondary roles in play rather than leadership roles, they can learn to be leaders, too, with adult support and encouragement. They can learn to be persuasive rather than threatening in their approaches and their suggestions, and they can be taught indirect methods of group entry.

YOUR ROLE IN HELPING CHILDREN PLAY

There are many things you can do to help children play. First, you can help children discover what interests they have in common. Hanson and Beckman (2001b) suggested the following activities:

- Ask parents to provide a list of their children's favorite things so you can see which children have similar interests. Try to incorporate the favorite topics of a child with disabilities in group activities to encourage the child to participate.

- Establish a time for show and tell. Children will be able to share their interests and connect with others who enjoy those things as well.

- Invite parents to volunteer so that other children can observe how the parent and child play together. The parent can also initiate group play activities that include the child.

- Explain any special equipment or language considerations (e.g., sign language, augmentative and alternative communication device) that a child with disabilities may have. Allow children to ask questions so that you can clear up any misconceptions that may be preventing the children from playing together.

- Approach the parents of a child who is having trouble making friends, and ask them to encourage the child's interest in popular music, books, characters, and toys. For example, the parents could take the child to a toy store and point out popular toys to familiarize the child with how to play with them. The parents could also rent a popular children's movie so the child can get to know the characters and catch phrases associated with that movie. These activities will help the child to develop common interests with peers.

- Teach the child social gestures (e.g., holding hands, waving hello, giving a high five) that will enable the child to communicate nonverbally with you and the child's peer.

Another option is to promote leadership. Consider the following scenario set in a preschool program with typically developing children and children with communication disorders. Marcia, the teacher, provides a valuable experience for

Table 16.2.   Strategies for bringing children with different abilities together in play

Assign group membership for certain activities. Make sure each group contains some children who are leaders and who can get the group started. Include two or three children who need extra assistance with expressive language or with motor skills. If possible, include a child in each group who works well with others and likes to cooperate.

Assign children to be buddies for a brief play activity each day; activities should be short to prevent resentment from developing. Try to pair children of differing abilities, with one child acting as peer mentor and the child with social difficulties as learner or imitator. Buddy pairings can be changed on a weekly basis, and make sure that the child with social difficulties sometimes gets a chance to be a peer mentor. Suggested play activities appropriate for buddies include the following:

Easel painting

Dress-up

Building activity

Bead stringing

Sand or water table play

"Reading" a story

Choose two children—one child with social difficulties and one typically developing child—to play with you in a special activity such as building with blocks. Encourage the typically developing child to interact with the second child, sharing blocks, demonstrating how to build a higher tower, or suggesting new ways to use the blocks. Make it a point to comment favorably on what the child with social difficulties contributes. Imitate the child with disabilities, and encourage the typically developing child to do the same.

Help the child with social difficulties practice group entry skills. Sit with the child beside a group of children playing at some activity. Make comments from time to time about what's taking place in the group play, directing your comments to the child as well as to members of the group. After several minutes, ask one of the children to include the child with social difficulties in the play activity. Use indirect language, for example, "I'll bet Janice could help you find the right block for that tower," or "What a great idea! You're making soup! May Janice and I have some soup?" Suggest that the child with social difficulties join the playgroup, giving him or her a specific role to carry out, for example, "Why don't you see if you can find a block for Jamie's tower?" or "Let's sit here and have a bowl of Karen's soup."

Andy, a child with cerebral palsy. Andy finds a drum in the block area of the prekindergarten classroom and sits down to pound on it with one hand. Marcia notices him, picks up another drum, sits down beside him, and begins pounding on the drum with both hands, following Andy's rhythm. Soon, Andy begins using both hands to pound his drum. Next, a typically developing child sits down beside Marcia. Marcia hands her drum to this child and reaches for a third drum.

Other children begin to notice the group. Attracted by the noise and the rhythmic pounding, they begin to join in, bringing other rhythm instruments or asking Marcia to find them instruments. Marcia keeps things going by supplying instruments and suggesting where children can sit, but she pays particular attention to Andy throughout the play session. She stays beside him and encourages him to take the lead. "Show me the beat," she says. "We'll follow your beat. Follow Andy's beat, everyone. Listen. It goes like this." The activity lasts about 10 minutes and includes seven children—three children with communication disorders and four typically developing children. The activity provides a rich opportunity for the children to experience a cooperative activity led by a child not accustomed to assuming a leadership role. It succeeds because Marcia is sensitive to the needs of all of the children and because she is willing to take a supportive, facilitative role.

Getting children of different ability levels to play together is often difficult. Table 16.2 provides some suggestions. This is an area that usually requires some adult intervention, but typically developing children will often follow an adult's lead in including their peers with disabilities in activities, especially if they are acknowledged for doing so. Use praise to reward children who take the initiative to play with others. This type of peer coaching usually works well for all children (Cook et al., 2000). You can also consider pairing a child with disabilities with a particularly social peer. The new "buddy" can introduce the child with disabilities to other children in the class or encourage the child with disabilities to participate in group activities (Hanson & Beckman, 2001b).

From the preceding discussion, you can see that taking an indirect role in promoting children's play is most successful. Your role should be as unobtrusive as possible, and you should decrease your involvement as the child's ability to make successful social overtures increases. You will want to praise children with special needs who play successfully, and sometimes you will need to intervene to prevent unsuccessful social interactions from occurring. You should support children's attempts to lead play activities, and teach children to be indirect and nonthreatening in their overtures. You can help by giving suggestions to get things started and modeling appropriate play activities when necessary.

Now that you know how to get children involved, how can you encourage parents to participate in the classroom and feel connected to the community? Chapter 17 offers suggestions for connecting a child's home life to his or her school and community life.

17

Connecting Home
to School and Beyond

Enabling Families to Participate
in the Classroom and Community

Communication and cooperation between parents and teachers is vital for children's success. Learning goals cannot be successfully achieved through play if what children learn at school is not carried over and practiced at home, and vice versa. Here are some ideas for achieving good cooperation.

MAINTAINING OPEN COMMUNICATION

Make time for communication. Allow time at the beginning and end of the day for parents to address any concerns. Find a time to call or speak to a parent after class on a regular basis to make sure you keep in touch (Hanson & Beckman, 2001a). Because parents love to know what their children do each day, encourage them to volunteer during class or help out at special events. Many parents would love to get more involved but aren't sure how. It may help to set up a display with a list of activities you have planned, what volunteering would entail, and how many volunteers you need. You can also set up an idea box for parents to suggest activities they could share with the class (e.g., teach children how to play with dreidels, put on a puppet show, teach a song in Spanish). The better you get to know the parents of the children you teach, the more willing they will be to work with you on their children's goals.

TOY LENDING LIBRARY

Nearly all families will take advantage of a toy lending library at their child's preschool. It is fairly easy to organize and run, and the benefits are numerous. You can start with toys purchased through the preschool program and gradually expand as you get donations from community organizations or businesses and from the parents themselves. You can add adaptive toys (e.g, toys operated by switches) if you can find someone to help you modify the toys.

Having a toy lending library gives you a natural opportunity to discuss with parents what types of toys might be suitable for their child to play with at home. You can also suggest ways to carry over the child's toy play from school to home. Adding toys to the classroom that children are familiar with from home will give children confidence in their play that may transfer to confidence in group play with the toy.

To begin a toy lending library, find a small space in the classroom that parents can gain access to on a regular basis. It need only be two or three shelves in a bookcase to begin with. Inventory all the toys that will be available for checkout, and keep the inventory in a notebook. Include a column in the inventory for keeping track of toys that need to be repaired. Figure 17.1 illustrates two simple forms you might use for checking toys in and out.

Example 1

Name	Toy	Date checked out	Date checked in
1.			
2.			
3.			
4.			
5.			

Example 2

Name: _____

Address: _____

_____

_____

Telehone: _____

Toy	Date checked out	Condition	Date checked in	Condition
1.				
2.				
3.				
4.				
5.				

Figure 17.1. Examples of toy lending library checkout forms.

The library should be open on a regular schedule but does not need to be open more than twice a week at the beginning. As parents request longer hours, you can open it on a more frequent basis. Ask parents when they prefer to check toys in and out, either first thing in the morning or last thing before leaving for the day. Usually one half-hour is sufficient for this process. It is best for the child if you can be available yourself to help parents choose toys so that you can match toys to learning goals and suggest ways for parents to use the toys at home.

Before the workshop

At least 2 weeks before the workshop, send out notices inviting parents. Ask each parent to bring one of his or her child's favorite toys to the workshop.

At the workshop

1. Begin by having all participants introduce themselves and, if appropriate, give their child's name.

2. As a warm-up activity, invite the parents one at a time to display the toys they brought. Ask each parent to describe how the child uses the toy, how or why the child likes to play with that toy, and what the parent believes the child learns from playing with the toy.

3. Make a wall chart listing some common learning goals of preschool children. Begin by writing two or three goals on the list, then invite parents to contribute their children's goals.

> *Learning Goals*
>
> 1. *Make a new friend*
> 2. *Understand "same" and "different"*
> 3. *Drink from a cup without help*
> 4.

4. With parents, brainstorm ways to address each learning goal through play. To start things off smoothly, have prepared ideas for the learning goals you contributed at the top of the list. That way, you can naturally take the lead at the beginning of the activity. Ask parents to talk about some ways they play with their children at home to work on their children's own learning goals. Parents often like to share with one another ideas that work. This activity also helps parents realize that playing with the child at home is not only fun but can also promote learning.

5. Present information concerning types of toys and various levels of toy use. Most toys fall into one of these three categories:

   • Exact-placement toys (e.g., stacking toys, puzzles, blocks)

   • Cause-and-effect toys (e.g., jack-in-the-boxes, spinning tops, wind-up toys such as music boxes)

   • Toys with barriers (e.g., toy barn with animals, toy school bus with passengers)

   Have examples of each of the three types of toys available to show parents.

Figure 17.2.   Sample agenda for a parent workshop on play and toy use. *Note:* This sample agenda gives you a few suggestions to get you started in planning a workshop about toys. You'll probably think of other activities to present, too. Workshops for parents that cover topics related to toys are a good way to involve parents in their children's learning program.

PARENT WORKSHOPS

Many parents enjoy attending workshops if the topics are specific enough and pertinent to their child's program. Workshops are not difficult to present if several people cooperate to plan and carry out the ideas. Possible topics for parent workshops follow.

6. Explain that each type of toy has a different purpose, and children learn different things from each type:

    Exact-placement toys

    Child learns

    - Fine motor skills (e.g., pincer grasp, picking up and releasing objects)
    - Cognitive skills (e.g., learning that small objects fit inside or on top of larger objects)

    Cause-and-effect toys

    Child learns

    - Fine motor skills (e.g., opening and closing doors, removing barrier to obtain small pieces)
    - Cognitive skills (e.g., mastery, cause-and-effect relationships)

    Toys with barriers

    Child learns

    - Fine motor skills (e.g., opening and closing doors, removing barrier to obtain small pieces)
    - Cognitive skills (e.g., problem solving)

7. Ask parents to think of everyday household items that could be used as exact-placement toys (e.g., kitchen pots and pans, plastic bowls that fit inside one another), as cause-and-effect toys (e.g., light switch, television, VCR, radio, faucets), or as barrier toys (e.g., food or juice cartons, boxes with lids, plastic food-storage containers).

8. Explain to parents that it is helpful for them to know their child's current level of toy use and what the next level is. That way, they can present toys that match the child's developmental level and encourage progress toward the next higher level.

    Levels of toy use

    Level 1   *Physical exploration:* The child mouths the toy or bangs it against the floor or a table.

    Level 2   *Uses toy as intended:* The child uses the toy as intended. The child uses the toy appropriately, such as stacking blocks or correctly completing a puzzle.

    Level 3   *Uses toy creatively:* The child incorporates the toy into creative or dramatic play. Examples are using farm animals to act out a story and using a block to represent the farmer's tractor.

9. For each level of play, talk about strategies you have found useful in the classroom for teaching children to use toys in that way.

Why Play Is Important for All Children

A workshop on why play is important for all children might help parents who question whether their child should be spending time playing instead of using the time to drill newly learned skills. The idea that children can practice new skills while playing, thus gaining mastery in a natural and enjoyable way, may never have occurred to some parents. A workshop about the benefits of play, the various types of play, and some of the ways adults can encourage children to play together would be of interest to many parents. Figure 17.2 gives a sample agenda for a workshop about play and toy use.

Making and Trading Toys

Some parents like to attend workshops that require more active participation. If you can locate a parent who would be willing to take on the responsibility of presenting a workshop about making toys from homemade materials, you are lucky! Perhaps someone would be willing to organize an afternoon devoted to a toy exchange among parents or an opportunity to trade in old toys for new ones. Any of these ideas would be welcomed by most parents.

For the toy exchange, ask each participant to bring three old toys to exchange with others. Set up large tables in the classroom, and lay out all the toys. Then, ask parents to circulate around the tables and choose one new toy. When everyone has selected one toy, repeat the process two more times. This gives all parents a fair chance to obtain toys they want, and if there are two particularly desirable toys, the same person won't end up with both of them.

For toy-making workshops, it is necessary to collect tools and whatever materials are required to construct the toy. You can ask the workshop participants to bring their own materials with them, or you can ask for donations from a local supplier. Better yet, assign a parent to carry out this chore if you can. If you type and photocopy complete instructions, then parents can work at their own speed.

How to Embed Learning Goals in Everyday Play (Using the Planning Matrix)

Parents are interested to learn how you work on their children's learning goals during the daily scheduled play activities. Because you hope they will work on the learning goals at home, a workshop on how to embed learning goals in everyday play using a planning matrix is a good opportunity to get them involved. This workshop should be required of all parents who have a child with disabilities or delays. It can be combined with the workshop on the importance of play, or it can be the second in a series on learning through play. Find a colleague to help you present these workshops.

How to Help Your Child Make Friends

An informative workshop on how to help your child make friends could present some interesting information about young children's friendships. Parents could share ideas about how to help their children make friends, as well as their success stories and problems. You could contribute information on the importance of having friends and specifics about how you encourage children to make friends in your classroom. See Chapter 16 for specific ideas.

Home–School Play Folders

It might be useful to present information about home–school play folders at one of the parent workshops held at the beginning of the year so that parents can

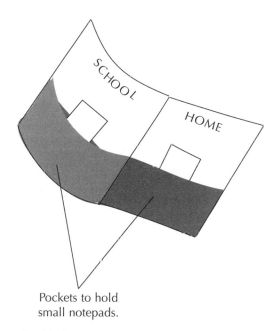

Pockets to hold
small notepads.

Figure 17.3. Example home–school folder.

become familiar with home–school communication at the beginning of their child's program. The folders would contain ongoing records of the child's learning goal achievements as well as the play activities used to accomplish the goals. You can let parents know about their child's play and playmates. The planning matrix should be included and updated on a regular basis. The home–school folder is not a substitute for parent visits but a supplement that is welcomed by many busy parents. An example of a home–school folder is shown in Figure 17.3.

Simple folders can be made of colored construction paper folded in half. Cut two strips about 4 inches wide from a manila folder. Place glue around three edges of each strip, and glue one strip in each half of the folder to form two pockets. Place a small notepad in each pocket. Each day, write a brief note to as many parents as you can. Ask parents to write back to you with their questions and concerns. Encourage them to share good news about their child with you, and ask them to tell you about their child's play activities at home.

PARENT NEWSLETTERS

For more general information, parents appreciate a regular newsletter. Although preparing a newsletter can be a time-consuming task, it is less so if the work of preparing it is shared. Either rotate the responsibility for the newsletter among all staff, each taking one issue, or ask everyone to donate an article each month, while you take responsibility for typing up the newsletter and making copies. It may be possible to enlist a parent to do the editorial work and even to write a monthly column describing how parents have been involved in the program that month. Distributing the newsletter is fairly simple because parents can pick it up at the same time they pick up their child, and children can sometimes be trusted to deliver it.

CONNECTION TO COMMUNITY RESOURCES

A good preschool program will invariably act as an information resource for the families it serves. There are community resources in most areas that can help families provide additional play opportunities for their children. These resources might include Lekotek toy lending libraries (see Appendix A for the address), public library story hours, computer lessons, playgroups, recreation programs sponsored by community recreation centers and swimming pools, and private neighborhood playgroups.

A good place to start when thinking about ways to involve a child in the community is to compile a list of activities you have observed the child actively participating in and to encourage parents to brainstorm about activities their child enjoys (Hanson & Beckman, 2001a). This will give you an idea of what types of organizations would most interest the child. For example, if the child loves the water table, swimming lessons or activities at the local pool may be a good match. If the child lights up when he or she enters the music area, perhaps music or dance lessons would be rewarding.

Offer to speak to staff members about modifications that should be made to include the child in the new activity (e.g., make sure a child who reads lips can always see the instructor's face, allow the child to observe a peer as a model). If you have the time and desire, you can volunteer to help out at the program to ease the child's transition. For example, you can attend the child's first few karate lessons and help as needed.

Playgroups are an excellent community activity for children with disabilities. If you notice that a few parents seem eager for their children to play with peers outside of class, ask them if it would be okay for you to give other parents their telephone number or e-mail address, or arrange for the parents to meet briefly when they drop off or pick up their children. Inform parents of any parent groups at school or in the community. You can ask parents to offer suggestions for support groups that may be helpful and include that information in the school newsletter or on a poster near the door of the classroom.

Now that you have learned about the many aspects involved in achieving learning goals through play, it's time to see how these ideas are applied. Chapter 18 provides a case study to illustrate how the information in this book was used to develop one child's individualized education program.

18

Achieving Jasmine's Learning Goals Through Play

The following is the story of Jasmine and how her parents and teachers developed her individualized education program (IEP), emphasizing learning through play. It is included here to help you understand how learning goals can be incorporated into play.

Jasmine is a 3-year-old preschool girl with mild cerebral palsy and delays in communication, fine and gross motor development, and self-care skills. She also has some mild cognitive delays. Jasmine began attending an infant intervention program when she was 6 months old. At the program, she received physical and occupational therapy twice a week, and she and her mother participated in group activities designed to improve communication and cognitive skills and to increase Jasmine's sense of independence. Now, Jasmine walks with a walker and can sit with support. She prefers to crawl when she is in the classroom because she can move more quickly that way. Sometimes she crawls, and sometimes she uses her walker.

Jasmine attends a morning preschool class taught by Annette and Richard. There are 23 children in the class, including Jasmine and two other children with disabilities. Annette has a master's degree in early childhood special education, and she acts as a special advisor for the children with disabilities in her classroom. She has worked closely with Jasmine's mother and father to plan Jasmine's educational program. Richard is an early childhood educator with considerable experience teaching groups of children with and without disabilities. Together Annette and Richard make a good team.

Jasmine's preschool classroom is part of the Middletown School District and is located in an elementary school building. Jasmine and the other children in her classroom have lunch in the school cafeteria every day, and they share the playground with children in kindergarten and first grade. Jasmine enjoys going to a "real" school. She says she likes having friends in preschool, and she especially likes eating lunch with her friends.

As a child with cerebral palsy and developmental delays, Jasmine was eligible for special education services when she entered preschool to continue the early intervention she received in her infant program. The school district assessment team gave her a series of tests before they made recommendations for her learning goals at an IEP meeting held before the school year started. Both parents attended her IEP meeting and agreed with the goals. They also suggested other learning goals to include in the IEP; they were particularly concerned about self-help and socialization goals. All of this was done during Jasmine's IEP meeting. Her IEP is shown in Figure 18.1.

Jasmine has been attending her preschool program for 4 months. Annette and Richard have incorporated her learning goals into the everyday play activities that take place in the classroom, being careful to make sure that Jasmine is paired with one or two other children for most of her play activities. Annette usually stays close by when Jasmine is beginning a new play activity, just to make sure that Jasmine is included in the activity. Richard or Annette often participate with Jasmine in her play activities whether she is playing by herself, with a friend, or

INDIVIDUALIZED EDUCATION PROGRAM

Student identification information

Student name _Jasmine Robertson_   Date of birth _4/7/2001_   Age _3 years; 4 months_

Parent/guardian/surrogate parent(s) _Mona and Jeffrey Robertson_

Address _1437 Third Street, Middletown, USA_   Date tested _August 15–18, 2004_

Background information

Jasmine attended Middletown Infant Services for 2 years. She had intensive physical and occupational therapy while enrolled in the infant program. Her parents wish therapy to continue but would like to enroll Jasmine in an inclusive preschool program so that she can attend school with her peers.

Current levels of functioning

At the time of testing, Jasmine was performing at the following developmental age levels:

Domain	Developmental age	Delay
Cognition	30 months	10 months
Communication	24 months	16 months
Gross motor	20 months	20 months
Fine motor	18 months	22 months
Social skills	30 months	10 months
Self-care skills	18 months	22 months

Jasmine is performing approximately 2 years below her chronological age level in motor and self-care skills and 1 year below age level in cognitive, communication, and social skills. She can successfully perform in an inclusive preschool classroom if she has special assistance and continues her physical, occupational, and speech therapies.

Annual goals and short-term objectives

The following goals will be reviewed in 1 year's time. To meet each goal, short-term objectives will be developed that will be measured weekly. As Jasmine achieves objectives, others at higher developmental levels will be substituted. The consensus of members of the assessment team and Jasmine's parents is that the objectives are best implemented when embedded in play activities that make up the inclusive preschool day.

1. **Cognition**—Jasmine will improve her concept of number, including *large* and *small, more* and *less,* and one-to-one correspondence.
2. **Communication**—Jasmine will increase her sentence length to three words or more. She will use *-ing* verb endings and add *-s* for plurals. She will combine action and object in the same sentence.
3. **Gross motor**—Jasmine will improve walking, standing, and sitting skills.
4. **Fine motor**—Jasmine will increase her ability to manipulate objects, including grasp and release.
5. **Socialization**—Jasmine will establish peer friendships by learning to give and take during play.
6. **Self-care**—Jasmine will learn to feed herself and assist with dressing herself.

Members of special education team

Annette Bridges   Classroom teacher
Janet Tillman   Speech-language pathologist
Lucas Rogers   Physical therapist
Sharon Jones   School nurse

Mona Robertson   _9-12-04_   _Rebecca Flynn_   _9-12-04_
Mona Robertson, Parent   Rebecca Flynn, Principal

John Robertson   _9-12-04_   _J Erhart_   _9-12-04_
John Robertson, Parent   Jordan Erhart, Team Coordinator

Figure 18.1. Jasmine's individualized education program.

INDIVIDUAL PLAY PLANNING MATRIX
Susan Sandall, Ph.D.

Child's name *Jasmine*

	Objective	Objective	Objective
	Cognitive: Understand "large," small," "more," and "less"	*Fine motor: Pick up and manipulate objects*	*Social: Share play activities with peers*
Arrival/free choice	• At breakfast, ask for "more" cereal, juice or toast	• Put together 2-or 3-piece puzzle with Annette's help	• Work on puzzles with friend Rebecca
Circle	• Listen as teachers talk about "big" and "little"	• Pick up/hold drum with one hand and play with other hand	• Sit next to Rebecca for rhythm time, play drums together
Free choice	*Sand table* • Use various-sized containers to fill and pour from one to another	• Pick up cups, bowls, and so forth to fill with sand, then dump and refill	• Play at sand table with Jeremiah and dump trucks
Outside	• On swings, ask for a "big" or "little" push; ask for "more"		• Sit in wagon with another child while adult pulls wagon
Bathroom			
Snack	• Adults encourage asking for "more," talking about "big" and "small" crackers	• Pick up finger foods and self-feed. pour milk and drink from cup	• Sit by Rebecca; talk about snacks with adult encouragement
Story	• Listen to examples of "big," "small," "more," and "less" in the story	• Hold book and turn pages	• Share picture book with peer; listen as adult reads or tells about book
Small groups	*Manipulatives* • With adult asistance, identify groups with "more" and "less" objects (beads)	• Place beads in cup or jar, dump and refill	• Make bead necklaces with peer, each wearing a necklace when finished
Music	• Play drums or shake tambourine with group		• Share rhythm instruments with peers

Figure 18.2.   Jasmine's play matrices.

GROUP PLAY PLANNING MATRIX

Susan Sandall, Ph.D.

Activity *Gluing shapes on large sheet of construction paper*

Child's name	Goal area *Communication*	Goal area *Social*	Goal area *Cognition*
Jasmine	Will use 3-word sentences to describe gluing activity to adult	Will work with Maria and Jeffrey, sharing glue and trading shapes	Will recognize differences in shape, size, and color of materials
Maria	Will ask for materials, using correct names of shapes and colors	Will give assistance to Jasmine when needed (adult facilitate)	Will correctly group triangles, squares, and circles
Jeffrey	Will tell adults and peers about his finished product	Will show his picture to Maria and Jasmine and look at theirs	Will correctly classify by color

with a small group of children. They keep track of her progress toward her learning goals by using the group and individual play matrices (see Figure 18.2) and encouraging her to work at her highest play levels.

A TYPICAL DAY IN JASMINE'S PRESCHOOL

Jasmine arrives at 8:30 in the morning after a short ride on the school bus. She is attending the school closest to her home, the same one other children in her neighborhood attend, but it is too far for her to walk by herself. Taking the bus is part of her IEP because it teaches her to be independent. The bus driver, Joe, regularly helps her on and off the bus.

Upon arrival, Jasmine joins her classmates for breakfast. She takes her turn helping to set the table or get the food ready. Sometimes, Annette or Richard help her if her walker gets stuck moving around the breakfast table. Jasmine eats breakfast at school, usually cereal, fruit, and toast or a muffin.

After breakfast, the children decide the area in which they want to spend time. Jasmine's favorite areas are the sand table and the creative area. Annette helps her into her standing frame when she plays at the sand table, and in the creative area, Jasmine uses a Rifton adaptive chair to sit at the table. The chair has been especially adjusted to fit her so that her back is firmly supported and her feet are always flat on the ground. The standing frame supports Jasmine in an upright position so that she can stand comfortably at the sand or water table, easel, or another play area.

Jasmine chooses the sand table today and notices that Richard has filled it with pinto beans. She decides she would like her doll to watch her as she plays with the beans, so her doll, named Dolly Debbie, sits on the side of the sand table as Jasmine fills the big red plastic bowl with beans, then scoops a handful out and lets them run through her fingers. She does this several times, enjoying the feeling of the beans as they fall back into the bowl. After she has done this for several minutes, Annette comes to the table and begins imitating Jasmine's action.

"That feels good," Annette says as the beans fall through her fingers into the bowl. "Do you think Dolly Debbie likes watching us play together?"

"Yes," replies Jasmine. "Nice dolly."

"Let's try filling this cup with beans, okay? Here's a good scoop to use. Will you help me?"

Annette shows Jasmine how to hold the plastic flour scoop, fill it with beans, and dump the beans into the measuring cup.

"Now, can you dump those beans from the cup into the bowl?" she asks.

As Annette and Jasmine play with the beans, Jeremiah comes to the table and wants to play, too. Jeremiah is a typically developing 3-year-old with whom Jasmine often plays. Annette invites him to join the bean play, and he puts the dump truck he was carrying into the bean table.

"I'm going to fill my truck with beans," he announces and proceeds to do so.

"That's great, Jeremiah," Annette confirms. "Oh, look, Jasmine. Jeremiah is filling his truck with beans. Shall we get a truck and do that, too? Wait a minute. I'll go get one."

Annette goes to find another dump truck, and soon the three are playing with the trucks, filling, dumping, and pretending there is a road for the trucks to move on.

Next, Jasmine moves to the creative area, using her walker. Here, she sits in her Rifton chair and tackles a gluing activity. She chooses from a pile of shapes cut from colored paper. She decides to use only red shapes, but she wants both circles and squares. She chooses a yellow sheet of construction paper for the background. She needs some help from Richard to squeeze the glue from the bottle, but after that, she works by herself. Jasmine looks around the table from time to time to see what others are doing, but she does not engage in conversation with the other children. Richard watches her at work, then sits next to her.

"What a beautiful picture, Jasmine. Why don't you show it to Alberto?"

Alberto is seated next to Jasmine, so she looks at him and points to her picture.

"Alberto, look at Jasmine's picture. Isn't it great? I'll bet Jasmine would like to see your picture, too," Richard announces.

As Richard encourages the interaction between the two children, Alberto looks at Jasmine, smiles at her, and holds up his picture. Then, Richard talks to Jasmine and Alberto about their pictures, asking questions about the shapes they have used, the colors they chose, and so forth. His goal is to expand their awareness of different shapes, sizes, and colors, as well as for them to notice when things are the same and when they are different.

Later in the morning, the children get ready to go outdoors to play. Annette places Jasmine in the wagon inside the classroom and wheels her outdoors. Although Jasmine cannot move on her own very well, she can ride a tricycle if someone helps her, and this is her favorite outdoor activity. Annette seats her on the tricycle, straps her feet to the special pedals, and supports her back and arms as Jasmine moves slowly around the play area. Jasmine also likes to swing if she is strapped into the swing and given gentle pushes. Annette is careful to check often with Jasmine to make sure she feels comfortable.

As the children return to the classroom for lunch, Richard makes sure they all have a chance to use the toilet and wash their hands. Jasmine needs assistance for both activities, but if Annette or Richard helps her into her stander at the sink, she can wash her hands with the other children. At the lunch table, Jasmine is able to pour her own milk with just a little spilling—much like some of the other 3-year-olds in the group.

After lunch, some of the children decide to take a walk with Richard. Jasmine is tired from her morning's work and elects to take a nap. Some of the children like to lie down after lunch or take picture books to their mats to look at. Not everyone needs a nap, and no one is forced to lie down if he or she would rather do something quiet. Jasmine usually does take a nap, but sometimes she likes to hear Annette read a story.

When it is time to go home, Annette collects Dolly Debbie and Jasmine's shapes picture to show Jasmine's mother and helps Jasmine put on her jacket. Jasmine's job is to put her arms straight above her head so Annette can slip the jacket over Jasmine's head. Now, she is ready for the school bus.

Jasmine's Learning Goals

This short case study describes Jasmine, a child with cerebral palsy and developmental delays. She gets along very well in her preschool classroom because she has the support of well-trained, positive teachers and informed, caring parents. Can you tell what learning goals were embedded in today's play activities?

Jasmine's story illustrates how early childhood special educators can work with early childhood educators to create a diverse and child-centered classroom while still maintaining the necessary emphasis on learning goals for the children with special needs. The adults involved in the early education of young children with and without disabilities can learn to collaborate and share each other's expertise for the benefit of all of the children in the classroom. With play as the medium, the possibilities for achieving learning goals are endless; every area of the classroom and every part of the daily schedule can be used to promote the children's progress!

References

Asher, S.R., Renshaw, P.D., & Hymel, S. (1982). Peer relations and the development of social skills. In S.G. Moore (Ed.), *The young child: Reviews of research* (Vol. 3, pp. 137–158). Washington, DC: National Association for the Education of Young Children.

Braun, S.J., & Edwards, E.P. (1972). *History and theory of early childhood education.* Worthington, OH: Charles A. Jones.

Bredekamp, S. (Ed.). (1987). *Developmentally appropriate practice for children birth through age 8.* Washington, DC: National Association for the Education of Young Children.

Bredekamp, S., & Copple, C. (Eds.). (1997). *Developmentally appropriate practice in early childhood programs.* Washington, DC: National Association for the Education of Young Children.

Bricker, D. (Series Ed.). (2002). *Assessment, Evaluation, and Programming System for Infants and Children (AEPS®)* (2nd ed., Vols. 1–4). Baltimore: Paul H. Brookes Publishing Co.

Brown, R. (1973). *A first language: The early stages.* Cambridge, MA: Harvard University Press.

Cavallaro, C.C., & Haney, M. (1999). *Preschool inclusion.* Baltimore: Paul H. Brookes Publishing Co.

Cook, R., Tessier, A., & Klein, D. (2000). *Adapting early childhood curricula for children in inclusive settings* (5th ed.). New York: Charles E. Merrill.

DEC Task Force on Recommended Practices. (1993). *DEC recommended practices: Indicators of quality in programs for infants and young children with special needs and their families.* Reston, VA: Council for Exceptional Children.

Dewey, J. (1902). *The child and the curriculum.* Chicago: University of Chicago Press.

Dewey, J. (1938). *Experience and education.* New York: Crowell-Collier-Macmillan.

Dickinson, D.K., & Tabors, P.O. (Eds.). (2001). *beginning literacy with language: Young children learning at home and school.* Baltimore: Paul H. Brookes Publishing Co.

Division for Early Childhood. (2000a). Concept paper on the identification of and intervention with challenging behavior. In S.R. Sandall, M. McLean, & B. Smith (Eds.), *DEC recommended practices in early intervention/early childhood special education.* Reston, VA: Council for Exceptional Children.

Division for Early Childhood. (2000b). Position on interventions for challenging behavior. In S.R. Sandall, M. McLean, & B. Smith (Eds.), *DEC Recommended practices in early intervention/early childhood special education.* Reston, VA: Council for Exceptional Children.

Eagen, C., & Toole, A. (1993). *Preschool play: Observation and intervention.* Yorktown Heights, NY: Board of Cooperative Educational Services.

Education for All Handicapped Children Act of 1975, PL 94-142, 20 U.S.C. §§ 1400 *et seq.*

Espinosa, L.M., & Burns, M.S. (2003). Early literacy for young children and English-language learners. In C. Howes (Ed.), *Teaching 4- to 8-year-olds: Literacy, math, multiculturalism, and classroom community* (pp. 47–69). Baltimore: Paul H. Brookes Publishing Co.

Evans, E.D. (1975). *Contemporary influences in early childhood education. (*2nd ed.). New York: Holt, Rinehart & Winston.

Guralnick, M.J. (Ed.). (1997). *The effectiveness of early intervention.* Baltimore: Paul H. Brookes Publishing Co.

Guralnick, M.J. (Ed.). (2001). *Early childhood inclusion: Focus on change.* Baltimore: Paul H. Brookes Publishing Co.

Hanson, M.J., & Beckman, P.J. (2001a). *Me, too! series: My community, my family.* Baltimore: Paul H. Brookes Publishing Co.

Hanson, M.J., & Beckman, P.J. (2001b). *Me, too! series: My new friends.* Baltimore: Paul H. Brookes Publishing Co.

Hanson, M.J., & Widerstrom, A.H. (1993). Consultation and collaboration: Essentials of integration efforts for young children. In C.A. Peck, S.L. Odom, & D.D. Bricker (Eds.), *Integrating young children with disabilities into community programs: Ecological perspectives on research and implementation* (pp. 149–168). Baltimore: Paul H. Brookes Publishing Co.

Hanson, M.J., & Zercher, C. (2001). The impact of cultural and linguistic diversity in inclusive preschool environments. In M.J. Guralnick (Ed.), *Early childhood inclusion: Focus on change.* Baltimore: Paul H. Brookes Publishing Co.

Haynes, W.O., & Shulman, B.B. (1994). *Communication development: Foundations, processes, and clinical applications.* Boston: Allyn & Bacon.

Hazen, N., Black, B., & Fleming-Johnson, F. (1984). Social acceptance. *Young Children, 39,* 26–36.

Heidemann, S., & Hewitt, D. (1992). *Pathways to play: Developing play skills in young children.* St. Paul, MN: Redleaf Press.

Hohmann, M., Banet, B., & Weikart, D. (1979). *Young children in action: A manual for preschool educators.* Ypsilanti, MI: The High/Scope Press.

Individuals with Disabilities Education Act Amendments of 1997, PL 105-17, 20 U.S.C. §§ 1400 *et seq.*

Individuals with Disabilities Education Act (IDEA) of 1990, PL 101-476, 20 U.S.C. §§ 1400 *et seq.*

Kamii, C., & DeVries, R. (1978). *Physical knowledge in preschool education: Implications of Piaget's theory.* Upper Saddle River, NJ: Prentice Hall.

Landy, S. (2002). *Pathways to competence: Encouraging healthy social and emotional development in young children.* Paul H. Brookes Publishing Co.

Lucyshyn, J.M., Dunlap, G., & Albin, R.W. (Eds.). (2002). *Families and positive behavior support: Addressing problem behaviors in family contexts.* Baltimore: Paul H. Brookes Publishing Co.

Mahler, M.S., Bergman, A., & Pine, F. (1975). *The psychological birth of the human infant.* New York: Basic Books.

McWilliam, R.A., & Strain, P.S. (1993). Service delivery models. In DEC Task Force on Recommended Practices, *DEC recommended practices: Indicators of quality in programs for infants and young children with special needs and their families.* (pp. 40–46). Reston, VA: Council for Exceptional Children

Montessori, M. (1912). *The Montessori method: Scientific pedagogy as applied to childhood education in Children's Houses.* New York: Frederick A. Stokes.

Morgan, H. (1999). *The imagination of early childhood education.* London: Bergin and Garvey.

Musselwhite, C. (1986). *Adaptive play for special needs children.* San Diego: College Hill Press.

National Association for the Education of Young Children. (1991). Guidelines for appropriate curriculum content and assessment in programs serving young children ages 3 through 8. *Young Children, 46*(3), 21–38.

National Association for the Education of Young Children. (1997). *Principles of child development and learning that inform developmentally appropriate practice: Developmentally appropriate practice in early childhood programs serving children from birth through age 8.* Available at http://www.naeyc.org/resources/position_statements/dap3.htm

Notari-Syverson, A., O'Connor, R.E., & Vadasy, P.F. (1998). *Ladders to literacy: A preschool activity book.* Baltimore: Paul H. Brookes Publishing Co.

Parten, M.B. (1932). Social participation among preschool children. *Journal of Abnormal and Social Psychology, 27,* 243–269.

Pestalozzi, J. (1890). Letter to Heinrich Gessner about his orphanage at Stanz, Switzerland. In R. de Guimps, *Pestalozzi, his life and work.* New York: Appleton. (Original work published 1799)

Piaget, J. (1962). *Play, dreams and imitation in childhood* (C. Gattegno & F.M. Hodgson, Trans.). New York: W. W. Norton.

Pretti-Frontczak, K., & Bricker, D. (2004). *An activity-based approach to early intervention* (3rd ed.). Baltimore: Paul H. Brookes Publishing Co.

Ritchie, S. (2003). Community-oriented classroom practices: Developing positive teacher–child relationships. In C. Howes (Ed.), *Teaching 4- to 8-year-olds: Literacy, math, multiculturalism, and classroom community* (pp. 2–46). Baltimore: Paul H. Brookes Publishing Co.

Ritchie, S., James-Szanton, J., & Howes, C. (2003). Emergent literacy practices in early childhood classrooms. In C. Howes (Ed.), *Teaching 4- to 8-year-olds: Literacy, math, multiculturalism, and classroom community* (pp. 71–92). Baltimore: Paul H. Brookes Publishing Co.

Rogers, S. (1988). Cognitive characteristics of handicapped children's play: A review. *Journal of the Division for Early Childhood, 12,* 161–168.

Sandall, S.R., McLean, M., & Smith, B. (Eds.). (2000). *DEC recommended practices in early intervention/early childhood special education.* Reston, VA: Council for Exceptional Children.

Sandall, S.R., & Ostrosky, M. (Eds.). (1999). *The young exceptional children monograph series: No. 1. Practical ideas for addressing challenging behavior.* Longmont, CO: Sopris West.

Sandall, S.R., & Schwartz, I.S. (with Joseph, G.E., Chou, H.-Y., Horn, E.M., Lieber, J., Odom, S.L., & Wolery, R.). (2002). *Building blocks for teaching preschoolers with special needs.* Baltimore: Paul H. Brookes Publishing Co.

Schaefer, C.E., Gitlin, K., & Sandgrund, A. (1988). *Play diagnosis and assessment.* New York: John Wiley & Sons.

Shapiro, E., & Biber, B. (1972). The education of young children: A developmental-interaction approach. *Teachers College Record, 74,* 55–79.

Smilansky, S. (1968). *The effects of sociodramatic play on disadvantaged preschool children.* New York: John Wiley & Sons.

Smith, M.W., & Dickinson, D.K. (with Sangeorge, A., & Anastasopoulos, L.). (2002). *User's guide to the Early Language and Literacy Classroom Observation (ELLCO) Toolkit* (Research ed.). Baltimore: Paul H. Brookes Publishing Co.

Thurman, S.K., & Widerstrom, A.H. (1990). *Infants and young children with special needs: A developmental and ecological approach.* Baltimore: Paul H. Brookes Publishing Co.

Widerstrom, A.H. (1986). How important is play for handicapped children? *Childhood Education, 59*(1), 39–49.

Widerstrom, A.H. (1991). *Adapting developmentally appropriate practice for children with special needs.* Workshop presented at the national conference of the Division for Early Childhood of the Council for Exceptional Children, St. Louis.

Williams, B., Briggs, N., & Williams, R. (1979). Selecting, adapting, and understanding toys and recreation materials. In P. Wehman (Ed.), *Recreation programming for developmentally disabled persons* (pp. 15–36). Baltimore: University Park Press.

Wolery, M., & Odom, S. (1991). Developmentally appropriate practice: Is it developmentally appropriate? *Topics in Early Childhood Special Education, 11*(1), 21–27.

Wolfberg, P.L., & Schuler, A.L. (1993). Integrated Play Groups: A model for promoting social and cognitive dimensions of play in children with autism. *Journal of Autism and Developmental Disorders, 23*(3), 467–489.

Sources for Adaptive Equipment and Learning Materials

This section is provided to acquaint first-time teachers of children with disabilities with the many materials and organizations that are available to support them. The following is a list of addresses for locating suppliers of adaptive equipment, such as the Rifton chair mentioned in Chapter 18, as well as software and hardware especially designed for children with special needs and toys appropriate for these children.

Most of the companies listed offer free or very inexpensive catalogues, and many have toll-free telephone or fax numbers and web sites. You are invited to explore this rich and varied field by browsing through some catalogs, then consulting with the child's parents before placing an order. The main organizations serving children with disabilities and how to get in touch with them are also given, with a line or two describing what they can provide. In addition, you will find publishers that produce resources for training teachers about disabilities.

ADAPTIVE EQUIPMENT

AbleNet
1081 Tenth Avenue, SE
Minneapolis, MN 55414-1312
(800) 322-0956 or FAX (612) 379-9143
http://www.ablenetinc.com

Communication Skill Builders and
Therapy Skill Builders products
(now owned by Harcourt Assessment)
19500 Bulverde Road
San Antonio, TX 78259
(800) 211-8378 or FAX (800) 232-1223
http://www.harcourt.com

Crestwood Communication Aids
6625 N. Sidney Place, Department 21F
Milwaukee, WI 53209-3259
(414) 352-5678 or FAX (414) 352-5679
http://www.communicationaids.com

Flaghouse
601 Flaghouse Drive
Hasbrouck Heights, NJ 07604-3116
(800) 793-7900 or FAX (800) 793-7922
http://www.flaghouse.com

Rifton Equipment
Community Products LLC
359 Gibson Hill Road
Chester, NY 10918-2321
(800) 777-4244 or FAX (800) 336-5948
http://www.riftonequipment.com

COMPUTER SOFTWARE AND ADAPTIVE HARDWARE

R. J. Cooper and Associates
27601 Forbes Road #39
Laguna Niguel, CA 92677
(800) 752-6673 or FAX (949) 582-3169
http://www.rjcooper.com

Dunamis
3545 Cruse Road, Suite 312
Lawrenceville, GA 30044
(770) 279-1144 or FAX (770) 279-0809
http://www.dunamisinc.com

Edmark
Riverdeep
500 Redwood Boulevard
Novato, CA 94947
(415) 763-4700
http://riverdeep.net/edmark

Laureate Learning Systems
110 East Spring Street
Winooski, VT 05404-1898
(800) 562-6801 or FAX (802) 655-4757
http://www.llsys.com

ADAPTIVE AND OTHER APPROPRIATE TOYS

Checkerboard Press
1560 Revere Road
Yardley, PA 19067
(215) 493-8228
http://www.abdopub.com

Constructive Playthings
U.S. Toy Company
13201 Arrington Road
Grandview, MO 64030
(800) 448-7830 or FAX (816) 761-9295
http://www.constplay.com

Kapable Kids
Post Office Box 250
Bohemia, NY 11716
(800) 356-1564

Kaplan Early Learning Company
1310 Lewisville-Clemmons Road
Lewisville, NC 27023
(800) 334-2014 or FAX (800) 452-7526
http://www.kaplanco.com

People of Every Stripe
P.O. Box 12505
Portland, OR 97212
(503) 282-0612

Redleaf Press
450 North Syndicate, Suite 5
St. Paul, MN 55104-4125
(612) 641-0305 or FAX (612) 645-0990
http://www.redleafpress.org

Toys for Special Children—Enabling Devices
385 Warburton Avenue
Hastings-on-Hudson, NY 10706
(800) 832-8697 or FAX (914) 479-1369

RESOURCE INFORMATION

American Foundation for the Blind
1 Pen Plaza, Suite 300
New York, NY 10001
(800) 232-5463
http://www.afb.org
The American Foundation for the Blind provides a variety of services and materials to assist people with visual impairments.

Division for Early Childhood
of the Council for Exceptional Children
634 Eddy Avenue
Missoula, MT 59812
(406) 243-5898 or FAX (406) 243-4730
http://www.dec-sped.org
The Division for Early Childhood of the Council for Exceptional Children offers professional development opportunities through publications and conferences for early childhood educators, early interventionists, and families, to improve the quality of services to all children from birth through age 8.

Easter Seals, Inc.
(formerly the National Easter Seal Society)
230 West Monroe Street, Suite 1800
Chicago, IL 60606
(800) 221-6827 or FAX (312) 726-1494
http://www.easterseals.com
Easter Seals, Inc. (formerly the National Easter Seal Society) is the headquarters for the federation of local and state organizations. It disseminates information and conducts national public awareness and fund-raising campaigns.

International Dyslexia Association
Chester Building, Suite 382
8600 LaSalle Road
Baltimore, MD 21286-2044
(410) 296-0232 or FAX (410) 321-5069
http://www.interdys.org
The International Dyslexia Association, formerly called the Orton Dyslexia Society, is an international membership organization dedicated to assisting people with reading disabilities.

The Leukemia and Lymphoma Society
1311 Mamaroneck Avenue
White Plains, NY 10605
(914) 949-5213 or FAX (914) 949-6691
http://www.leukemia.org

The Leukemia and Lymphoma Society works to provide supplementary assistance to people with leukemia, the lymphomas, and Hodgkin's disease, as well as to find cures for these diseases.

National Association for the Education of Young Children (NAEYC)
1509 16th Street, NW
Washington, DC 20036
(800) 424-2460
http://www.naeyc.org
NAEYC offers professional development opportunities through publications, conferences, and grants to early childhood educators to improve the quality of services to children from birth through age 8.

National Down Syndrome Society
666 Broadway
New York, NY 10012
(800) 221-4602
http://www.ndss.org
The National Down Syndrome Society was founded to educate the public, serve people who were referred for help, and raise money for further research on Down syndrome.

National Early Childhood Technical Assistance Center (NECTAC)
University of North Carolina at Chapel Hill
Campus Box 8040
Chapel Hill, NC 27599-8040
(919) 962-2001 or FAX (919) 966-7463
http://www.nectac.org
NECTAC is a collaborative system coordinated by the Frank Porter Graham Child Development Institute at the University of North Carolina at Chapel Hill.

National Lekotek Center
3204 W. Armitage Avenue
Chicago, IL 60647
(773) 276-5164 or FAX (773) 276-8644
http://www.lekotek.org
Lekotek is a toy library program for families of children with disabilities. It has toy libraries throughout the United States.

Spina Bifida Association of America
4590 MacArthur Boulevard, NW, Suite 250
Washington, DC 20007-4226
(800) 621-3141 or FAX (202) 944-3295
http://www.sbaa.org
The Spina Bifida Association assists local parent and support groups and provides assistance with public education and advocacy.

BOOKS AND TRAINING MATERIALS

Communication Skill Builders and
Therapy Skill Builders products
(now owned by Harcourt Assessment)
19500 Bulverde Road
San Antonio, TX 78259
(800) 211-8378 or FAX (800) 232-1223
http://www.harcourt.com

Educational Productions
9000 SW Gemini Drive
Beaverton, OR 97008
(800) 950-4949
http://www.edpro.com

Paul H. Brookes Publishing Co.
P.O. Box 10624
Baltimore, MD 21285
(800) 638-3775 or FAX (410) 337-8539
http://www.brookespublishing.com

Redleaf Press
450 North Syndicate, Suite 5
St. Paul, MN 55104-4125
(612) 641-0305 or FAX (612) 645-0990
http://www.redleafpress.org

Research Press
Department 24W
P.O. Box 9177
Champaign, IL 61826
(217) 352-3273 or FAX (217) 352-1221
http://www.researchpress.com

Young Adult Institute/National Institute for People with Disabilities
460 West 34th Street
New York, NY 10001
(212) 273-6182
http://www.yai.org

B

Guidelines for Developmentally Appropriate Practice

Adaptations for Preschool Children with Disabilities

In this appendix, you will find an abbreviated and adapted version of the guidelines developed by the National Association for the Education of Young Children (NAEYC). The adaptations consist mainly of simple additions or explanations to make the guidelines more appropriate for children who are not developing in a typical way (Widerstrom, 1991). For a complete discussion of the guidelines, see the excellent overview published by NAEYC (Bredekamp 1987).

Appropriate practice for 3-year-olds	Adaptation
Adults provide affection and support, comforting children when they cry and reassuring them when they are fearful. Adults plan experiences to alleviate children's fears.	No adaptation is necessary. Appropriate for all children.
Adults support 3-year-olds' play and developing independence, helping when needed but allowing them to do what they are capable of doing and what they want to do for themselves.	No adaptation necessary for children with mild or moderate delays. For children with severe needs, it may be necessary to lead them in play, take a more active role in play, or model appropriate behaviors more often. *Caution:* Adults must not do tasks for children with disabilities that the children could do for themselves.
Adults recognize that although 3-year-olds are usually more cooperative than toddlers and want to please adults, they may revert to toddler behavior (thumb sucking, crying, hitting, baby talk) when they are feeling shy and upset, especially in new situations. Adults know that 3-year-olds' interest in babies, and especially their own recent infancy, is an opportunity for children to learn about themselves and human development.	Three-year-olds with delays may exhibit toddler behaviors frequently. For them, these behaviors are developmentally appropriate and should be viewed as such by adults. Children should never be reprimanded or ridiculed for immature behavior.
Adults provide opportunities for 3-year-olds to demonstrate and practice their newly developed self-help skills and their desire to help adults with dressing and undressing, toileting, feeding themselves (including help with pouring milk or setting the table), brushing teeth, washing hands, and helping to pick up toys. Adults are patient with occasional toileting accidents, spilled food, and unfinished jobs.	No adaptation is necessary. Adults who work with children with delays or disabilities should have as a primary goal the encouragement of independence in all developmental areas to the greatest extent possible. Children should be allowed to play with their food or to have accidents in toileting. Adults should not insist that children always pick up their toys.
Adults know that growth rates may slow down and appetites decrease at this age. Children are encouraged to eat "tastes" in small portions with the possibility of more servings if desired.	No adaptation is necessary. Appropriate for all children.
Adults guide 3-year-olds to take naps or do restful activities periodically throughout the day, recognizing that younger children may exhaust themselves—especially when trying to keep up with older children in the group.	No adaptation is necessary. Keep in mind that young children with disabilities may tire more easily than typical peers and, therefore, should be offered the choice of a daily nap.
Adults provide many opportunities for 3-year-olds to play by themselves next to another child (parallel play) or with one or two other children. Adults recognize that 3-year-olds are not comfortable with much group participation. Adults read a story or play music with small groups and allow children to enter and leave the group at will.	Three-year-olds with mild or moderate delays may need no adaptations. Children with attention deficits or problems of distractibility may need adults to use more directive strategies, such as sitting beside the child during story reading or interacting one-to-one with the child during larger group play. Adults should not expect all children to participate in every whole-group activity.

Figure B.1. Developmentally appropriate practice for children 3 years of age. Adapted for children with special needs by Anne H. Widerstrom, Ph.D. *Note:* The appropriate practices listed here are taken from *Developmentally Appropriate Practice in Early Childhood Programs Serving Children Birth Through Age 8,* edited by Sue Bredekamp. Washington, DC: National Association for the Education of Young Children, 1987.

Appropriate practice for 3-year-olds	Adaptation
Adults support children's beginning friendships, recognizing that such relationships ("my best friend") are short-lived and may consist of acting silly together or chasing for a few minutes. When conflicts arise, 3-year-olds will often return to playing alone. Adults encourage children to take turns and share but do not always expect children to give up favored items.	Children with disabilities may need assistance making friends. Typically developing peers may not readily choose them as friends, so adults can facilitate the process by suggesting activities for pairs of children to do. The children's own choices for friends should always receive first consideration. Children with disabilities should not be expected to give up favorite toys or take turns consistently.
Adults provide plenty of space and time indoors and outdoors for children to explore and exercise their large muscle skills through running, jumping, galloping, riding a tricycle, or catching a ball, with adults close by to offer assistance as needed.	No adaptation is necessary. Appropriate for all children, although some with motor problems may be able to participate less actively. Adaptive equipment, such as adaptive tricycles, wagons, and swings with seat and shoulder belts, should be available for these children.
Adults provide large amounts of uninterrupted time for children to persist at self-chosen tasks and activities and to practice and perfect their newly developed physical skills if they choose.	No adaptation necessary for children with mild or moderate delays. All children should be allowed to work at their own pace, repeat some activities many times (if learning is taking place), and choose their own activities for at least part of every day.
Adults provide many materials and opportunities for children to develop fine motor skills through puzzles, pegboards, beads to string, construction sets, and art materials (crayons, brushes, paints, markers, modeling clay, blunt scissors). Adults do not expect a representational product even though children's scribbles are more controlled than those of toddlers, children will create designs with horizontal and vertical strokes, and children will sometimes name their drawings and paintings. Art is viewed as creative expression and exploration of materials.	No adaptation is necessary. All children enjoy some type of creative expression.
Adults provide plenty of materials and time for children to explore and learn about the environment, to exercise their natural curiosity, and to experiment with cause-and-effect relationships. For example, they provide 1) blocks (that children first line up and later build into towers); 2) more complex dramatic play props (for role-playing work and family roles and animals); 3) sand and water with tools for pouring, measuring, and scooping; 4) many toys and tools to experiment with, including knobs, latches, and any toys that open and close or can be taken apart; and 5) simple science activities like blowing bubbles, flying kites, or planting seeds.	No adaptation is necessary for children with mild delays. For children with moderate to severe needs, adults may need to encourage exploration and experimentation because they may not occur spontaneously. Adults should be sensitive to how much supervision each child needs to become actively engaged and should back off as soon as possible. Adults should adopt a reactive stance in their interactions with children of all developmental levels.

(continued)

Figure B.1. *(continued)*

Appropriate practice for 3-year-olds	Adaptation
Adults encourage children's developing language by speaking clearly and frequently to individual children and listening to their responses. Adults respond quickly and appropriately to children's verbal initiatives. They recognize that talking may be more important than listening for 3-year-olds. Adults patiently answer children's questions ("Why?" "How come?") and recognize that 3-year-olds often ask questions they know the answers to in order to open a discussion or practice giving answers themselves. Adults know that children are rapidly acquiring language, experimenting with verbal sounds, and beginning to use language to solve problems and learn concepts.	No adaptation is necessary. Adults can encourage children with disabilities to communicate verbally or nonverbally by responding quickly and effectively to their attempts at communication. They can help children learn to resolve conflicts verbally instead of physically.
Adults provide many experiences and opportunities to extend children's language and musical abilities. Adults 1) read books to a single child or a small group; 2) recite simple poems, nursery rhymes, and fingerplays; 3) encourage children to sing songs and listen to recordings; 4) facilitate children's play of circle and movement games like "London Bridge," "Farmer in the Dell," and "Ring Around the Rosy"; 5) provide simple rhythm instruments; 6) listen to stories that children tell or write down stories they dictate; and 7) enjoy 3-year-olds' sense of humor.	No adaptation is necessary. These practices are appropriate for all preschool children.
Adults know that 3-year-olds do not usually understand or remember rules. Rules that are specific to a real situation and that are demonstrated repeatedly are more likely to impress young children.	Three-year olds with disabilities may need additional reminders to obey classroom rules. Rules should be simple and few in number. Adults should be able to tolerate moderately noisy classrooms and should be comfortable giving children room to express themselves freely. Children should not be required to line up when they leave the classroom.
Adults provide a safe, hazard-free environment and careful supervision. Adults recognize that 3-year-olds often overestimate their newly developed physical powers and will try activities that are unsafe or beyond their abilities (especially in multi-age groups in which they may model 4- and 5-year olds). Adults protect children's safety in these situations while helping them deal with their frustrations and maintain their self-confidence. For example, "Joel can tie his shoe because he's 5; when you're 5, you'll probably know how to tie, too."	No adaptation is necessary.

Appropriate practice for 4- and 5-year-olds	Adaptation
Experiences are provided that meet children's needs and stimulate learning in all developmental areas—physical, social, emotional, and intellectual.	No adaptation is necessary.
Each child is viewed as a unique person with an individual pattern and timing of growth and development. The curriculum and adults' interactions are responsive to individual differences in daily life and interests. Different levels of ability and development and different learning styles are expected, accepted, and used to design appropriate activities.	No adaptation is necessary. Responding to each child's individual strengths and needs is an accepted principle in early childhood special education.
Interactions and activities are designed to develop children's self-esteem and positive feelings toward learning.	No adaptation is necessary. This is appropriate for all children.
Teachers prepare the environment for children to learn through active exploration and interaction with adults, other children, and materials.	No adaptation is necessary. All children learn through active exploration and interaction with adults, other children, and materials. Preparing the environment to encourage active learning encourages children with disabilities to become independent and self-reliant.
Children select many of their own activities from among a variety of learning areas the teacher prepares, including dramatic play, blocks, science, math, games, puzzles, books, recordings, art, and music.	Children with disabilities must learn to make their own decisions to the greatest extent possible. They should be encouraged to make choices among activities that are either developmentally or age appropriate. They should be allowed to initiate their own learning and go at their own pace, regardless of their developmental levels.
Children are expected to be physically and mentally active. Children choose from among activities the teacher has set up or that they spontaneously initiate.	No adaptation is necessary. Children with mild or moderate delays can initiate their own activities, especially in small-group play, in which typically developing peers provide leadership. Children with severe disabilities are more dependent on teacher initiation.
Children work individually or in small, informal groups most of the time.	No adaptation is necessary. Most children with disabilities do not perform as well in large groups as they do in small ones.
Children are provided concrete learning activities with materials and people relevant to their own life experiences.	No adaptation is necessary.
Teachers move toward groups and individuals to facilitate children's involvement with materials and activities by asking questions, offering sug- *(continued)*	No adaptation is necessary for children with mild to moderate delays. Children with more severe disabilities may require more one-to-one *(continued)*

Figure B.2. Developmentally appropriate practice for children 4 and 5 years of age. Adapted for children with special needs by Anne H. Widerstrom, Ph.D. *Note:* The appropriate practices listed here are taken from *Developmentally Appropriate Practice in Early Childhood Programs Serving Children Birth Through Age 8,* edited by Sue Bredekamp. Washington, DC: National Association for the Education of Young Children, 1987.

Figure B.2.   *(continued)*

Appropriate practice for 4- and 5-year-olds	Adaptation
gestions, or adding more complex materials or ideas to a situation.	interaction with an adult, combined with some small-group experiences. Teachers avoid dominating the environment or telling children what to do.
Teachers accept that there is often more than one right answer. Teachers recognize that children learn from self-directed problem-solving and experimentation.	No adaptation is necessary. All children learn from self-directed problem solving and experimentation. Like all children, children with disabilities learn from their mistakes.
Teachers facilitate the development of self-control in children by using positive guidance techniques such as modeling and encouraging expected behaviors, redirecting children to more acceptable activities, and setting clear limits. Teachers' expectations match and respect children's developing capabilities.	No adaptation is necessary.
Children are provided many opportunities to develop social skills such as cooperating, helping, negotiating, and solving interpersonal problems by talking with the person involved. Teachers facilitate the development of positive social skills at all times.	To the greatest extent possible, children with disabilities should be given the same opportunities as typically developing children to develop social skills. Children with more severe disabilities may need more adult assistance in resolving conflicts, communicating with peers, and other social interactions than do children with mild or moderate delays.
Children are provided many opportunities to see how reading and writing are useful before they are instructed in letter names, sounds, and word identification. Basic skills develop when they are meaningful to children. The teacher provides an abundance of these types of activities to develop children's language and literacy through meaningful experiences: 1) listening to and reading stories and poems; 2) taking field trips; 3) dictating stories; 4) seeing classroom charts and other print in use; 5) participating in dramatic play and other experiences requiring communication; 6) talking informally with other children and adults; and 7) experimenting with writing by drawing, copying, and inventing their own spellings.	Language and the beginnings of literacy are developed through meaningful experiences: 1) listening to stories and poems, 2) going on field trips, 3) dictating stories, 4) seeing classroom charts and other print in use, 5) participating in dramatic play and other experiences requiring communication, 6) talking informally with other children and adults, and 7) experimenting with writing by drawing and copying.
Children develop an understanding of information about themselves, others, and the world around them through observation, interacting with people and real objects, and seeking solutions to concrete problems. Learning about math, science, social studies, health, and other	Children with delays learn through concrete experiences just as typically developing children do. The experiences may need to be simplified and supported by more adult facilitation and by smaller adult-child ratios. Rote learning acquisition of isolated (splinter) skills, meaningless
(continued)	*(continued)*

Appropriate practice for 4- and 5-year-olds	Adaptation
content areas is integrated into meaningful activities such as 1) building with blocks; 2) measuring sand, water, or ingredients for cooking; observing changes in the environment; 3) working with wood and tools; 4) sorting objects for a purpose; 5) exploring animals, plants, water, wheels, and gears; 6) singing and listening to music from various cultures; 7) drawing; 8) painting; or 9) working with clay. Teachers follow routines that help children keep themselves healthy and safe.	drills, and sole reliance on adult-directed instruction or therapy do not constitute appropriate practice for children with disabilities.
Children have daily opportunities to use large muscles through activities such as running, jumping, and balancing. Outdoor activity is planned daily so children can develop large muscle skills, learn about outdoor environments, and express themselves freely and loudly.	No adaptation is necessary. Even children with physical disabilities need opportunities and encouragement to use their bodies as much as possible.
Children have daily opportunities to develop small muscle skills through play activities such as pegboards, puzzles, painting, and cutting.	No adaptation is necessary.
Children have daily opportunities for aesthetic expression and appreciation of art and music. Children experiment with and enjoy various forms of music. A variety of art forms are available for creative expression, such as easel painting, fingerpainting, and clay sculpture.	No adaptation is necessary. Aesthetic development is important for all children.
Children's natural curiosity and desire to make sense of their work are used to motivate them to become involved in learning activities.	To the greatest extent possible, a child's natural desire to learn should be the primary motivation for any activity. Sometimes external rewards are necessary for children who have not yet developed internal motivation.
Teachers work in partnership with parents, communicating regularly to build mutual understanding and greater consistency for children.	No adaptation is necessary. Early childhood special educators have extensive experience in working with parents as partners in early intervention programs.
Decisions that have a major impact on children (e.g, enrollment, retention, or assignment to remedial classes) are based primarily on information obtained from observations by teachers and parents, not on the basis of a single test score. *(continued)*	Decisions regarding provision of special educational and related services to children with disabilities are regulated by state and federal laws, which require the use of standardized test scores to determine eligibility for services. Diagnosis *(continued)*

(continued)

Figure B.2.   *(continued)*

Appropriate practice for 4- and 5-year-olds	Adaptation
Developmental assessment of children's progress and achievement is used to plan the curriculum, identify children with special needs, communicate with parents, and evaluate the program's effectiveness.	cannot be based on a single test score. Developmental assessment is appropriate for developing individualized education program goals, curriculum planning, communicating with parents, and evaluating program effectiveness.
In public schools, there is a place for every child of legal entry age, regardless of the developmental level of the child. No public school program should deny access to children on the basis of results of screening or other arbitrary determinations regarding the child's lack of readiness. The educational system adjusts to the developmental needs and levels of the children it serves; children are not expected to adapt to an inappropriate system.	No adaptation is necessary. Appropriate practice dictates that every child shall have a school program that meets his or her individual needs, whatever the child's developmental level. Children must not be made to feel they have failed by being denied admission to an age-appropriate public school program. For children with disabilities, this principle is encoded in federal legislation.
Teachers become qualified to work with 4- and 5-year-olds through college preparation in early childhood education or child development and supervised experience with this age group.	Teachers of young children with disabilities are qualified to work with 4- and 5-year-olds through graduate work in early childhood special education, including theory and supervised practice.
The group size and ratio of teachers to children are limited to enable individualized and age-appropriate programming. Children 4–5 years of age are in groups of no more than 20 children with 2 adults.	Children with disabilities 4–5 years of age are included in groups of no more than 20 typically developing children and children with disabilities with 3 adults.

Resources for Including Children with Special Needs

Appendix C contains guidelines to help teachers easily include children with special needs in preschool programs. First are some suggestions for including children with hearing or visual impairments in play activities. Next are guidelines for positioning and handling a child with physical disabilities. These guidelines and suggestions are intended to help preschool teachers who may lack training in special education to feel confident enough to truly involve children with disabilities in their program. Finally, there is a list of principles for play intervention and suggestions for adapting play materials. Table C.1 provides some strategies for adapting play materials for children with disabilities. Table C.2. gives a list of general rules of play intervention.

Musselwhite's (1986) information on adapting play materials for children with special needs has been adapted and included here. It contains many useful suggestions for preschool teachers. Refer to her excellent book for a more detailed discussion of these strategies.

CHILDREN WITH HEARING IMPAIRMENTS

- Consult the child's audiologist (with written permission) to find out what kind of hearing aid the child is wearing and how to care for it. Ask the parents for as much information as they can give you about the child's hearing ability. Find out whether the child should wear the aid all the time and whether not doing so could cause problems.

- Help other children to understand what the hearing aid is, why the child wears it, and how it works. If the child with a hearing impairment uses some sign language, make sure the other children know at least those signs the child commonly uses. Suggestions are MORE, YES, NO, STOP, BOY, GIRL, and GOOD-BYE.

- Help the child develop a special friendship with a hearing child by placing the two children together for play activities. Use some of the suggestions in Chapter 16 to facilitate friendships.

CHILDREN WITH VISUAL IMPAIRMENTS

- Consult the child's parents and physician (with written permission) to learn as much as you can about the visual problem. Find out what is being done to correct or compensate for it.

- On entry into the preschool program, the child will need a thorough orientation to the layout of the room. An orientation and mobility specialist can assist in this process. Find out from the child's parents how to arrange a consultation with this specialist or call the American Federation for the Blind at (800) AFBLIND (232-5463) for information.

- Leave at least part of the room unchanged from week to week so the child will have a familiar territory within which to work and play.

- Help the other children understand that having blindness or visual impairment is not a reason to be isolated or avoided, nor a reason to be less able than other children. Encourage special friendships with typically developing peers by arranging play activities in groups of two or three.

CHILDREN WITH VISUAL AND HEARING IMPAIRMENTS

- Make sure structured activities take place during a part of every day in large or small groups. This will ensure some time when auditory and visual distractions are kept to a minimum.

- Include friendship goals in the child's indivualized education program (IEP). This suggestion applies to all children with disabilities, but it is particularly important for children with sensory impairments. These children, because of their disabilities, may be more socially isolated than others without visual or hearing impairments.

- Arrange small-group and one-to-one learning sessions more frequently than for other children. Allow additional response time for children with sensory impairments. Do not supply "correct" information too quickly because the child may process information more slowly and may need extra time to respond.

CHILDREN WITH PHYSICAL DISABILITIES

For children with physical disabilities to successfully attend preschools with typically developing children, teachers and other adults must know how to take care of their physical needs. Consultation with an occupational or physical therapist is invaluable but is not always possible, especially in private schools that operate on limited budgets. Because consultation with a specialist may not be possible, some general guidelines for positioning and handling the child with physical impairments are given here. Some children also require other physical procedures such as gavage feeding. Although educational staff can easily learn these techniques—as many parents do—it is best to learn them from a professional who knows and works with the child.

First, it is important to keep in mind the following principles of typical physical development:

- The child develops from *head to toe;* that is, development occurs from the head downward. This means that head control is achieved before trunk control and before crawling or walking.

- The child develops from the *central trunk outward.* This means that trunk stability—in shoulders and hips—must be achieved before the child can use the arms, hands, legs, and feet effectively.

- Smooth, efficient movement requires good *muscle tone.* If muscles are too tight or rigid (hypertonic), the child lacks the strength for good movement. Massaging tight muscles can reduce tone and encourage more natural movement. Physical therapists have many good suggestions for increasing or decreasing a child's muscle tone.

- Muscles work in pairs. Smooth, efficient movement requires good *extension* and *flexion.* Extension refers to stretching out away from the body. Flexion refers to bending inward toward the body. With good muscle control and normal tone, the child can extend and flex muscles equally well. Many children with cerebral palsy have trouble flexing (bending) their trunks, arms, and legs because they have too much muscle extension.

- As children develop physically, they increase their ability to move *voluntarily* as opposed to involuntarily (reflex movements). Children with cerebral palsy often become locked into atypical reflex patterns that inhibit normal movement. The goal of therapy in this case is to reduce reflex movements and allow typical voluntary movement patterns to develop.

Positioning Techniques

- Make sure the child is comfortable, whether sitting, standing with support, or lying down.

- Make sure the child's trunk is stable and well supported. Use special equipment (e.g., Rifton chair, which has shoulder and hip straps) for sitting or standing. Place pillows or small cushions behind the child's back to maintain as upright a posture as possible. Notice especially whether the hips and shoulders are supported. *Only when the trunk is stable can the child have free use of the arms and hands for reaching, holding, or handling objects.*

Table C.1. Strategies for adapting play materials

Strategy	Description	Example
Stabilize	Attach play material to steady play surface.	Affix playhouse to lap tray with C-clamp.
Enlarge	Enlarge materials to enhance visual perception.	Use large puzzle pieces.
Prosthetize	Enlarge key parts to enhance toy manipulation.	Affix large Plexiglas "button" over small Push 'n Go button.
	Affix parts to allow access for children with physical disabilities.	Use foam hair curlers (without the tubes) to add grip to a brush handle.
Reduce required response	Minimize the distance, range of motion, and complexity of response.	Place a doll on an elevated tray. Use a tray to keep cars within range. Use a plate switch rather than an on–off switch.
Make more familiar	Relate to the environment.	Select symbols that reflect the child's world.
Make more concrete	Reduce abstract quality.	Demonstrate the activity and toy play. Add clues to graphic symbols.
Remove extraneous cues	Consider the goal, and remove unrelated cues.	If the task is shape recognition, do not simultaneously color-code items to be sorted.
Remove distracting stimuli	Simplify busy backgrounds.	Use dark background behind objects being visually tracked or as a backdrop for puzzles.
Add or enhance cues	Increase visual stimuli.	Use bright, contrasting colors.
	Increase tactile stimuli.	Affix fabrics to adaptive switches.
Improve safety and durability	Avoid sharp objects.	Round off or pad corners.
	Protect objects from drool.	Laminate materials or coat them with nontoxic sealant.
	Increase strength of toys.	Replace cardboard with triwall. Replace staples or nails with screws.

From Musselwhite, C. (1986). *Adaptive play for special needs children.* San Diego: College Hill Press; adapted by permission. Categories are from Williams, B., Briggs, N., & Williams, R. (1979). Selecting, adapting, and understanding toys and recreation materials. In P. Wehman (Ed.), *Recreation programming for developmentally disabled persons* (pp. 15–36). Baltimore: University Park Press; reprinted by permission.

- Make sure the child's feet are flat and supported in sitting position. Make sure the child's chair is the right size to allow the feet to rest flat on the ground, or choose a special chair with an elevated footrest. Never allow feet to dangle unsupported.

- An effective position for a child with too much muscle tone is *sidelying.* Place the child on the floor lying on one side with both arms extended in front of the

Table C.2. General rules of play intervention

Facilitate play. Don't direct it.
Expand play. Don't interrupt it.
Encourage an appropriate play level.
Provide appropriate materials.
Create an environment that stimulates good play.
Create a successful atmosphere.
Encourage play.
Attend play preferences.
Allow overlearning.
Task-analyze behavior.

From Eagen, C., & Toole, A. (1993). *Preschool play: Observation and intervention.* Yorktown Heights, NY: Board of Cooperative Educational Services, p. 5; adapted by permission.

body and the top leg flexed. Place a cushion or pillow behind the child to support the back, and place another under the head. In this position, the child has good trunk support and use of the hands and is able to see what is going on in the area.

- Change the child's position frequently—from sitting to standing, then to lying down, then back to sitting. The child will probably let you know when a position is becoming tiring, but be ready to anticipate the child's need to change in any case. Frequent position changes are important to prevent the child from becoming locked into any one position.

- Children with too much muscle tone are better in flexed positions, which allow them to overextend. Although it is important to maintain the child's head upright, make sure the child's neck is not overextended, causing the head to tilt back and leaving the child looking at the ceiling. Try to keep the child's head perpendicular to the ground so the child can look straight ahead and all around. Keep the child's arms and legs bent some of the time.

- Massaging tight muscles can make it easier for the child to move voluntarily. Massage reduces the effect of reflexes on tight muscles, making it easier for the child to control movements.

Handling Techniques

- Use a firm, sure touch when handling a child with physical disabilities. This is reassuring to the child and more comfortable than a tentative or light touch.

- Place your hands on the child's hips or shoulders to provide maximum trunk support, rather than holding the arms or legs.

- When carrying a child, hold him or her in a flexed position. Lay the child on one side rather than on the back.

- Don't be afraid to handle the child. If you feel unsure of yourself, get some advice from a physical or occupational therapist or the parents. Remember that your positioning and handling make it possible for the child to spend time in your classroom instead of being isolated in a special class. You are performing a valuable service!

- Always let the child lead the way in moving or changing positions. Allow the child the greatest possible opportunity to use whatever voluntary movement is available, then use your own hands to continue the movement as naturally as possible.

D

Play Checklists

Three play checklists and one summary that may be useful for observing children with developmental delays in play are included in this appendix. All of these items are intended to help preschool teachers determine children's current level of play in order to plan appropriate play activities. These tools also assist teachers in organizing and making sense of the information collected during an observation. The skills on the checklists and summary are organized in developmental order.

The first two checklists, Developmental Sequences of Play Checklist (Figure D.1) and Play Checklist (Figure D.2), are designed for classroom use and are probably the easiest to use. Next is the Summary of Symbolic Play Development (Figure D.3) by Carol Westby. The last item is Westby's Symbolic Play Scale (Figure D.4), which is very popular with preschool educators and addresses language development as well as play development.

DEVELOPMENTAL SEQUENCES OF PLAY CHECKLIST

Child's name _____

Date _____

Description	Achieved	Not achieved
Developmental sequence of block play		
Level 1: Picks up a block and puts in mouth		
Level 2: Bangs two blocks together		
Level 3: Stacks one block on top of the other		
Level 4: Uses blocks to stand for other objects		
Level 5: Builds simple structures with blocks		
Level 6: Builds complex structures with blocks		
Developmental sequence of sand and water play		
Level 1: Sensorimotor exploration		
Level 2: Simple exploration		
Level 3: Beginning conservation		
Level 4: Beginning symbolic play		
Level 5: Full conservation		
Developmental sequence of pretend play skills		
Level 1: Substitutes one object for another		
Level 2: Uses toys in simple play routines		
Level 3: Engages in more complex routines with order		
Level 4: Engages in pretend play with roles		

Achieving Learning Goals Through Play: Teaching Young Children with Special Needs, Second Edition, by Anne H. Widerstrom

Figure D.1. Developmental Sequences of Play Checklist by Anne Widerstrom, Ph.D.

Child's name _____

Description	Achieved	Not achieved
Developmental sequence of play with manipulatives		
Level 1: Puts together simple one- or two-piece puzzles		
Level 2: Completes more complex puzzles		
Level 3 Works independently on manipulative tasks		
Developmental sequence of common outdoor activities		
Playground vehicles		
Level 1: Sits in a wagon while someone pulls it		
Level 2: Rides a tricycle or truck without pedals		
Level 3: Rides a tricycle with pedals		
Level 4: Pulls someone in a wagon		
Level 5: Can do activities independently		
Swings and slides		
Level 1: With assistance, swings in a swing with a safety bar		
Level 2: Goes down a slide with assistance		
Level 3: With assistance, swings in a swing without a safety bar		
Level 4: Swings and slides with limited assistance		
Level 5: Can swing and slide independently		

(continued)

Figure D.1. *(continued)*

Child's name _____

Description	Achieved	Not achieved
Developmental sequence of common outdoor activities (continued)		
Ball skills		
Level 1: Rolls a ball to an adult or another child		
Level 2: Throws a large ball with both hands		
Level 3: Attempts to kick a ball		
Level 4: Attempts to catch a ball with both hands		
Level 5: Throws a ball with one hand		
Level 6: Kicks a ball to an adult or another child		
Level 7: Catches a ball		
Developmental sequence of rhythm skills		
Level 1: Bangs or shakes an object to mark time with music		
Level 2: Bounces in place to music		
Level 3: Uses both hands to play a rhythm instrument		
Level 4: Marches to music, keeping time with both feet		
Level 5: Dances simple steps to music		
Level 6: Leads dancing or rhythm activity		

Child's name _____

Description	Achieved	Not achieved
Developmental sequence of music skills		
Level 1: Listens to adults singing a song		
Level 2: Sings some of the words during group singing		
Level 3: Sings the whole song during group singing		
Level 4: Sings a song alone		
Level 5: Sings a song with accompanying finger-play		
Level 6: Makes up songs and sings them alone		
Developmental sequence of creative skills		
Level 1: Sensorimotor exploration		
Level 2: Simple use of materials		
Level 3: Simple creative play		
Level 4: Complex creative play		
Developmental sequence of literacy		
Level 1: Awareness of print		
Level 2: Awareness of the relationship between oral and written language		
Level 3: Knowledge of letters, their names, and their sounds		
Level 4: Phonological awareness		
Level 5: Developing vocabulary, both oral and written		
Level 6: Development of narrative skills and discourse		

PLAY CHECKLIST

Child's name _____ Date of birth _____ Today's date _____

Check the highest level skills you consistently observe.

1. **Pretending with objects***
   - ☐ Does not use objects to pretend
   - ☐ Uses real objects
   - ☐ Substitutes objects for other objects
   - ☐ Uses imaginary objects

2. **Role playing***
   - ☐ No role play
   - ☐ Uses one sequence of play
   - ☐ Combines sequences
   - ☐ Uses verbal declaration (e.g., "I'm a doctor.")
   - ☐ Imitates actions of role, including dress

3. **Verbalizations about play scenario***
   - ☐ Does not use pretend words during play
   - ☐ Uses words to describe substitute objects
   - ☐ Uses words to describe imaginary objects and actions (e.g., "I'm painting a house.")
   - ☐ Uses words to create a play scenario (e.g., "Let's say we're being taken by a monster.")

4. **Verbal communication during a play episode***
   - ☐ Does not verbally communicate during play
   - ☐ Talks during play only to self
   - ☐ Talks only to adults in play
   - ☐ Talks with peers in play by stepping outside of role
   - ☐ Talks with peers from within role (e.g., "Eat your dinner before your dad comes home.")

5. **Persistence in play***
   - ☐ Less than five minutes
   - ☐ Six to nine minutes
   - ☐ Ten minutes or longer

6. **Interactions**
   - ☐ Plays alone
   - ☐ Plays only with adults
   - ☐ Plays with one child, always the same person
   - ☐ Plays with one child, can be different partners
   - ☐ Can play with two or three children all together

7. **Entrance to a playgroup#**
   - ☐ Does not attempt to enter playgroup
   - ☐ Uses force to enter playgroup
   - ☐ Stands near group and watches
   - ☐ Imitates behavior of group
   - ☐ Makes comments related to play theme
   - ☐ Gets attention of another child before commenting

8. **Conflict management**
   - ☐ Gives in during conflict
   - ☐ Uses force to solve conflicts
   - ☐ Seeks adult assistance
   - ☐ Imitates verbal solutions provided by adults
   - ☐ Recalls words to use when reminded
   - ☐ Initiates use of words
   - ☐ Accepts reasonable compromises

9. **Turn taking**
   - ☐ Refuses to take turns
   - ☐ Leaves toys; protests when others pick them up
   - ☐ Gives up toy easily if done with it
   - ☐ Gives up toy if another child asks for it
   - ☐ Takes turns if arranged and directed by an adult
   - ☐ Asks for turn; does not wait for a response
   - ☐ Proposes turn taking; will take and give turns

10. **Support of peers**
    - ☐ Shows no interest in peers
    - ☐ Directs attention to distress of peers
    - ☐ Offers help
    - ☐ Offers and takes suggestions of peers at times
    - ☐ Encourages or praises peers

Figure D.2. Play Checklist. Adapted from *Pathways to play: Developing play skills in young children,* by Sandra Heidemann and Deborah Hewitt with permission from the publisher: Redleaf Press, 450 N. Syndicate, Suite 5, St. Paul, MN 55104. Copyright 1992. *Note:* The developmental progression outlined in each segment of the play checklist can be used as a guideline when assessing most children's development. However, not all individuals will go through the same steps in development nor through the same developmental sequence.
*Sections are adapted from Smilansky, S. (1968). *The effects of sociodramatic play on disadvantaged preschool children.* New York: John Wiley and Sons.
#Section is adapted from Hazen, Black, and Fleming-Johnson. (1984). Social acceptance. *Young Children, 39,* 26–36.

EXPLANATION OF THE PLAY CHECKLIST

The following is a detailed explanation for the Play Checklist (Figure D.2). Remember to complete the checklist based on two to three observations, rather than during a direct observation. Information from several observations helps provide a complete picture of a child. Be sure the observations are in varied settings, with opportunities for a variety of play for the child.

1. Pretending with Objects

Pretending with objects is one of the first skills a child acquires in play. At around 12–18 months of age, a child begins to use objects in a dramatically new way. Instead of just exploring objects' physical properties, a child begins to pretend with them. For example, a young girl in this stage not only picks up and puts down the telephone, but she also *talks* when the receiver is near her mouth. Now, she is beginning to symbolize. The smooth transition between these two stages underplays the truly dramatic and exciting beginnings of pretending.

It may be difficult to always interpret accurately how a child is using an object. Because you cannot see inside the child's mind, you need to observe the child's behaviors and listen to his or her language. Most of the time, if you understand the child's frame of reference, you will be able to see how he or she is pretending with objects.

Does Not Use Objects to Pretend

If the child does not use objects to pretend, he or she simply uses objects to bang, roll, drop, or push. All of the actions are done to explore physical properties, *not* to pretend.

Uses Real Objects

By 18 months old, most children begin to use real objects or child-size replicas to pretend. For example, a child may use a bottle to feed a doll or may pretend to cook by stirring with a spoon in a pan. At this level, the child almost always needs an object that looks like the real thing to pretend. If given substitutes, the child may ignore them.

Substitutes Objects for Other Objects

A child can increasingly use more dissimilar objects to pretend. For instance, a child may use a block as a bed for the baby and a few months later use a blanket or rug as a bed. A child who cannot do this will seek out a more realistic prop to use.

Uses Imaginary Objects

By age 4, most children no longer need an object to pretend. They use actions and words to indicate imaginary objects. In our experience, many children do this first with imaginary food or imaginary money. Gradually, the child learns that even if he or she doesn't have an object, the play doesn't have to stop. The child can *pretend* to have the object.

2. Role Playing

Role playing is a child's ability to act out a role in play. Certainly, most children find role-playing to be delightful. They quickly don the firefighter hats and coats to fight the fire. This requires a complex understanding of *how* the role is played. Children use voice, dress, body language, and props to communicate that understanding.

No Role Play

If a child uses no props, language, or actions to play a role, he or she may lack the cognitive understanding of what a role is or may be afraid to risk role playing in a group.

Uses One Sequence of Play

In early role playing, toddlers pretend just one incident. For example, a 2-year-old may pick up the telephone, say hello, and hang up. Or the child may put a bottle to a doll's mouth for a few seconds and then throw the bottle and the doll aside.

Combines Sequences

As a child matures, he or she learns to combine play events so they become more complex. For example, Monica stirs a spoon in a pan at the stove in the house corner and then sets the table. Combining these distinct and separate events into one continuous flow builds up to playing a role in an elaborate and unique style.

Uses Verbal Declaration

Children may verbally indicate that they are a dad or a firefighter; however, this may or may not be supported by dress, actions, and language appropriate to that role. If a child does not elaborate beyond the verbal declaration, he or she may need help to further play out the role. For example, Ali would run into the doctor play and say, "I'm the doctor." He would then run out. His caregiver helped him do the actions of a doctor by encouraging him to put on the white coat, take a blood pressure reading, and give a shot.

Imitates Actions of Role, Including Dress

If a child has the ability to imitate roles (e.g., doctor, parent, superhero, baby) in play, he or she will use dress, actions or body language, props, voice, and words to play out his or her understanding of what others in that role *do*. The child learns what each role requires by watching adults, watching television or movies, and reading books. Unless a child can succeed in role-playing, he or she will have real difficulty with sociodramatic play in a group. He or she will be quickly left behind in the ongoing action.

3. Verbalizations About Play Scenario

Children use language during play to let their play partners know where the play is going. Without words, children lose track of the collective play theme, and play disintegrates. Verbalizations about play scenario looks at the child's use of words that build the pretend theme. These words may or may not be spoken to others in play.

Does Not Use Pretend Words During Play

Marking "does not use pretend words during play" on a child's Play Checklist means that the child probably is not talking much during play. A child with a language delay or a shy temperament may have difficulty with verbalizations.

Uses Words to Describe Substitute Objects

Using words to describe substitute objects means that the child will use words to communicate to other children or adults what a substitute object represents. For instance, a child may put a piece of paper in another child's hand and state, "Here's a rock for the wall."

Uses Words to Describe Imaginary Objects and Actions

Using words to describe imaginary objects and actions means that the child will use words to communicate what an object or action is. For instance, a child may stand in front of the wall and move his or her arm up and down the wall, saying, "I'm painting now."

Uses Words to Create a Play Scenario

Using words to create a play scenario is the most difficult skill in the Verbalizations About Play Scenario section. You may see a child outline a scene that a group of children then enter. For example, Sarah says loudly, "Let's say this is an ocean and we are on this boat and there's a whole bunch of sharks after us." If the group of children agrees to this scene, the play begins.

4. Verbal Communication During a Play Episode

Not only do children use words to create agreement on actions and themes, but they also use language to direct others or communicate with others during play. Unless this verbal interaction occurs, children play their roles alone with little communication between them. Gestural language such as sign language can perform the same function. Language or gestural communication becomes the glue that holds the play together.

Does Not Verbally Communicate During Play

If a child does not speak during play episodes, he or she may be an onlooker. Other times, a child may be in the middle of a playgroup but attempt no verbal communication.

Talks During Play Only to Self

A child may talk during play, but the words may not be directed or intended as communication. The child may simply talk to him- or herself. This type of verbal communication is used by many children to further their individual play, but it doesn't help the child integrate into the group play.

Talks Only to Adults in Play

Children who talk only to adults during play may ask adults for toys or materials. They may also describe to adults what they are doing or ask for help with sensorimotor tasks like buttoning a doll's shirt.

Talks with Peers in Play by Stepping Outside of Role

A child may direct comments to others but step out of a role temporarily to do it. He or she may tell another child how to play a role or correct the other child's actions. For example, Mary stops feeding the baby long enough to tell John, "No, John! That's not where the daddy sits."

Talks with Peers from within Role

The most sophisticated way to verbally communicate during play is to talk from inside the role. A skilled child will be able to give suggestions or direct others in their respective roles by playing the mom, teacher, or doctor. In the previous example, Mary would have demonstrated this skill if she had said in her mommy voice, "No, dear, you sit over here." When this skill is achieved, there are fewer breaks in the play.

5. Persistence in Play

Persistence in play examines how long a child plays *in a group* as part of a sociodramatic play theme. A child with a short attention span will have difficulty staying in one place, much less playing with a group. Although a child may play alone longer than he or she plays with a group, use this section of the Play Checklist only to measure time in a group play episode.

Less than Five Minutes

Toddlers flit from activity to activity, but most 3-year-olds should be able to join in group play for as long as 4 minutes.

Six to Nine Minutes

Four-year-olds should increasingly expand their group play times to 9 minutes.

Ten Minutes or Longer

Most 5-year-olds can sustain a sociodramatic play episode with other children for 10 minutes or longer.

6. Interactions

In sociodramatic play, a child will interact with at least one other child. The children exchange ideas, have conversations, and share materials as they work together to create playful scenes.

Plays Alone

A child who plays alone is sometimes thought of as a loner or a withdrawn child. He or she may tend to be on the outskirts of the group's activities and may isolate him- or herself further by choosing activities and materials that are typically used by one person at a time, such as easel painting or working with beads.

Plays Only with Adults

Adults can become a child's primary play partners if the child is uncomfortable with his or her peers. Such a child can be quite demanding of adult attention and unsure of what to do with him- or herself when the adult is unavailable. The child might look to the adult to provide play ideas and to keep play going. For example, Michael prefers to be with Ms. Jody and follows her around the classroom during free time. When Ms. Jody is busy helping another student, Michael can't think of any appropriate play ideas and goes to the water table to play alone.

Plays with One Child, Always the Same Person

People consider a child who always plays with the same person to have a best friend. Although the child has learned to get along adequately with this best friend, he or she may be unable to transfer the interaction skills to play with any other children.

Plays with One Child, Can Be Different Partners

A child interacting at this level plays with a number of different children but only one at a time. The child's partners may switch from day to day or from activity to activity, but the child is unable to play in groups of three and may reject others.

Can Play with Two or Three Children All Together

Playing with two or three others in a group is the most sophisticated level of interaction. A child who knows how to do this pays attention to the other children and is capable of some give and take.

7. Entrance to a Playgroup

Skills required for entrance to a playgroup differ in a subtle way from the interaction skills discussed previously. Entrance to a playgroup refers specifically to a child's ability to enter into a group of children who have already established a play scenario. This category was adapted from Hazan, Black, and Fleming-Johnson (1984).

Does Not Attempt to Enter Playgroup

A child who does not attempt to enter a playgroup may be somewhat disconnected from other children. He or she may not attend to others' behavior or verbalizations. The child may play alone frequently and may decline the play invitations of other children.

Uses Force to Enter Playgroup

Children may mistakenly try many types of force in an attempt to enter the play of others. Children may initiate contacts with others by patting them on the back, poking their arm, wrestling them to the ground, or making verbal threats such as, "I'm not going to be your friend anymore." These attempts to make contact are rarely successful.

Stands Near Group and Watches

Sometimes standing near the group and watching the established play can be an effective method of gaining entry. The child becomes enveloped as the play of the group surrounds him or her.

Imitates Behavior of Group

As in the previous response, the child stands near the group but begins to perform the same type of activities. The child is usually on the outskirts of the group, but instead of just watching, he or she imitates the group's behaviors. Once again, the play of the group surrounds the child.

Makes Comments Related to Play Theme

A child uses the strategy of making comments related to play by going into the group and saying something related to what the other children are doing. For example, when Marie comes up to a group of children playing school, she says, "How about we go on a field trip to the zoo?"

Gets Attention of Another Child Before Commenting

The most effective strategy a child can use is to call another child's name, establish eye contact with another child, or tap another child on the shoulder to get his or her attention before making a comment that is related to the existing play. Building on the previous example, Marie could have used this strategy if she had said, "Josh, how about if we go on a field trip to the zoo?"

8. Conflict Management

For many preschoolers, conflicts occur because they don't agree about who should play with a toy or what to play. If problems cannot be resolved in a way that is acceptable to all those involved, play will fall apart or individuals will be left out.

Gives in During Conflict

Some children respond to conflict in a passive manner. A child who gives in will leave the area or go on to another activity when someone takes his or her toy. Sometimes this child looks very surprised that another person would take the toy and may look as if he or she doesn't know what to do in a conflict situation. Another child may choose not to respond to a conflict situation.

Uses Force to Solve Conflicts

Preschoolers often try to solve problems through the use of force. Force can mean physical aggression, verbal aggression, manipulation, or physical intimidation. Preschoolers with poor language skills are more likely to try to get a new toy by using aggression because of the difficulty they have in making themselves understood. Others may verbally threaten their peers by saying, "I'm going to let you have it if you don't give me the Big Wheel." A child may even try to bully someone by standing over him and puffing out his chest while showing his clenched fist.

Seeks Adult Assistance

A child with little problem-solving ability may rely on adults to solve a conflict. The child might start crying when he or she has a problem and look toward the adult, or the child might come to the adult to complain about a situation that he or she doesn't know how to handle. Most often, the adult must go with the child to assist him or her in solving the problem.

Imitates Verbal Solutions Provided by Adults

Although a child may not be able to solve a conflict by him- or herself, he or she may be able to use words given by an adult. The adult must provide the child with the appropriate words to use in the situation. The child is responsible for going back to the conflict situation and imitating the words given.

Recalls Words to Use When Reminded

A child at the Recalls Words to Use When Reminded level still goes to an adult for help when faced with a problem. The adult reminds him or her of how to solve the problem by giving a direction such as, "Use your words." The child is then able to go back to the situation and use some of the words he or she recalls having learned in the past.

Initiates Use of Words

After much practice, a child learns to use words to solve conflicts on his or her own. The child needs no reminders or help in thinking of the words to use, but he or she may need help getting the other child to listen to or follow through with his or her request.

Accepts Reasonable Compromises

Children who are able to accept reasonable compromises in their problem-solving situations know how to use words to get their needs met and can sometimes do what another child asks in order to solve a conflict.

9. Turn Taking

In group child care settings, children are asked to share at a very early age. Because of a limited number of resources, children must learn to take turns with toys, equipment, and adult attention. In order to successfully take turns, a child must understand give and take. He or she must learn to temporarily delay personal satisfaction in order to coordinate his or her behavior with others. In addition, the child must learn how to negotiate a trade or a deal and sometimes accept the suggestions made by others. These skills are closely related to the child's ability to manage conflict.

Refuses to Take Turns

It is not uncommon for a child to refuse to take turns. If the child is forced to share a possession, he or she may prefer to leave the area than share something that he or she is not ready to give up. A young child may have a tantrum when asked to share an item. An older child may say, "I'm not playing if I can't have the one I want."

Leaves Toys; Protests When Others Pick Them Up

Children may leave a toy that they have been playing with but still feel that it is theirs. They may become upset and demand a toy back that someone else has picked up. For example, D.J. is using a yellow truck in the sand but leaves the area to greet another child who has just arrived. When D.J. returns, he finds out that Jeremy has picked up the yellow truck and is driving it around. D.J. yells, "Hey, I was using that."

Gives Up Toy Easily if Done with It

As a child matures, he or she may leave a toy when finished with it. The child understands that the toy might not be in the same place when he or she returns and that others may use the toy.

Gives Up Toy if Another Child Asks for It

A child may share a toy or a material when asked if the child feels that he or she is done with it. A typical response would be, "That's okay; I'm done anyway," or "Sure, I'm going to play with the dump truck now."

Takes Turns if Arranged and Directed by Adult

Some children need an adult to structure turn taking. For instance, the adult may tell the child to judge when the other is done, set limits on the number of children using a material, or divide up toys among the players. Whatever type of adult intervention is used, a child at this level will be able to agree on the turn-taking propositions.

Asks for Turn; Does Not Wait for a Response

When a child begins to learn to ask for a turn, he or she uses words to ask but sometimes leaves out the pause that gives the other person a chance to respond. The child does not understand that he or she needs to wait for the other person, so the words and the taking of the item take place simultaneously. For instance, when Jackie asks for a towel, she says, "Can I have a towel, Ellie?" At the same time, she takes the towel from Ellie's hand.

Proposes Turn Taking; Will Take and Give Turns

Play can proceed smoothly when a child has successfully learned to share a piece of equipment. Learning to share means being able to both give and take turns.

10. Support of Peers

Being able to support your peers is important to starting and maintaining friendships. This is difficult for many younger children, who may be at a very egocentric stage in their development. It requires that a child learn to look at a situation from another person's position, empathize with others' feelings, offer comfort or help, establish a balance in giving and taking suggestions that help play to continue, and develop positive attitudes toward others (Asher, Renshaw, & Hymel, 1982).

Shows No Interest in Peers

To stand and watch others seems simple enough, yet some children do not notice the actions and expressions of others. An impulsive, active, or self-absorbed child may have difficulty showing interest in peers.

Directs Attention to Distress of Peers

Young children will pay attention to others in the room who are crying or upset. They may stop what they are doing momentarily and look in the direction of the other child. They may even move closer to the child who is upset.

Offers Help

Once children pay attention to another child in the room who is crying or upset, they may try to help. They may hold out a cuddly, stuffed animal or a blanket to provide comfort, or they may try to hug or pat the back of the child who is upset. Their actions suggest that they understand how the other child feels and want to help him or her feel better.

Offers and Takes Suggestions of Peers at Times

When two or three children are playing together, they must share in the planning and leadership roles of play. A child capable of this will go along with the suggestions of others and may say something like, "Yeah, let's do that," or "That's a good idea." At other times, the child will offer play ideas by saying, "Let's pretend . . . ," or "How about if we . . . " There should be some balance in suggesting scenes to play and accepting those of others.

Encourages or Praises Peers

A child who encourages or praises peers is able to recognize the strengths of other children and comment on them or to notice and say something about a child who is working hard or doing a good job. For instance, as Marcia arrives at the child care center, Lexi says, "That's a neat sweatshirt, Marcia."

SUMMARY OF SYMBOLIC PLAY DEVELOPMENT

Age	Props	Themes	Organization	Roles	Language use in play
By 18 months	Uses one realistic object at a time	Familiar activities in which the child is an active participant (e.g., eating, sleeping)	Short, isolated pretend actions	Autosymbolic pretend (e.g., child feeds self pretend food)	Gets and maintains toys and seeks assistance operating toys (e.g., "baby," "mine," "help")
By 22 months	Uses two realistic objects at a time	Familiar activities that caregivers do (e.g., cooking, reading)	Two related toys combined or actions performed on two people (e.g., uses spoon to eat from plate, feeds mother, then doll)	Acting on dolls and others (e.g., child feeds doll or caregiver)	Occasional comment on toy or action
By 24 months	Uses several realistic objects		Multischeme combinations of steps (e.g., puts doll in tub, applies soap, takes doll out and dries)		Talks to doll briefly, describes some of the doll's actions (e.g., "baby sleeping")
By 30 months		Common but less frequently experienced or especially traumatic experiences (e.g., shopping, doctor)		Emerging limited doll actions (e.g., doll cries)	Talking to doll and commenting on doll's actions increase in frequency
By 3 years		Observed but not personally experienced activities (e.g., police, firefighter)	Sequences of multischeme events (e.g., prepare food, set table, clear table, wash dishes)	Talking to a doll in response to the doll's actions (e.g., "Don't cry now," "I'll get you a cookie.") Brief complementary role-play with peers (e.g., mother and child, doctor and patient)	May comment on what he or she has just completed or what he or she will do next ("Dolly ate the cake," "I'm gonna wash dishes.")
By 3½ years	Uses miniature props, small figures, and object substitutions			Attributing emotions and desires to dolls; reciprocal role taking with dolls (e.g., treats doll as partner; talks for doll and caregiver)	Uses dialogue for dolls and metalinguistic markers (e.g., "he said"); refers to emotions
By 4 years	Uses imaginary props (language and gesture help set the scene)	Familiar fantasy themes (e.g., Batman, Wonder Woman, Cinderella)	Planned play events (e.g., child decides to play a birthday party and gathers necessary props and assigns roles)	Assigning multiple roles to child or doll (e.g., mother, wife, doctor, firefighter, husband, father) Handling two or more dolls in complementary roles (dolls are doctor and patient) Attributing thoughts and plans to dolls	Uses language to plan and narrate the story line
By 6 years	Uses language and gesture to carry the play without props	Novel fantasy characters and plots	Multiple planned sequences (plans for self and other players)	Assigning more than one role per doll (e.g., doll is mother, wife, doctor)	Elaborates planning and narrative story line

Figure D.3. Summary of symbolic play development by Carol Westby, Ph.D. From Haynes, W.O., & Shulman, B.B. (1994). *Communication development: Foundations, processes, and clinical applications.* Boston: Allyn & Bacon; reprinted by permission.

SYMBOLIC PLAY SCALE

	Play		Language
Object permanence	Means–end/problem solving	Object use	Communication

A. Presymbolic levels

Presymbolic Level I: 8 to 12 months

Object permanence	Means–end/problem solving	Object use	Communication
— Aware that objects exist when not seen; finds a toy hidden under cloth, box, etc.; associates object with location	— Attains toy by pulling cloth on which toy is resting — Attains toy by pulling string — Touches adult to continue activity	— Explores moveable parts of toy — Does not mouth all toys. Uses several different schemas (patting, turning, throwing, etc.); uses some differential schemas on familiar objects	— No true language; may have performative words that are associated with action or the total situation — Shows and gives objects Exhibits the following communicative intents: — Request (instrumental) — Command (regulatory)

Presymbolic Level II: 13 to 17 months

Object permanence	Means–end/problem solving	Object use	Communication
— Aware that objects exist separate from location; finds objects hidden in first one location and then in a second or third location	— Understands "in-ness"; dumps objects out of bottle — Hands toy to adult if unable to operate it — Hands toy to adult to gain attention — Uses index finger to point to desired objects	— Recognizes operating parts of toys (attends to knobs, levers, buttons) — Discovers operation of toys through trial and error — Uses familiar objects appropriately	— Context-dependent single words (e.g., child may use the word "car" when riding in a car but not when he sees a car); words tend to come and go in child's vocabulary Exhibits the following communicative functions: — Request — Protest — Command — Label — Interactional — Response — Personal — Greeting

Figure D.4. Symbolic Play Scale by Carol Westby, Ph.D. From *Play Diagnosis and Assessment*, edited by Charles E. Schaefer, Karen Gitlin, and Alice Sandgrund. Copyright © 1988 by John Wiley & Sons, Inc. Reprinted by permission of John Wiley & Sons, Inc. Copying these pages is expressly forbidden.

	Play				Language	
Decontextualization (What props are used in pretend play?)	Thematic content (What schemas/scripts does the child represent?)	Organization (How coherent and logical are the child's schemas/scripts?)	Self-other relations (What roles does the child take and give to toys and other people?)	Function	Form and content

B. Symbolic levels

Symbolic Level I: 17 to 19 months

Decontextualization	Thematic content	Organization	Self-other relations	Function	Form and content
— Child exhibits internal mental representation — Tool use (uses stick to reach toy) — Find a toy invisibly hidden when placed in box and box emptied under scarf — Pretends, using life-like props — Does not stack solid ring	— Familiar, everyday activities, (e.g., eating, sleeping) in which child has been an active participant	— Short, isolated schemas (single pretend actions)	— Self as agent (autosymbolic or self-representational play; e.g., child pretends to go to sleep; to eat from spoon; to drink from cup)	Directing — Requesting — Commanding — Interactional Self-maintaining — Protesting — Protecting self and self-interests Commenting — Labeling (objects and activity) — Indicating personal feeling	Beginning of true verbal communication. Words have following functional and semantic relations: — Recurrence — Existence — Nonexistence — Rejection — Denial — Agent — Object — Action or state — Location — Object or person associated with object or person

Symbolic Level II: 19 to 22 months

Decontextualization	Thematic content	Organization	Self-other relations	Function	Form and content
	— Activities of familiar other's (e.g., cooking, reading, cleaning)	— Short, isolated schema combinations (child combines two actions or toys in pretend play; e.g., rocking doll and putting it to bed; pouring from pitcher into cup; or feeding doll from plate with spoon)	— Child acts on doll (doll is passive recipient of action); brushes doll's hair; feeds doll; covers doll with blanket — Child performs pretend actions on more than one object or person (e.g., feeds self, a doll, mother, and another child)	— Refers to objects and persons not present — Requests information	Beginning of word combinations with the following semantic relations: — Agent–action — Action–object — Agent–object — Attributive — Dative — Action–location — Possessive

(continued)

Figure D.4. *(continued)*

	Play			Language	
Decontextualization (*What props are used in pretend play?*)	Thematic content (*What schemas/scripts does the child represent?*)	Organization (*How coherent and logical are the child's schemas/scripts?*)	Self-other relations (*What roles does the child take and give to toys and other people?*)	Function	Form and content

B. Symbolic levels
Symbolic Level III: 2 years

| | | — Elaborated single schemas (represents daily experiences with details, e.g., puts lids on pan, puts pan on stove; collects items associated with cooking/ eating such as dishes, pans, silverware, glasses, high chair) | | — Comments on activity of self (get apple)

— Comments on doll (baby sleep) | — Uses phrases and short sentences

Appearance of morphological markers:

— Present progressive (*-ing*) on verbs

— Plural

— Possessive |

Symbolic Level IV: 2½ years

| Represents personally experienced events that occur less frequently, particularly those that are memorable because they are pleasurable or traumatic:

— Store shopping

— Doctor–nurse– sick child | | — Evolving episode sequences (e.g., child mixes cake, bakes it, serves it, washes dishes; or doctor checks patient, calls ambulance, takes patient to hospital); sequence is not planned | —Talks to doll | | Responds appropriately to the following *wh-* questions in context:

— What   — Where
— Who   — Whose
— What...do

— Asks *wh-* questions (generally puts *wh-* at beginning of sentence)

— Responses to *why* questions inappropriate except for well-known routines

— Asks why, but often inappropriate and does not attend to answer |

	Play			Language	
Decontextualization (What props are used in pretend play?)	Thematic content (What schemas/scripts does the child represent?)	Organization (How coherent and logical are the child's schemas/scripts?)	Self-other relations (What roles does the child take and give to toys and other people?)	Function	Form and content

B. Symbolic levels

Symbolic Level V: 3 years

	Thematic content		Self-other relations	Function	Form and content
	— Compensatory play: Reenacts experienced events, but modifies original outcomes		— Transforms self into role — Engages in associative play (i.e., children do similar activities, may share same role, but no organized goal)	— Reporting — Predicting — Narrating or story-telling	— Uses past tense, such as "I ate the cake," "I walked" — Uses future aspect (particularly "gonna") forms, such as "I'm gonna wash dishes."

Symbolic Level VI: 3 to 3½ years

Decontextualization	Thematic content		Self-other relations	Function	Form and content
— Carries out pretend activities with replica toys (Fisher-Price/ Playmobil doll-house, barn, garage, village, airport) — Uses one object to represent another (e.g., stick can be a comb, chair can be a car) — Uses blocks and sandbox for imaginative play. Blocks used as enclosures (fences, houses) for animals and dolls.	— Observed events (i.e., events in which child was not an active participant—e.g., police officer, firefighter, war, cowhard, schemas/scripts from television shows—Superman, Wonder Woman, He-Man) — Highly imaginative activities that integrate parts of known schemas/scripts for events child has never participated in or observed (e.g., astronaut builds ship, flies to strange planet, explores, eats unusual food, talks with creatures on planet)		Uses doll or puppet as participant in play: — Child talks to doll — Reciprocal role taking—child talks for doll and as parent of doll — Child assigns roles to other children — Uses dolls and puppets to act out schemas/scripts	— Projecting — Gives desires, thoughts, feelings to doll or puppet — Uses indirect requests (e.g., "Mommy lets me have cookies for breakfast") — Changes speech depending on listener — Reasoning (integrates reporting, predicting, projecting information)	Descriptive vocabulary expands as child becomes more aware of perceptual attributes. Uses terms for the following concepts (not always correctly): — Shapes — Sizes — Colors — Textures — Spatial relations — Uses metalinguistic and metacognitive language (e.g., "He said...," "I know...")

(continued)

Figure D.4. (continued)

Play				Language	
Decontextualization (*What props are used in pretend play?*)	Thematic content (*What schemas/scripts does the child represent?*)	Self-other relations (*What roles does the child take and give to toys and other people?*)	Organization (*How coherent and logical are the child's schemas/scripts?*)	Function	Form and content

B. Symbolic levels

Symbolic Level VII: 3½ to 4 years

Decontextualization	Self-other relations	Organization	Function	Form and content
— Uses language to invent props and set scene — Builds 3-dimensional structures with blocks	— Child or doll has multiple roles (e.g., mother and wife; fireman, husband, father)	— Schemas/scripts are planned — Child hypothesizes, "What would happen if…"	— Uses language to take roles of character in the play, stage manager for the props, or as author of the play story	— Uses modals (can, may, might, will, would, could) — Uses conjunctions (and, but, so, if, because) *Note:* Full competence for modals and conjunctions does not develop until 10–12 years of age. — Begins to respond appropriately to why and how questions that require reasoning

Symbolic Level VIII: 5 years

Decontextualization	Self-other relations	Organization	Form and content
— Can use language to set the scene, actions, and roles in the play	— Engages in collaborative play (i.e., play roles coordinated and themes are goal-directed)	— Plans several sequences of pretend events; organizes what is needed—both objects and other children; coordinates several scripts occurring simultaneously	— Uses relational terms (then, when, first, last, next, while, before, after) *Note:* Full competence does not develop until 10–12 years of age.

Reproducible
Planning Matrices and Play Quiz

Appendix E contains the planning matrices introduced in Chapter 4. These items may be reproduced for administrative use. Also included is a short play quiz, which you may use to find out how much you remember about children's play from that child development course you took several years ago! It also is a good introductory warm-up activity for a parent or teacher workshop on play.

INDIVIDUAL PLAY PLANNING MATRIX

Susan Sandall, Ph.D.

Child's name _____

	Objective	Objective	Objective
Arrival/free choice			
Circle			
Free choice			
Outside			
Bathroom			
Snack			
Story			
Small groups			
Music			

GROUP PLAY PLANNING MATRIX

Susan Sandall, Ph.D.

Activity _____

Child's name	*Goal area*	*Goal area*	*Goal area*

PLAY QUIZ

This is a true-and-false quiz. Place a **T** beside each statement that is true. Place an **F** beside each statement that is false.

_____ 1.   Children begin playing at about age 2.

_____ 2.   Play is always goal-directed.

_____ 3.   Playing dress-up is an example of symbolic play.

_____ 4.   Play can serve as an outlet for expressing anger or aggression or working through feelings.

_____ 5.   Toddlers would be likely to engage in parallel play.

_____ 6.   In associative play, each child takes a different role, and children must demonstrate a high level of cooperation.

_____ 7.   An advantage of play is that it is failure-proof for the child.

_____ 8.   Play is primarily for fun; children don't really learn anything from it.

_____ 9.   The most complex type of play is probably a game with rules.

_____ 10. A characteristic of more cooperative types of play is that they always exclude some children.

_____ 11. Solitary independent play represents a relatively low level of play.

PLAY QUIZ—ANSWER KEY

F 1. Children begin playing at about age 2.

F 2. Play is always goal-directed.

T 3. Playing dress-up is an example of symbolic play.

T 4. Play can serve as an outlet for expressing anger or aggression or working through feelings.

T 5. Toddlers would be likely to engage in parallel play.

F 6. In associative play, each child takes a different role, and children must demonstrate a high level of cooperation.

T 7. An advantage of play is that it is failure-proof for the child.

F 8. Play is primarily for fun; children don't really learn anything from it.

T 9. The most complex type of play is probably a game with rules.

T 10. A characteristic of more cooperative types of play is that they always exclude some children.

F 11. Solitary independent play represents a relatively low level of play.

Index

Page numbers followed by *f* indicate figures; those followed by *t* indicate tables.